JUST LAW

By the same author

EVE WAS FRAMED: WOMEN AND THE LAW

JUST LAW

HELENA KENNEDY

Chatto & Windus
LONDON

Published by Chatto & Windus 2004

2 4 6 8 10 9 7 5 3

First published in Great Britain in 2004 by
Chatto & Windus
Random House, 20 Vauxhall Bridge Road,
London SW1V 2SA

Random House Australia (Pty) Limited
20 Alfred Street, Milsons Point, Sydney,
New South Wales 2061, Australia

Random House New Zealand Limited
18 Poland Road, Glenfield,
Auckland 10, New Zealand

Random House (Pty) Limited
Endulini, 5A Jubilee Road, Parktown 2193, South Africa

The Random House Group Limited Reg. No. 954009
www.randomhouse.co.uk

A CIP catalogue record for this book is available from the British Library

ISBN 0 7011 7506 0

Papers used by The Random House Group Limited are natural, recyclable products made from wood grown in sustainable forests; the manufacturing processes conform to the environmental regulations of the country of origin

Typeset by SX Composing DTP, Rayleigh, Essex
Printed and bound in Great Britain by
Clays Ltd, St Ives Plc

For my friend Angelica Mitchell

CONTENTS

ACKNOWLEDGEMENTS

WHENEVER I WAS studying for exams I used to find myself saying 'Dammit, if only I had more time.' I feel that about this book. It has been written with a sense of urgency because principles of such importance are being abandoned with very little time for people to consider the consequences. I found it hard to place a final full stop because it seemed that every week an announcement was being made of yet another erosion of civil liberties. Given that I had so many other commitments, I could never have written this book if it had not been for the unswerving support of my great circle of friends and my family, who loved and encouraged me through it all.

I especially want to thank the woman who is my right arm, Hilary Hard. She has been my personal assistant for 12 years and is an extraordinary, warm, resourceful human being who could really run the World Bank but instead runs me. Along with the glorious secretariat at the British Council – Rebecca Walton, Mona Lotten and Jessica Shepherd, Hilary had the tough task of squeezing time out of a diary that screams for mercy. I could not have been more fortunate in my management team.

There is another posse of fantastic women friends to whom I am indebted and who have been an enduring network of support, supplying information and notes to help – Angelica Mitchell, Madeleine Colvin, Reggie Nadelson, Leora Mosston, Eleanor Stein, Jane Hoyal, Bianca Jagger, and Estela Welldon. I have also been greatly assisted by conversations with Professor Pat Carlen, Michael Ratner, Michael Boudin, David Blackburn, Phillipe Sands QC, Nicholas Blake QC, Stephanie Irwin QC, Chris Sallon, the late Dick Neustadt, Richard Swinney, Jon Snow and colleagues in the House of Lords, Shirley Williams, Ann Mallelieu, Frank Judd, Conrad Russell, Navnit Dholakia and Martin Thomas. And by missives from my friends at Southall Black Sisters, from None Ardill of Legal Action Group, Zoe Gillard of Liberty, and Ruth Brander who is a member of my chambers. A special thanks to two great friends, Vivien Stern and Jeffrey Bindman, who painstakingly read the manuscript and commented so helpfully on the book. Two young academic lawyers deserve special gratitude, Emily Cheffin and Kathy Liddell, both of whom were involved in some earlier research for me when I gave the Hamlyn lectures on which I have drawn for two chapters. And a huge thank-you for ideas, enthusiasm and google-searching, to my friend, Rebecca Lee, who is one of the best and brightest of a committed new generation of lawyers coming to the Bar.

There were several occasions while writing this book when my technical skills fell short of the mark and I managed to freeze the computer or send whole pages of work off into the ether. At those suicidal moments I was rescued by the genius of Dr Patrick Magennis who, as a surgeon colleague of my husband, has far more important things to do. However, he patiently saved the day and the book. So if you ever need your face reconstructed and your computer mended, he is your man.

I would also like to thank Faith Evans, my agent, who has been urging me to write another book for the last ten years. Her patient care and wise counsel have been invaluable. Thanks go also to the copy-editor, Beth Humphries, and to Poppy Hampson of Chatto & Windus, who were midwives in the final processes of publication. And to my Chatto publisher Alison Samuel who convinced me that this was a book that I had to write.

A special tribute to Jenny Uglow, who is the most brilliant of women and the editor from heaven. She not only helped me to hone this book into existence but she was a constant source of encouragement, intelligent comment and gentle harrying.

To Keir, Clio and Roland, my children, I am grateful for the pleasure of their interest and encouragement and for reminding me that they are the best thing that I have ever done. And to my husband, Iain Hutchison, my thanks – for his humour, his optimism and his love, without which nothing would be possible.

I have had some dark moments over the last few years. It is never easy being in conflict with your own political party and to find yourself at such odds with many people whom you love and who have been such close friends. But my life has been the law and I believe in the law's role in safeguarding those who are vulnerable and marginalised. These are the people to whom my loyalty lies.

Roof it again. Batten down. Dig in.
Drink out of tin. Know the scullery cold.
A latch, a door bar, forged tongs and a grate.

Touch the cross-beam, drive iron in a wall,
Hang a line to verify the plumb
From lintel, coping stone and chimney breast.

Relocate the bedrock in the threshold.
Take squarings from the recessed gable pane.
Make your study the unregarded floor . . .

'Seeing Things' by Seamus Heaney

INTRODUCTION: THE RETREAT FROM PRINCIPLE

THE LAW IS the bedrock of a nation; it tells us who we are, what we value, who has power and who hasn't.

Almost nothing has more impact on our lives. The law is entangled with our everyday existence, regulating our social relations and business dealings, controlling conduct which could threaten our safety and security, establishing the rules by which we live. It is the baseline.

The message of this book is simple. Law matters. Civil liberties matter. The world is going through a period of dynamic change, presenting entirely new problems to nations and to the international community. Societies are now more complex and mixed than they were in the twentieth century; people are better educated, more demanding and much more conscious of their rights. The position of women has changed radically. Attitudes to homosexuality, marriage and illegitimacy have all altered. The rigid divisions between classes have broken down. The police and security agencies now have an incredible array of technology at their disposal, which makes questions of privacy now more pressing.

Law has a central role to play in this new landscape, and legal systems must learn to adapt or they will lose the confidence of the public. It is, however, vital that any process of modernisation or reform must take place against a backdrop of principle: a retreat from the rule of law, human rights and civil liberties is short-sighted and unthinkable. Yet such a retreat is precisely what is taking place. A quiet and relentless war is being waged on our rights. One individual encroachment on freedom can seem inconsequential or even justifiable if the reasons given are sufficiently seductive, but taken as a whole a pattern begins to emerge which should leave none of us feeling sanguine. The catalogue of inroads into our liberty is shocking when we take stock:

- Internment without trial for non-citizens suspected of terrorist links.
- Repeated efforts to reduce trial by jury for citizens on a whole range of issues.
- Retrial of those who have been acquitted, thus eroding the double jeopardy principle.
- Attacks on the independence of the judiciary.
- Serious limits on access to justice through cuts to legal aid.
- Abandonment of safeguards for accused people, which means increasingly placing previous convictions before the courts and shifting the burden of proof to the accused.
- Severe limitation on the right to silence.
- Imprisonment of more people for longer.
- 'Pre-emptive strike' incarceration of the mentally ill.
- Special punishments for the poor.
- Neighbourhood curfews against young people.
- Huge expansion in the powers of the state to invade privacy.
- Subversion of new technology such as telecommunications and DNA for undeclared ends.
- Co-option of the victims' movement and women's groups to expand state power.
- Streamlining of extradition processes so that British citizens can be removed abroad with insufficient protections.
- Incitement of public fear of terrorism, crime, asylum seekers, immigrants and paedophiles to justify serious erosions of civil liberty.
- Introduction of identity cards so that people can be monitored at all times.
- Removal of judicial review in asylum cases.

This is the roll-call as I write this book but the assault will undoubtedly continue unless we resist it.

It seems inconceivable that such attrition could take place as we enter a new millennium with the cry of human rights on the lips of leaders everywhere. Yet the twenty-first century brings the world to a new place. For many the century did not begin with millennium celebrations but with the horror of 11 September. We are now at a crossroads where either we take the opportunity to restate loudly the imperatives of a world based on law, consent and collective responses to threat, or we retreat from principle and perhaps return to the law of the mightiest as it existed before Hobbes and Thomas Paine, or a situation where there is a selective use of law in a universe dominated by a single superpower, the United States of America.

No one would doubt that institutions created 50 years ago, like the United Nations, should be shaken free of their bureaucratic ethos. Some international conventions should be revisited, not to be abandoned but to be made more effective in a changed environment. For example, we need one international agreement relating to terrorism; we need to recognise that new threats may come not from states but people and organisations who could acquire access to weapons of mass destruction; we should aim towards international collaboration to deal with the great divisions between rich and poor. There should also be clear protection for those fleeing persecution; well established, shared principles on asylum and more transparent policies on immigration. We should also seek ways to deal effectively with despots who abuse human rights. But change should not be an empty show of activity by governments, divorced from real values and principles, merely designed to signal to the public that something is being done. No programme of modernisation and reform should take place without the non-negotiables first being identified. Certainly we must modernise the law – but without jettisoning our core civil liberties and without an abrogation of human rights.

I am not attempting in this book to look at the whole world stage or to examine law's failures globally. If I did, British readers might take comfort and congratulate themselves on the success of our legal system. Instead I want to point out that our own retreat from human rights and civil liberties undermines the rule of law at home and internationally. Human rights activists abroad are devastated when they see us loosen the constraints we have placed upon the state because they lose one of their strongest arguments for change within their own systems.

It is important to recognise that law is cultural and located in deeper soil than many politicians understand. To be effective, laws have to resonate with the value system of a people and with their historic pulse. Harmonisation or homogenising of law even within

Europe poses problems when approaches come out of very different traditions. We should always be open about purposes if we are making changes to ease collaboration. The British establishment has a tendency towards secrecy. This stems from the arrogance of knowing what is good for the rest of us, a desire to avoid full frontal disagreements and a belief that more can be achieved by stealth. In the past few years there is no doubt that technician lawyers from the bureaucratic mould have thought that the failure of British juries to give a reasoned explanation for their verdicts affronted the approach taken in Europe, where all judgments must be explained with reasoning. This literalism about the meaning of due process was then married to other concerns to justify jury erosion. For example, lobby groups on child abuse can often be persuaded that the European system of trial would be more sympathetic because of the absence of the jury and non-adversarial methods. However, it is not the case that the inquisitorial system is more effective in bringing abusers to book. In the Nordic states it may be true because of a high level of sexual awareness and the sensitisation of judges but in many southern European countries the taboos around sexual abuse have yet to be lifted and their laws' failures are much more marked than ours. The factors that improve systems are awareness, good training and changes in court behaviour, not lowering of the standards of evidence or undermining the rules to get easier convictions or, indeed, looking to other systems for quick fixes. However, there is a momentum gathering around 'legal regime change' based on fallacious ideas that a new hybrid should be created, marrying up European civil law approaches to our own common law system without any thought as to the consequences.

Successful law builds on customs, habits and traditions. Law in democratic societies receives legitimacy from the consent of the people. But it should be informed consent, not a consent based on questionable facts or encouraged by fear. Greater harmonisation is not best achieved by bolting on legal rules which belong to a completely different system, or by jettisoning laws and practices which are the product of accumulated legal wisdom within a nation's tradition. We have to take account of domestic as well as international needs.

Citizens within a disturbingly uncertain world do seek areas of certainty. While 'the state' may be in the process of change the idea of 'the nation' is being reclaimed with enthusiasm all over the world; people are seeking the comfort of national identity, retiring into smaller and tighter groupings, exhibiting what the political commentator Michael Ignatieff calls 'the narcissism of minor difference'. People are easily alarmed by the idea that barbarians are at every gate, including their own, in the form of asylum seekers and criminals. As a result they are prepared to sacrifice a significant level of freedom and privacy in exchange for greater security. The temptation is for governments to read expressions of public fear and the willingness of citizens to make sacrifices as giving them *carte blanche* to rewrite underlying principles of law. Instead of making the political weather, devising policies for which they then seek public endorsement, governments increasingly see citizens as consumers, to be listened to through the marketing device of focus groups and to whom policy must be tailored. Government-as-product-supplier means pursuing market share, redesigning the brand and purveying policy on a 'what works' basis rather than principle. But there are some areas of our lives, including the justice system, which are not susceptible to market forces, where to rely on economic drivers or populist desires creates distortions, injustice and outcomes which take no account of the 'common good'. The move towards a market state may be unsettling but the move towards a market society, where all human interaction takes on a quasi-commercial spin, is even more alarming.

In Britain, the public worry greatly about crime and the police failure to catch criminals and about the treatment of victims within the system. Government should feel required to respond; but the current strapline of 'rebalancing the system in favour of victims' has all the hallmarks of the advertising agency. In fact, people are perfectly capable of hearing a more nuanced debate about crime and alternatives to prison, yet the great fear of governments is that they may hand their political opponents a trump card if they are not seen to be punitive.

Do we need to rebalance the court system by jettisoning well-established rules? And is the government looking for quick and cheap fixes for problems of crime which essentially need investment and a far more considered response?

Clearly, the law has to be fine-tuned to fit a changing world. If law is completely out of touch with public opinion it will be held in contempt; but if it were to respond to every tabloid editorial, it would become manipulated by our worst impulses. This two-step which the law has to conduct, of leading public opinion yet also reflecting it, is a difficult manoeuvre. While the system cannot dismiss public concerns out of hand, it is unconscionable for governments to pursue populist reform programmes which are based on a desire to appease important sections of the electorate at the expense of the most vulnerable.

Law reform is not easy and politicians must remember the reasons for protecting the marginalised. The safeguards for accused people are there for good reason and they have to keep being re-argued. Each new generation must learn why the system is balanced in the way that it is. We must always keep an eye to what an uneasy future might bring.

The removal of civil liberties by governments is not new. The public has always been sold erosion on the basis that the new restrictions are designed to convict the guilty, and that decent citizens have nothing to fear. The rhetoric of all governments who reduce rights is that they are doing so for good reason, in the interests of the people and to counter disruptive elements in society. And we, the citizens, can easily feel that the current move is all about the 'other' – terrorists, criminals, paedophiles, prostitutes, the mentally ill, Muslims, young blacks. We always think it is *other* people's liberty that is being traded, which somehow makes it all right. We do not realise that liberty is not divisible in this way.

In a globalised world we have to find a common language of law: not creating one universal system but establishing shared principles and fundamental values. All societies have legal systems but not all of them command international respect. The basic principles which should underlie any legal system are equality before the law, fairness and respect for human dignity. Yet, even our system can fail those tests. How else can we explain that five times more black people go to prison than white? That, while crime has reduced overall, prisons are now at breaking point? That the victims of child abuse and rape still fail to get justice? That encroachments on our privacy are taken for granted? That we are creating a hierarchy, deciding whose human rights matter and whose do not?

Over the last five years I have been involved in depressing and wretched disagreements with government over their retreat from civil liberties. On one of the occasions when I was called to book by a whip for voting against the government, he said to me that my concerns were completely out of touch with voters for whom it was 'just law'. Not anything serious like health or education or the economy. Just law. I left the meeting with my heart as heavy as a stone.

Yet law is at the heart of every inspired project to strengthen and protect peaceful human relations. Law matters. And if it is not too important to be left to lawyers, it is certainly too important to be left to politicians, whose desire for short-term gains makes them cavalier with long-term interests. As Seamus Heaney says in his wonderful poem 'Seeing Things', before any process of renovation, we should take stock and shore up the vital foundations. Law is a cornerstone. And unless we are prepared to revert to the continuous use of force, law is the supreme regulator. Whether nationally or internationally, it is the glue that holds together the constituent parts of society, a civilising force. Law is what makes the centre hold, the mortar that fills the gaps between people and communities, creating a social bond without which the quality of our lives would be greatly undermined. Just law is the invisible substance which sustains social well-being, moral consensus, mutuality of interest and trust. If we interfere with the principles which underpin law, fritter them away, pick them out of the crannies of our political and social architecture, restoration is impossible. Our only hope is an order governed by law and consent.

I

THE BENIGN STATE – A MODERN MYTH

WE ARE TOLD that today the state is increasingly 'benign', yet this is a modern myth.

'It is perhaps the biggest miscarriage of justice in today's system when the guilty walk away unpunished.' In a single sentence in a pronouncement on criminal justice reforms on 18 June 2002, the Prime Minister sought to overturn centuries of legal principle, a complete reversal of the approach to justice that every mature democracy in the world respects, whereby the conviction of an innocent man is deemed the greatest miscarriage of justice. Borrowing a soundbite from the Conservatives, Tony Blair explained that his legislative programme in criminal justice for 2002/2003 was 'to rebalance the system emphatically in favour of the victims of crime'.

Concern for victims is timely and right but it is not the same as justice. In this populist programme of reform the Prime Minister failed to appreciate that risking the conviction of the innocent does not solve crime. However, amongst his many attributes, the Prime Minister is not a liberal. He has brought a strong authoritarian streak to government and licenses his Home Secretaries to implement deeply illiberal policies. He wants more convictions and feeds the myth that the faults all lie in the safeguards currently provided for those who are accused.

I have spent my life in the law arguing as vigorously for the rights of those who suffer because of crime as for the accused. I like to think that it is this dual perspective which I can bring to the debate. Improving the system, particularly for women and children when they are complainants in cases of rape, sexual assault and abuse, has been a central plank of my work. But we must guard against campaigns to improve the position of victims by reducing defendants' rights. Maintaining that justice for victims can only be purchased at the expense of the accused is as dishonest as the claim that jurors are the source of miscarriages of justice. Those who claim that we need a levelling of the playing field between victims and defendants are deluding the public about the role of the state. The state is the real beneficiary when power is shifted.

Criminal practitioners, who prosecute and defend, know why civil liberties matter. The principles seep into the bones with every day in court. As Oliver Wendell Holmes, the American Supreme Court Justice said of his career: 'The life of the law has not been logic. It has been experience.' We know how devastating wrong judgments can be. Experience has taught us that rights are indispensable to democracy. However, it is not always simple to make the arguments, because civil liberties constrain the state from enforcing certain majority preferences. If you live by opinion polls and focus groups, they will tell you that there is too much crime, the system is soft on criminals and something ought to be done. There is nothing new in most of the public holding those views. But the risks attached to following the majority are precisely why protections and safeguards have to exist. Majorities can demand the death penalty, the majority resisted votes for women, the majority once thought slavery no bad thing. What is new is for a Labour government to mount such a wholesale assault on the underpinnings of the rule of law.

Why is this government attacking civil liberties? Are we seeing a case of wilful amnesia?

In the adversarial criminal justice system we do not start off from a position of neutrality. We start off with a preferred truth – that the accused is innocent – and we ask the jury to err on the side of that preferred truth, even if they think she probably did do it. I explain to juries that if they find themselves in the jury room saying I think she probably committed the offence or she may well have done it, they have to stop themselves short, because probabilities are not good enough. The criminal justice system is based on the fundamental value that it is far worse to convict an innocent person than to let a guilty one walk free. It is that fundamental value which is now in jeopardy.

In the wake of 11 September 2001, still reeling from the horrifying events, I received a telephone call from an American friend – a passionately liberal New Yorker – whose first words to me were, 'To hell with civil liberties.' It was a carefully designed curse because we both knew that surrender of such a household god could not come easily. However, in the face of such a devastating assault upon ordinary, decent people in her city, she wanted no truck with the cool reason of law and rights. She was still listening to the long moan of pain from those whose husbands, sisters, sons and lovers were killed. She wanted every young Arab on the turnpike rounded up and she boldly declared she was not averse to a bit of cruel and inhumane treatment if it drew intelligence of future attacks.

In debates about civil liberties the emotional power is always on the side of the victims. How could it be otherwise? We can all put ourselves in their place. Supporting civil liberties is not to stand in the opposite corner to victims, but to caution against the creation of yet more victims. But it is never easy to make the argument. People who have had no brush with the law find it hard to imagine what it might be like to be wrongly accused, how it might feel to be the young Arab on the turnpike; much easier to imagine the smoke filling our lungs, the heat of the flames on our skin, the crushing fall of masonry, the leap from skyscraper heights into oblivion.

The challenge for civil libertarians is that authoritarians always have the best rhetoric. They claim the songs, the flags, the pictures of the dead and the dying. They claim the role of protector and patriot. They promise a comforting paternalism to which we can surrender and they persuade us that the sacrifice of liberty is worth the warm blanket of security. They will not allow us to become victims of crime or terrorism. That is why Tony Blair chooses to come armoured to fight on behalf of victims. With the taste of fear in our mouths, who are we to mount a challenge?

The arguments for civil liberties are not the stuff of the easy soundbite and can be readily caricatured as the luxury of cushioned intellectuals. A discourse on rights can also seem cold, abstract and legalistic because that is law's purpose: to introduce reason and rationality into the passionate stuff of human existence. However, the arguments can seem bereft of the necessary empathy, unless you yourself are an Arab or black and closer to the risk of suspicion. Most often the prosecution case is the one that captures the headlines – woman raped in her own bed, child abducted, old lady robbed, wedding party bombed.

All of us agree that preventing terrorism, combating crime and securing justice for victims are clear moral imperatives; arguments about civil liberties and human rights are vulnerable to dismissive accusations of abstraction and vagueness when compared with the tangible effects of violence on the lives of real people. Yet the importance of that role of the law – providing us with a dispassionate set of rules when powerful emotions are unleashed – cannot be overstated. The whole function of law is to set an effective regime for the resolution of conflict, whether between nations or individuals or individuals and the state. Ill-considered laws introduced in the face of subversion or clamour about perceived levels of crime can be seriously counter-productive because they help to keep alive, and in some cases exacerbate, distrust amongst sections of the community. In fact, they make people less safe. But in periods of perceived emergency an Executive can use its control over a legislative chamber – particularly when a nation is in the grip of shock – to introduce repressive laws. An Executive with a large majority can translate its will into law with little challenge, by curtailing debate and by the liberal use of party whips who use every wile to persuade MPs to support the Executive line. Additionally, a climate can be created where any dissent is deemed unsupportive, soft on crime or terrorism; even unpatriotic.

One of the reasons why it is now so hard to engage popular support for the protection of civil liberties is that we are also losing our historic memory of the need for such safeguards. As the journalist Jenni Russell honestly conceded in a *New Statesman* piece on 6 October 2003, for at least twenty years she had felt that civil liberties was a specialised interest like golf or architecture, which she did not have to share. 'In the west, surely all the arguments and most of the battles had been won. I could leave it to groups such as Liberty to deal with the skirmishes.' It was attacks upon liberty in the USA that sensitised her antennae.

In the main, the lives of middle-class white people in the West have not been directly affected by anything that creates the visceral feel for what such protection really means. The Jews and the Irish, black people, homosexuals and other minorities may still have some sense of what it is like to be powerless and marginalised, at risk of being caught up in a backlash where the law may be your only shield. Michael Ratner, Director of the Centre for Constitutional Rights in the United States, and I both tell very similar stories when reminding an audience of the need to place a finger in the dike to stop the flood of state encroachment. We both recognise from experience how scapegoating can lead to injustice. As a Jew, Michael describes very powerfully the way that Jewish people were blamed for the Black Death in medieval Europe. A number of rabbis were rounded up and after torture swore on the Torah that they had poisoned the wells in many major cities. They were executed. It is now known that the plague was caused by a bacillus transmitted by rat fleas.

My Catholic story is about the Great Fire of London, when a rumour caught the public imagination that it was started by Catholics who were suspected of disloyalty to the Crown because of their overriding loyalty to Rome. A young man was arrested, interrogated, and after signing a confession was hanged, only for it to be discovered that he was out of the country when the fire began. Many foreigners were accused, Dutch Protestants as well as French papists, showing there is nothing new about a culture of blame.

But even minorities who have been at the receiving end of state abuse in the past have been drawn into the warm embrace of 'us' as distinct from 'them'. Even members of the 1960s generation which campaigned so vociferously for civil rights and liberties are themselves the authors of many incursions; now in positions of power, they are no longer able to identify with those who suffer. In the current backlash occasioned by the attacks on the United States one of the central barriers to securing support against encroachment on liberty is that fundamentalist Islam is so illiberal and alien ideologically that erstwhile liberal Western hegemony feels distinctly preferable to Islamic fundamentalist hegemony – at any price.

Collective memory about abuse of power, from the Tolpuddle Martyrs, the early trade unionists of 1834, to the use of 'Suspected Persons' laws against black people in the 1960s and '70s, fired a belief that civil liberties mattered. Knowledge of these battles gives us the power to say 'no' and the ability to give reasons for the rejection: if we do not understand past struggle we are much more likely to be taken in by newfangled dogma. In order to renew or reform effectively, you need to understand the old. If the urgently evanescent – tomorrow's headline, the next poll or the next vote – is all that matters, discernment drops away.

We should have learned from history that in the long run abuses by the state are far more dangerous to liberty and democracy than individual criminal conduct, dangerous and disturbing as that is.

The rule of law is one of the tools we use in our stumbling progress towards civilising the human condition: a structure of law, with proper methods and independent judges, before whom even a government must be answerable. It is the only restraint upon the tendency of power to debase its holders. History is dogged by the tragic fact that whenever individuals, political parties or countries become too powerful they are tempted to refuse to subordinate that power to wider and higher law. We have seen it recently with the United States picking and choosing when to apply the Geneva Convention.

The important thing for all of us to remember is that the rule of law is not simply what a government says it is: obeying rules that you have formulated yourself is no great discipline. In 2003 the Italian parliament passed laws which will have the practical effect of preventing Prime Minister Berlusconi from being effectively prosecuted for criminal charges: there is profound concern that the rule of law is being held up to ridicule, with a premier and his party making laws for their own protection.

It is precisely when there is high political fever that the controlling power of the judiciary and lawyers becomes so important. The judges have to curb governmental excess; they are the guardians of the rule of law, and it is crucial that they do not allow themselves to be co-opted by the Executive.

Democratic societies display their commitment to the rule of law in a number of different ways. In the area of crime this is done by having clearly defined laws, circumscribed police powers, access to lawyers, an open trial process, rules of evidence, the right of appeal and an onerous burden of proof shouldered by the state. The accused is presumed innocent. In international dialogue, adherence to such due process is urged upon every nascent democracy, and Britain and the United States are admired as model states where the rule of law is paramount. That is one reason why it matters so much when we are cavalier with the principles of justice and due process: every president or prime minister around the world sees parallels which would justify their abandonment of principle and process too.

The rules on inadmissible evidence have been virtually jettisoned in civil cases. However, in civil cases factual errors or prejudicial material will not result in the convicting of the innocent. Unfortunately, civil lawyers in the judiciary and in the government think the same abandonment of procedural rules can be transferred without any consequence into the criminal courts. The burden of proof in criminal cases is 'beyond reasonable doubt', while the burden of proof in civil cases is 'the balance of probabilities' – is it more probable than not that something happened?

This means that it takes more and better proof to convict a criminal defendant of a crime than to hold a civil defendant liable for financial damages. The reasons have always seemed obvious to me and they all return to the fact that the greater value of liberty has to be protected.

In the early days of New Labour I tended to think that, as with the economy, the government was anxious to show that it too could play hardball. Labour governments have always had to prove that they are as financially astute as Conservatives, that they can run the military and are not afraid of war, and when it come to law and order they really have to show their mettle, not so much taking no prisoners as taking lots of prisoners. So when I was feeling very pessimistic, I thought the tough talk on criminal justice was just a display of machismo by the boys with a touch of magisterial snobbery about criminal lawyers thrown in. The caravan of commercial lawyers who now inhabit the corridors of power grandly think that those who practise criminal law are lesser mortals. For them, no one would be a criminal lawyer by choice when the financial rewards are so much higher elsewhere in the law. Some of these men, although very familiar with financial deal-making, would not recognise a civil liberty if it jumped on them.

But rather than seeing the Labour stand as a symptom of wayward testosterone, I think something more complex is taking place. With the arrival of Margaret Thatcher as Prime Minister in 1979 we started to see the slow abandonment of the embedded liberalism that had been a diffuse presence in British politics since the war. There were shared assumptions about the value of the welfare state, about the necessary independence of the Civil Service, about protecting the special role of the judiciary, maintaining safeguards for those accused of crime, and imprisoning as a last resort. Cultural swings take time and the Thatcher assault upon liberalism is now coming into stark relief. Rather than reversing that pendulum, Blairism has accelerated the pace.

All governments can be seduced by power; it has a mesmerising quality. 'Power is delightful and absolute power is absolutely delightful,' as Lord Lester the great human rights lawyer has been known to say in parody of Lord Acton, an eminent judge who took a stand against the Executive. Those in positions of power can become short-sighted about the risks they are taking with other people's liberty. On top of that, no contemporary government identifies itself with a potentially oppressive state. Part of the problem is that our governors see themselves as the good guys. 'So what is all this old-hat business about the malign power of the state? People who share our values should know that we would not use our power to bad ends. Trust us.' They insist the new powers will be used rarely. I think they are good guys, but it is still essential to have serious restraints on power in place.

Once people 'are the state' or have their hands on the levers of the state they forget the basic lessons that safeguards and legal protections are there for the bad times which could confront us, when a government may be less hospitable, or when social pressures make law our only lifeline. Governments should always be looking in their wing mirrors for the spectre of what may follow them into office. They should never ignore the fact that once liberties have been lost they are almost impossible to restore.

We are supposed to be living in a post-modernist, post-ideological state where the potential for extremes of any kind has moved off the political radar. History has ended, as Francis Fukuyama asserted in his seminal book after the end of the Cold War, with victory to the free market and parliamentary democracy. In such a world, politics has apparently ended up in the centre ground, with parties only pitching slightly leftwards or rightwards. The Western state in such a configured world, our political class would have us believe, is benign and vanilla-flavoured, posing no real threat to any citizen that cannot be remedied by making an application to the courts under the Human Rights Act.

In his own writings on politics David Blunkett, the Home Secretary, presses this delusion. The state, he told us in the *Guardian* on Saturday, 14 September 2002, is not some bogey of which we should be afraid. It is in fact you and me, the community.

> I still find it surprising that so many people who consider themselves to be on the left of the political spectrum find themselves

> instinctively aggressive about the role of the state and insist on their absolute protection against it. Those of us on the centre left must remember that the state can be a positive force, empowering and enabling people to shape their lives, a collective vehicle to achieve progressive change.

Civil liberties, he says, are as much about the needs of citizens to be protected from crime and to live in security as about the civil liberties of a person accused. And of course he is right, but he is only partly right. The welfare state provided my family with housing as I was growing up, made it possible for me to have a higher education by giving me a grant, and is currently providing wonderful care for my elderly mother in Scotland. The rest of the United Kingdom may not be so lucky. Many of us regret that those life-enhancing opportunities are no longer available for a host of people. We can see the positive role that can be played by the state in the hands of visionary politicians – providing security and guarding our human rights. We must be protected from the predations of criminals. The state should prosecute wrongs with vigour but state power must be kept in check. When politicians say 'trust us' they usually speak in good faith but we should always exercise caution. We have to be sure that such trust is justified and not being sought for short-term gains.

In this brave new world New Labour in its early days was seeking to find a coherent philosophy. Anthony Giddens is a gifted sociologist and his defining book *The Third Way* published in 1998 provided an interesting analysis of social developments in contemporary Western societies: changes in the status of women, family forms, acceptance of homosexuality, the emergence of different class alignments. He advocated a rethink of social democracy to take account of these social shifts. Social liberalism and political pluralism will always have my support but justice and liberty ominously received little mention in these pronouncements. Instead, they implied a colonising of conservative policies and while this is clear in many policy areas nowhere has it been more vivid than in law and order. But there is no Third Way when it comes to liberty. It is a critique, not an intellectually coherent philosophy. Its major purpose seemed to be providing policy absent of ideology in order to extinguish any whiff of old-fashioned socialism.

Yet amongst the hype, Tony Blair at one time seemed to be on to something. There is a need to reposition left politics in a way that makes more room for civil society and the participation of citizens in the solution of social problems. Ways should be found to engage people. Markets, contracts, law and economic rationality provide a necessary but insufficient basis for the stability and prosperity of post-industrial societies; these must be leavened with reciprocity, moral obligation, duty to the community and trust. Political thinkers like Robert Putnam in his book *Bowling Alone* (2000) describe this as 'social capital', which has a large and measurable economic value. A nation's well-being as well as its ability to compete is conditioned by a single pervasive cultural characteristic – the level of social capital inherent in a society.

Traditionally Britain has been rich in social capital, with high levels of voluntary work, and lots of networks from the Women's Institute to youth groups to social clubs, all based on mutuality and trust. Britain has also been inventive in finding ways of drawing the public into participatory, civic roles as school governors, lay magistrates or volunteers at Citizens' Advice Bureaux, but the bank of such capital has to keep receiving deposits and better ways must be found of encouraging that engagement. I had once thought that an appealing plank of the Third Way might be about finding a new grammar for co-operative living, particularly in a society becoming more diverse, sharing less common history and where there is greater variety of religion and culture. As well as finding ways of creating 'bonding social capital' where groups come together on the basis of common value systems like religion or a common interest like a sport, we also have to find ways of creating 'bridging social capital' which cross the divides in society whether of class, race or religion. Yet the Prime Minister seems to have a very shallow idea of what democracy means. When Blair or Blunkett fumbles for ideas about community the best they can present are feeble or even alarming ideas about local communities electing chiefs of police or prosecutors, who would no doubt stand for election on the basis of their high conviction ratios. We never hear talk of strengthening local authority democracy, and too rare are the utterances about revitalising community by encouraging voluntarism.

When people trust government to act in their interests and for the common good, they themselves are happy to give something in return. When people join together in a common endeavour, they create the subsoil from which growth and development can emerge.

What Labour has brought to government which is so distinctive is a real commitment to end discrimination against women and minorities, whether black or homosexual; a widening of opportunities, and some serious and imaginative strategies for tackling poverty, not just at home but also in the developing world. This government has been brave and reforming on a number of fronts, from devolution to the minimum wage. Tony Blair's determination and skills have been central to the peace process in Northern Ireland. The introduction of the Human Rights Act is an impressive and powerful reform. The government is also trying to modernise institutions that have become moribund and creaky – and the legal system is certainly one of those.

However, New Labour's warm embrace of the market, and its endeavour to thin out the role of the state in the delivery of public services and welfare, calls upon it to chart new waters. Unfortunately, when Labour politicians do that they often slide into right of centre positions rather than progressive ones – Thatcherism with superior public relations. Instead of gathering people in, some at the top show a disdain for ordinary folk. As Professor Colin Crouch described it in his Fabian Society pamphlet in 2001, 'politics and government are increasingly slipping back into the control of privileged elites in the manner characteristic of pre-democratic times'. We saw it with the arrogant reluctance of key figures to embrace democratic reform of the House of Lords and we see it in the repeated efforts to reduce jury trial.

The government describes its vision as a shift away from the Big State, the nanny state, to the enabling state, which will put more choice in the hands of individuals. In the sweep of reform crossing all ministries, the challenge, as they see it, is to reduce to a minimum what is delivered by government; citizens themselves or the private sector can assume many of the roles formerly undertaken by the state. The state is to step back. However, if you want to draw people around a distinct and urgent common purpose your message has to be clear and inviting. Too often people are evicted from the processes when the message should be one of invitation to join in.

In the view of New Labour the welfare state had created its own vested interests. These now have to be tackled head on – and they involve not just the recipients of benefits but hospital consultants, public service unions, legal aid lawyers and state school teachers.

There is much that the public sector has to learn from the world of business but the mistake that is too often made is to expect public services to be businesses rather than businesslike, to be competitive in ways which are wholly inappropriate if the needs of the community are to be served. All the public services – the National Health Service, social, educational and legal services – are struggling to forge a new synthesis, a blend which is true to the public service ethos with its commitment to 'the public good' but at the same time exploits business as a model of effectiveness. Policy makers too often emphasise the side of strategies which devalue and sap public sector workers' commitment and morale. Increasingly, we hear accounts of teachers or doctors talking about 'getting out'. The same is true of legal aid lawyers or people involved in the running of the courts. Contemporary politicians often lose the awareness of how much our society depends on the public service ethos which motivates teachers, health professionals, social workers, policemen, and others who make choices to their material disadvantage because they want to do something good, something that makes a difference. It is this ethos which helps to earn public trust, esteem and support.

In New Labour's 'post-state' vision, criminal justice can look like another aspect of state provision, ripe for rebalancing, giving more power to the consumer, who is identified as the victim. The problem with this analysis is that the accused is also a consumer of the criminal justice system. Indeed, since the criminal justice system is a 'social good' belonging to us all, it does not lend itself to 'customer' analogies. The rhetoric of 'rebalancing the system' as between victims and the accused disingenuously presents the criminal trial as a contest between these two parties, thus denying the central role of the state. We are beginning to see a semi-privatisation of the criminal justice process, with the victim, the private individual, being used to disguise the reality of the powerplay.

This may not have been the original design but such distortions take place if reform is embarked upon without consideration of wider consequences. Successful reform is not possible without seeing that there are qualitative differences between substantive reform, which goes to the founding principles of the law, and process reform, which is about procedural change. The substantive changes can have disturbing implications for other parts of our carefully knit checks and balances and should be only undertaken with caution; alterations in procedure are of less consequence. But ministers behave as if there was no difference between the two.

The famous leaked documents between the Prime Minister and

his polling *meister*, Phillip Gould, revealed in July 2000, gave an alarming insight into the impulses behind policy. 'Find me an eyecatching initiative on crime', was the message. The preference always seems to be for highly visible projects which can be set up easily so that the leadership can be seen to be doing something. We saw this with the idea of frogmarching yobs to cashpoints for instant fines showcased in a speech in Germany on 30 June 2000, or the setting up of night courts in the 2001 manifesto so that anti-social louts can be dealt with immediately. Both notions provided catchy tabloid headlines and conveyed the notion of toughness but displayed a cataclysmic ignorance of social reality and practical problems. Drunks and misfits are unlikely to be proud possessors of the magical plastic. Those who have cards would have to be capable of remembering PIN numbers in their drunken state. Policemen immediately stamped on the idea, pointing out that they did not want to handle money or go in search of machines in the company of marauders.

As for night courts, the government's £5.4 million experiment starting in late 2002 in London and Manchester ended in disaster. It proved to be forty times more expensive to process a defendant through the night court than through the ordinary magistrates' court the following morning, and the Lord Chancellor's Department had to announce an abandonment of the scheme in January 2003.

Solicitors, magistrates and probation officers spoke out against the scheme, 'but they would, wouldn't they,' went the government mantra 'They have a vested interest therefore their views have no value.' The Prison Service also pointed out that the scheme was misconceived because receiving people into custody after sentencing late at night would compromise prison security. Having magistrates, clerks, the Crown Prosecuting Service (CPS), a duty solicitor, two security guards and probation officers all sitting around on overtime on the off chance of arrests was never viable.

Night courts were only introduced in New York because locking people up overnight or over a weekend without a hearing was a violation of their constitutional rights under American law. They also work there because of the institutionalised use of plea bargaining, which means most of those arrested will cop a plea to a lesser charge and walk off with a fine. Although instant justice may have great appeal, it often fails to be just. The vast majority of people likely to appear before night courts are those with drink or drug problems, people who are mentally ill or homeless, prostitutes, vagrants and those who are living on the margins. They will rarely be the terrible villains the public have in their mind's eye and their cases will often require adjournment for a pre-sentencing report to ensure that those in need of support do not slip through the net. Alternatively, an adjournment will be needed for the preparation of a defence if they have pleaded not guilty. It may be inconvenient but that is how a decent society handles criminal cases. Even lawyers from the United States cautioned against embarking on the project because of the conveyor belt quality of what takes place but no one would listen. In pure cost terms the whole scheme was crazy.

There is a restless quality about our Prime Minister. Modernisation has to mean constant activity. 'New, new, new, everything new,' he chirped on arrival in Downing Street in 1997. Almost 700 new criminal laws have been introduced in his period in office according to the Liberal Democrat MP Simon Hughes, who kept tally when he was spokesman on Home Affairs. Many of the new offences are completely unnecessary but the intention is to feed the perception that something is being done. There have been 16 Criminal Justice Acts so far and over 100 initiatives. (Khrushchev once described politicians as people who build bridges where there are no rivers.) Blair wants instant fines to curb crime – having to take people to court and go through due process is such a nuisance. Yet where reform is needed, for example in conspiracy to defraud, nothing is done because this area of law is complicated and unsexy. There are other much-needed reforms. Children under 14 should be taken out of the criminal justice system completely, however serious their offences, and an entirely new process invented which acknowledges that children who offend need serious help and understanding. The crime of corporate manslaughter should be sharpened, making company directors take responsibility for deaths caused by their corporations' criminal negligence, but governments are too afraid to upset the business world. Crown immunity should be abolished. The mandatory life sentence should be ended – if any political party has the gumption – and replaced with discretionary sentences reflecting the different aggravating factors in homicides and other serious crime. That way judges would not be required to pass the life sentence on battered women who kill, and Home Secretaries and tabloid newspapers would have no hand in saying what a life sentence should automatically mean. Instead we have the

Home Secretary seeking to hobble judicial discretion dramatically and impose mandatory minimum sentences for different kinds of murder to win public accolade.

The other folly is the tendency to use a megaphone for profoundly illiberal actions on crime and asylum in the hope that this will provide cover for saner, more liberal steps. We saw this with the amnesty for 15,000 asylum seekers followed quickly with the toughest crackdown yet, including the threat to take the children of refused asylum seekers into care. The problem with such strategies to appease the right is that they destroy a progressive climate so that creative measures become almost impossible. The Courts which have heard so much on the loudhailer about toughness will not be as inclined towards alternative sentences in the community. Asylum adjudicators caught up in this policy schizophrenia are uncertain which government steer to follow. Police officers tutored on anti-racism forget it all in the pressure to reach targets. Worst of all, decent ministers intent on outflanking the right become the right, moving so successfully into that political space that they lose their political as well as their moral compass.

Who pays for these follies? We do.

As I have said, one of the reasons for the existence of the criminal justice system is to create distance from the grief, anger and understandably vengeful human emotions felt by a victim. The decoupling of the victim's intimate engagement from the prosecution allows rationality and rules of law to intervene.

It is in cases where there are overwhelming feelings of repugnance that the system is most tested. All of us – police, lawyers, judges and juries – all feel our detachment challenged when confronted with brutal killing or terrorism or paedophilia, and it is in these very cases that the innocent are most at risk. Here is where most miscarriages of justice take place. The impulse for vengeance and the desire to punish is present in most of us: those who govern should recognise that succumbing to populist desires to avenge nourishes a dark part of our soul. Since most of us also recoil from the possibility of a person being punished for something they did not do, the instinct for justice should receive reinforcement.

An intemperate rhetoric of punishment, the promotion of the short term over the long term, a penchant for quippy formulations ('a nineteenth-century legal system unfit for the twentieth century', 'rebalancing the system in favour of victims', 'airy-fairy civil liberties') impoverish the debate and foster public nervousness that our legal institutions do not work at all. Which is not true. Attacking lawyers who speak out about civil liberties or human rights as 'fat cats', implying that they are only expressing a view out of self-interest, may just be a bit of debating society joshing but repeated relentlessly it adds to public distrust of the whole legal system. (It is especially rich coming from lawyers in government who were previously the fattest cats in the business.) Fulminating against judges when they give judgments against the government also feeds into public consciousness so that the entire system is ultimately seen as untrustworthy.

The majority of offenders are not trying to pull the wool over the eyes of courts. Indeed most plead guilty. According to the Department for Constitutional Affairs, formerly the Lord Chancellor's Department, 95% of criminal cases are disposed of in the magistrates' courts and most by way of guilty plea, and of the remaining 5% only a quarter end up in a contested jury trial. Of that quarter, over half of the defendants are convicted. Someone who is innocent will most likely insist on a contested trial. Of course, there are always a few guilty chancers who try their luck in a contested trial, as well as some people who cannot acknowledge their own wrongdoing because of shame or fear of the personal consequences. However, among the accused are those who are not guilty: these are the people we have to keep in our sights when we consider reform.

When an individual suffers a loss or is harmed in some way, they seek redress through the civil courts using the law of torts. In civil litigation the claimant and defendant come before the courts as equals, so here we *can* talk about balance as between the parties. Though it may not feel very evenly balanced if you, the individual, are suing some huge corporation. (If a government was really interested in a degree of 'rebalancing', here would be fruitful territory. However, it might mean upsetting some corporate friends.) In the civil courts, the remedy comes in the form of compensation, not loss of liberty.

The role of the criminal courts is different. Certain wrongs offend not just against the individual but against society as a whole, undermining the values and mores which bind the nation, putting at risk social order and community well-being. Citizens sign up to a social contract which means acknowledging that their suffering is not just a private matter but one affecting the community as a whole. Individuals are not entitled to punish or exact revenge. The state, however, is entitled to marshal all its resources to prove the crime in a court of law and is entitled to punish – subcontracting the determination of appropriate punishment to an independent judiciary. Because there is such inequality of arms between the state and the individual, the scales must be balanced in an accused person's favour. The state is like a supercharged juggernaut bearing down on a man with a bike. The protections and safeguards are just the provision of a crash helmet.

In the criminal courts the victim is a witness, a crucial and central witness for the state. So when the government talks about rebalancing the system, it is really about a rebalancing in favour of the state, giving more power to the state. That is the fraud in the government's rhetoric, the sleight of hand.

Solutions to crime are never easy. The government has been reasonably good at diagnosis of the problems, particularly relating to drug abuse and the new gun culture associated with it, but it is less good at the prescription. It should stop pursuing high-profile simplistic solutions which pander to the baying crowd, such as mandatory minimum sentences for gun possession, because they do not provide the flexibility judges [illegible] imprisoned for a long time and those who need treatment and diversion from crime. It also requires an attack on the social problems which are the seedbed of so much crime, even if this does not play so well with the right-wing press. The mantra which Gordon Brown invented for Tony Blair contains the answer: being tough on crime and on the causes of crime.

The justice system depends on memory.

The memory is an extraordinary repository. Witnesses arrive at court and recount events stored away in their personal mental computers. Their recollection is then prodded and tested by lawyers.

Sometimes people misremember or pick up pieces of information from other witnesses and unwittingly make them their own. Groups of people witnessing the same event remember it differently. Recall will be affected by the circumstances in which a memory is laid down. Quick sightings or swift incidents affect the quality of the retrieval. A singular event can be unforgettable but just as frequently a rare and horrifying happening can be so traumatic that solid recollection is impossible. Sometimes people suffer areas of amnesia occasioned by this trauma. Occasionally, the amnesia is wilful.

Even events which seared our national conscience are quickly forgotten. It is little more than a decade since the unravelling of a shocking catalogue of injustice in the cases of the Birmingham Six, the Guildford Four, the Maguires, the Tottenham Three, Stefan Kiszco, Judith Ward and a whole legion of men wrongly convicted at the hands of the West Midland Crime Squad. Then there were those wrongly convicted of the M3 murder, and the Bridgewater Three. I thought the lessons we learned were that terrible crimes and public outrage can place intolerable pressure on the police, prosecutors and experts to nail people. In such circumstances the innocent can be swept up in the maelstrom and if the safeguards are not strong enough they may be destroyed. Human beings are frail and corrupt, capable of mistakes but also capable of dishonesty and it is human beings who people the justice system. I thought we had also learned that by introducing special policing methods and accepting lower standards to deal with Irish terrorism, we had created a poison which leached into everyday policing conduct and contaminated the culture of policing and investigation. That was why we had seen such a spread of other miscarriages of justice in the 1970s and '80s. I thought we had learned that liberty mattered. Forcing people to lose large chunks of their lives to imprisonment for something they had not done was a crime by the state of such monumental importance it reinforced our belief that the system had to be weighted in such a way as to prevent this happening as far as was humanly possible. Where was Jack Straw? Or David Blunkett? Did Tony Blair read those columns of the newspapers? Surely as Shadow Home Secretary from 1992 till 1994, Tony Blair received the same letters I received from people in prison explaining urgently that something had gone badly wrong.

Non-lawyers always want to know how advocates feel about representing the guilty. The stock answer is that we do a professional job representing an accused as they would represent themselves were they schooled in the law, and it is not for us to sit in judgment but for the judge and jury. However, a powerful addendum is that it is actually nothing like as hard as representing someone you know to be innocent. That is the worst hell, when you are tormented by sleepless nights and stress-filled days.

We have to remind ourselves regularly about Giuseppe Conlon, one of the accused in the Maguire case, who protested his innocence to Cardinal Hume even on his prison deathbed in January 1980 and whose palpable honesty initiated the unravelling of so many of the Irish cases, including that of the Guildford Four. We should frequently bring to mind the image of Stefan Kiszco on his release in 1992. He was the mentally disabled man who was imprisoned for 16 years for the sexual murder of a young girl. He confessed but the police and Crown failed to disclose vital evidence that swabs taken from the victim showed active sperm whereas Stefan had a zero sperm count. His elderly, lone, widowed mother died before his release and he went mad inside: it's not much fun being a convicted child-killer in prison. He died just two years after his conviction was quashed. Judith Ward was also convicted of crimes she did not commit, serving 17 years in prison before her release on 11 May 1992: again evidence showing her mental vulnerabilities was never [illegible] Nadia Zekra, a middle-class mother of two teenage sons who was charged with blowing up the Israeli Embassy in July 1994. Halfway through the trial the case against her was dismissed by the judge. It became clear to everyone, including the officer in charge and counsel for the Crown, that she was innocent, a cruel case of mistaken identity, but not before she had spent months in Holloway Prison and virtually had a breakdown. She has never fully recovered.

Then there was Mary Druhan, a woman whose life fell apart when her husband died. She had ended up with a drink problem and homeless. She was convicted of setting fire to a dosshouse, causing the death of two other alcoholics. Again, mistaken identity and questionable forensic evidence led to a wrongful conviction. She spent 11 years in prison and came out blinking into the sun on 16 July 1999, unsure how to manage her money or even how to use public transport. I am haunted by the way in which she had become like a little girl in the prison environment, asking permission even to sit or stand.

It needs little imagination to realise the horror of what it means to be given a life sentence for a crime you did not commit. Before I ever dealt with the serious end of crime I spent many years in lower courts and there I also saw people wrongly convicted. The injustice had less grave consequences but it still sears the hearts of those who experience it. Let it also be clear that I saw guilty people unfairly acquitted, that other miscarriage of justice. This happened particularly in sex cases, a problem that has to be met with better investigation and evidence-gathering, better lawyering and judging. The answer is not to meet it with legal adjustments which risk wrongful convictions. That provides no peace for those who have been wronged.

Justice is not only a result; it is a process. People insist that the purpose of a trial is to get at the truth and, of course, truth is one of the important goals of the criminal trial but it is not its only goal. If the only goal of our trial system was to unearth the truth we would allow the torture of suspects, we would arrest mothers and lovers to apply pressure to the accused, we would allow the police any power they needed to gather evidence, even if it meant breaking into homes. For most of us these methods are unacceptable because they would make our lives intolerable. We also know that oppressive methods produce false outcomes. Our system balances inconsistent goals. We want truth but we also want to respect human rights. We want truth but we also want privacy, fairness, equality and finality. In the running of our criminal justice system we recognise that there is another set of values that has to be served as well as truth because they determine the kind of society we live in and the quality of our lives. This means that sometimes the guilty will walk free because there is insufficient evidence on which to found a conviction or they will walk free in order to send a message to the state and the police that their methods are unacceptable.

There are miscarriages of justice in the freeing of the guilty and in the convicting of the innocent. The problem is that, other than by better police investigation, there is no way of reducing the former without increasing the latter. Every time we play with the rules to make it easier to convict the guilty, we make it easier to convict the innocent. We also increase the violation of individual rights. One of the things I have learned is that you have to go on fighting for liberal values. The battle never stops. We can never reassure ourselves that they have finally been well and truly won.

2

THE CHALLENGE OF TERRORISM

> He that would make his own liberty secure must guard even his enemy from repression.
>
> Thomas Paine

WHEN GEORGE BUSH declared a war on terrorism in September 2001 he was not displaying his usual waywardness with the English language. The word 'war' was chosen with care. War offers opportunities not otherwise available even to a president. The climate becomes more favourable for repressive legislation which would never be countenanced during peacetime. Our own history is littered with examples. The xenophobic Defence of the Realm Act was ushered into being during the First World War and the War Powers (Defence) Act, which hugely expanded censorship and definitions of official secrets, arrived with the Second World War but remained on the statute book long after peace returned.

Back in 1974 after the horror of the Birmingham bombing, a Labour government created Prevention of Terrorism legislation which was supposed to be a 'strictly temporary measure', but it was never repealed. It gave the police extensive special powers to intern without trial, to exclude people from mainland Britain even if they were citizens, to question suspects for up to four days without access to lawyers and to spy upon a whole community. It ran a railroad through our basic liberties and protections but it was such a boon for the powers that be that they clung to it like molluscs. No matter the complexion of government, they all fell in love with the idea of emergency powers. Bold Labour in opposition promised to repeal the Act and it did. However, what was put in its place was even more offensive to civil liberties and even more draconian, with district judges able to authorise detention for up to seven days on far more relaxed criteria. And although now there is access to lawyers, inferences of guilt can be drawn from silence even if this course is taken on the advice of a lawyer. The presumption of guilt permeates the Terrorism Act 2000. It enshrines a reversal of the burden of proof, with accused persons having to show beyond reasonable doubt that they did not have items for terrorist purposes. Suspected terrorists can now be stripped of their citizenship and under the latest Criminal Justice Act, 2003, police powers are being extended yet again so that people can be held for interrogation without charge for up to 14 days. The 'abolition' of the right to silence, which entitled people to refuse to answer questions and which was opposed by Labour in opposition, has been extended. It used to be inapplicable to children under 14 but even children can now have an adverse inference drawn from their failure to answer questions. Ministers who had been champions of civil liberties themselves fell silent on the subject once in office.

Of course, principles are easy until they are put to the test. The phenomenon of terrorism is one of the great challenges to the rule of law. In the face of such provocation the temptation to erode civil liberties is great but this is precisely the repression terrorists seek to stimulate, and if great care is not taken, emergency measures to combat terrorism end up undermining the very freedoms we value.

Bad law is counter-productive. It often keeps alive and in some cases exacerbates the antagonisms which underpin political violence. It is widely believed now that internment in Northern Ireland was the best recruiting sergeant the IRA ever had. Repressive special laws also make it easier for those who have bombed and maimed to claim to be political prisoners rather than criminals because they have already been given special treatment by the state.

Yet we rarely see that there is another cost. Counter-terrorist laws giving the police and courts special powers set up a contagion which seeps into the bloodstream of the legal and political system. They play havoc with the mindset of police officers and people working in the legal system, even lawyers and judges. As a result standards shift and we begin to lose sight of liberty's meaning in areas of criminal justice quite unconnected with terrorism. It is no accident that so many miscarriages of justice took place back in the 1970s and early

'80s, especially in the West Midlands and the Metropolitan Police, and they were not all related to subversion. These forces dealt with the bulk of terrorism cases and a culture was created that fostered a particular kind of policing while a neglectful, cynical political class turned its back on what was happening.

One of the reasons why we are seeing a more general assault upon civil liberties is because our guard has been so effectively lowered over the years in response to our own experiences of subversion. Over three decades, under governments of different hue, we have seen the steady attrition of our liberties, largely because of the situation in Northern Ireland. We have become used to a person having fewer rights and we have accepted unprecedented inroads into our own privacy. Fear has lulled our vigilance.

For example, the right to silence was emasculated first in Northern Ireland in 1988 after Britain was hauled over the coals at the European Court of Human Rights for using inhumane methods of interrogation. The right to silence was founded on the basis that it was for the state to prove wrongdoing, not for accused people to provide evidence against themselves. The powers that be felt that if securing confessions was going to be hampered, remaining silent had to be punished by allowing courts to assume the worst of those who claimed it. The problem is that many people do not speak out because of fear that their family will experience reprisals if they do. The erosion of the right to silence was then extended into the general criminal domestic law of the UK in the Criminal Justice and Public Order Act 1994. It is now possible for a court to draw an adverse inference from the silence of an accused either during interrogation or at trial in any criminal case. The arguments for extending detention without charging to 14 days in terrorist cases is that the suspects are now foreign and inquiries take time and interpreters are needed and computers have to be disembowelled for evidence. All are reasons that could apply in many drug importation cases, which means that in the near future we are also likely to see a creeping of these special measures into the system as a whole.

This is not to say that a democratic society has to roll over when bombs are placed in public buildings or politicians are assassinated. Of course, the state can respond to political violence by the enactment of special laws or the modification of certain evidential rules; it would be perverse if a democratic nation had to prove its liberal bona fides by allowing itself to be destroyed by its enemies.

Justice Jackson of the US Supreme Court made the same point decades ago, saying that Americans should not allow their constitution and their shared sense of decency to become 'a suicide pact'. However, any changes or responses to terrorism which are introduced must conform to the rule of law.

Law is there to provide an effective regime for the resolution of conflict even in the heat of passions. As Lord Atkin, one of our most senior judges, famously explained during the Second World War, 'amidst the clash of arms the law is not silent'. But when some terrible event like the destruction of the Twin Towers has taken place, it is tempting to introduce repressive laws, with an undertow of hostility towards anyone who seeks to question the rush to legislation. The climate can silence many who are anxious not to be seen as appeasers or as sympathisers with those who are perpetrating the outrages.

Systems of law are many and various but it must be possible to identify a set of principles which would define the investigation of terrorism and the detention and trial of terror suspects, even after an event as horrifying as the attack on Manhattan or the bombing in Bali and the consequent loss of lives.

The concept of the rule of law has an evaluative as well as a purely descriptive dimension. It is supposed to have started its life here in England in the sixteenth century with Lord Coke insisting that even the King, the sovereign lord, is subject to law. However the historian GM Trevelyan saw the roots of the rule of law and jury trial in Magna Carta: 'No freeman shall be taken or imprisoned . . . or exiled or in any way destroyed . . . except by the lawful judgment of his peers or the law of the land.'

Not surprisingly, other countries which adopted common law systems, usually as a result of colonialism, absorbed these notions. However, the central theses that those who govern should not be outside law's disciplines and that there should be restraint upon the arbitrary use of power was very compelling, even beyond common law shores. By the twentieth century these had become adopted as central pillars of all democracies. Human rights activists across the world use our system as the model.

Democratic societies display their commitment to the rule of law in a number of different ways. In the area of crime this is done by having clearly defined laws, circumscribed police powers, access to lawyers, an open trial process, rules of evidence, right of appeal and an onerous burden of proof shouldered by the state. In international dialogue, adherence to such due process is urged upon every nascent democracy.

Politicians the world over pay lip service to the rule of law but half the time it is a formulaic mantra, meaning we pass laws and the courts uphold the laws we pass. Even sophisticated democratic nations, which recognise that courts should check the power of the state, have reservations about what that should mean when the state itself is under threat.

In our contemporary world, the rule of law has to mean more than the requirement that laws be clear and precise and that procedures are available for every eventuality. Although countries assert their commitment to the principle of 'fairness', in different countries the notion of 'fair' has different meanings. There is no single judicial space. Some countries think nothing of holding people for years before trial. Others provide such low levels of legal aid that practical justice is denied. Some systems have jury trials; others do not. But the crucial fact is that the United States and Britain are held up as the paradigm.

In any real debate about the response to terrorism the 'wicked issue' invariably arises of when the use of violence might be permissible and morally legitimate. It is an issue which cannot be ducked. Certain types of resistance may be morally right and it is unhelpful to label all political violence as terrorism. However, it is impossible to reconcile the different perspectives on who is or is not a freedom fighter and whether certain forms of political violence are legitimate.

Scholarship on the nature of the 'just war', which has its roots in the theology of Thomas Aquinas and St Augustine, makes a distinction between *ius ad bellum* – the right to wage war – with *ius in bello* – the rights and duties of those engaged in war, whether it's a just war or not. We do not have to be talking about formal wars to recognise that the way in which a military campaign or armed struggle is conducted is a separate moral question from whether the war or struggle itself is justified. Many may have sympathy with a cause but abhor, for example, the use of suicide bombing on a civilian population. Whatever arguments groups may have about the legitimacy of their grievances they are usually at their most exposed on the issue of *ius in bello*. People reach their own opinions one way or the other on the morality of the goals of different political organisations or their historical or cultural claims to legitimacy. There will always be disagreements about political struggles but we ought to be able to secure consensus on the fact that too often struggles are conducted on a battlefield strewn with innocent victims.

The moral principles of *ius in bello* do not apply to violent subversive groups alone. The state too is duty bound to behave in morally consistent ways, whether or not the decision to defend itself is morally defensible. Recent international politics is littered with examples of states that have engaged in terrorist campaigns to preserve their own power. Huge attention is given to subversive terrorism, yet in fact the majority of innocent victims of indiscriminate political violence worldwide in the past forty years have been killed by state forces. States confronted with terror all too often respond by becoming terrorists themselves.

If we apply *ius in bello* to the liberal democratic state, the moral dimension is even greater than elsewhere. Governments that claim a strong moral distinction between their authority and that of the subversive groups that oppose them must be judged by higher standards than their opponents. What distinguishes the state from the subversive in a liberal democracy lies in the existence in the former of an independent rule of law to which the authorities are [illegible] This [illegible] mil[illegible] and [illegible] ntal [illegible] uire [illegible] ot b[illegible]

[illegible] mer to the law of human rights. In most liberal democratic nations, the written constitution of the country concerned sets out the basic principles by which all state agencies are explicitly declared to be bound. Most such documents include a code of basic human rights, and the authorities are only permitted to depart from this code in the narrowest of circumstances. In these countries, therefore, the idea of the rule of law is inseparable both from the written constitution and from the courts where it is further defined. In the UK, where there is no written constitution, we look to the common law and now to the Human Rights Act. International conventions and protocols also serve as our touchstones.

Britain has had experience of terrorism. The UK should have learned through her own mistakes in Ireland that taking shortcuts with the rules leads to miscarriages of justice, fuels distrust, and can make a whole community feel suspected and undermined. My fear is we are now repeating this process with those who are Muslim immigrants. As I have pointed out, the UK was taken before the European Court for Human Rights in the case of *Ireland* v. *United Kingdom 1978* for the cruel and inhumane treatment of suspects in interrogation centres in Northern Ireland and found wanting. Police put hoods over the heads of suspects, depriving them of light and disorienting them. They were made to stand for hours on end against walls, limbs outspread. They were beaten and humiliated in our efforts to obtain intelligence. The government extended periods of detention for the purpose of interrogation, it allowed no access to lawyers and as a result a whole plethora of confessions were made under duress and there were consequent wrongful convictions. Having had our eyes opened to all this, the UK should be in a position to lend experience to other countries about what not to do and it should be working with them to establish ground rules. Perhaps our American cousins dealing with prisoners in Guantanamo Bay should be told these stories as they quiz Taliban suspects to establish Al-Qaida links.

In Northern Ireland, the British allowed intelligence operations to get completely out of control, as the Stevens Inquiry showed when its report was published on 17 April 2003. A dirty war was waged during the 1980s and '90s in which a covert army unit and elements in the Royal Ulster Constabulary passed details of suspected IRA members to loyalist death squads. Amongst those killed was Pat Finucane, a Catholic solicitor, who was shot in his own home in front of his wife and children on 12 February 1989 but was later shown to have no connections with the IRA. Intelligence dossiers were compiled full of misinformation on the basis of which many innocent people were assassinated. The inquiry, which lasted for four years, was at times blocked by sections of the security forces, and the office used as the inquiry centre, where confidential papers were stored, was mysteriously burned down. The investigations uncovered widespread collusion between special branch police, who were responsible for running agents, and loyalist paramilitaries. The special branch totally ignored the rule of law and operated by its own rules. The experience does not inspire total confidence in the integrity of the intelligence services and, while it may only be 'rogue elements' which behave in unacceptable ways, it is a cautionary reminder of why open justice and high standards of proof are essential. The other concern, when we think of the Stevens Inquiry, should be that intelligence reports can be used for political ends. In 2003, the débâcle over the Iraq war, as demonstrated in the Hutton Inquiry, suggested that intelligence reports can be presented in a particular way for maximum impact or 'sexed-up' when it is deemed to be in the interests of government.

With others in the international community we should be settling on principles which are inviolable even in the face of terrorist atrocities, when rational consideration is in danger of being overwhelmed by the desire for revenge.

Preventing terrorism is a moral imperative. We only have to think of the bombing at Omagh and the emotions surge back. In 1995, Professor Conor Gearty and his colleague John Kimbell of King's College, London reviewed emergency legislation in *Terrorism and the Rule of Law*, a Civil Liberties Research Unit publication. The new laws had been introduced in the UK to deal with the 'Irish Troubles'. Gearty and Kimbell argued that the rule book could not be thrown away just because we felt so incensed by the horror of terrorist acts, and they evolved the three principles of equality, fairness and human dignity as the objective and immutable yardsticks against which the legitimacy of any special legislation must be judged. Together these principles represent the basic common denominator of a civilised rule of law and in my view they encapsulate the idea of justice. Even in the environment of international, border-crossing terrorism, they remain the best set of principles. Yet within a couple of years of the creation of our own Human Rights Act, inaugurating a new culture of rights, the government was prepared to trim the whole concept.

The clearest illustration of this is the power vested in the Home Secretary to detain foreign nationals indefinitely without charge or trial, a measure that the government pushed through a hesitant parliament in December 2001. This is plainly incompatible with human rights obligations, particularly Article 5 of the European Convention and Article 9 of the International Covenant on Civil and Political Rights, which entitle people to an open and fair trial. The government claimed a derogation or exemption from Article 5.

Derogation is permitted only in time of war or other public emergency threatening the life of the nation and even then only to a minimum extent and consistently with other international obligations. (In Belgium, Germany and Italy, men have already been put on trial and convicted of offences connected to 11 September and Al-Qaida without any need to derogate from the European Convention on Human Rights.) Mr Justice Andrew Collins sitting in the Special Immigration Appeals Commission held that the attempted derogation failed because it was not only discriminatory – failing the test of equality before the law – but also disproportionate. He did not uphold an additional argument that there was no state of emergency in the UK (although it was hard to see that Britain was in the sights of Islamic terrorists at that time whereas it most certainly is now as a result of support for the war in Iraq).

This brave decision, however, was overturned by the Court of Appeal and at the time of writing the case is journeying to the House of Lords. The judiciary and lawyers have a crucial function when the political temperature goes up. The judges have to curb governmental excess; they are the guardians of the rule of law, and must not allow themselves to be co-opted by the Executive. Detention without trial can become punishment and only judges should be able to punish.

During the Second World War a regulation was introduced with no regard to civil liberties at all and no effect whatsoever on the war. It was designed by the then Home Office to confer absolute power on the Home Secretary to detain without charge or trial anyone who in his opinion needed to be prevented from acting in any manner prejudicial to public safety. Most of the people detained posed no threat to security and one of them brought a case all the way to the House of Lords. Jack Perlsweig was a Jewish émigré, who had changed his name to Robert Liversidge to avoid anti-semitism. A successful businessman, at the outbreak of war he had joined the airforce; he later became an officer. Because he had not applied in his original name and had some unsavoury business connections before the war, he was detained under the regulation, 18b. In the case of *Liversidge* v. *Anderson* the judges in the House of Lords decided they were powerless to intervene, however unreasonable the Home Secretary might have been. Lord Atkin – whom I have already quoted – dissented, pointing out that the judges were supposed to be the lions under the British throne, protecting liberty and justice. In his view this regulation turned them into nothing more than 'mice squeaking in the Home Office', a role for the judiciary which some subsequent Home Secretaries have tried to entrench.

Sometimes, judges can collude unwittingly in the erosion of the rule of law. They can do so by allowing themselves to be appointed to quasi-judicial bodies which adjudicate in camera on issues which should be in the public domain. In this position, they become unable to give due regard to the principles which should be the muscle within the rule of law because, unconsciously, they identify too readily with the state or the government of the day, and the balancing of human rights considerations against those of state security becomes impossible. Fortunately some judges resist.

An article in the *New York Times* on 2 September 2002 started: 'You want an American hero? A real hero? I nominate Judge Damon Keith of the United States Court of Appeals Sixth Circuit.' Judge Keith had led a three-judge panel in Cincinnati, which gave a judgment that clarified and reaffirmed some crucially important democratic principles that have been in danger of being discarded after the terrorist attacks on 11 September 2001. The opinion was a reflection of true patriotism, a twenty-first-century echo of a pair of comments by John Adams nearly two centuries ago. 'Liberty,' said Adams, 'cannot be preserved without a general knowledge among the people.' And in a letter to Thomas Jefferson, Adams said 'Power [illegible] eck.'

[illegible]

The administration argued that opening up the hearings would compromise its fight against terrorism. Judge Keith and the two concurring judges in the unanimous ruling took the position that excessive secrecy compromised the very principles of free and open government that the fight against terror was meant to protect. 'Democracies die behind closed doors,' wrote Judge Keith. The court accepted that there might be points within hearings when the administration could argue for the court to go into camera but that should be decided on a case by case basis.

That case shifted the climate of silence in the United States where people have felt afraid to speak out about what was happening to their legal system; there is now much more open debate. Judge Keith was lauded as a hero; we have our equivalent heroes, reminding government that judicial independence is necessary to curb abuse of power and to protect the rights of those who might be unpopular and marginalised. Asserting their independence may make the judiciary unpopular at times but that is their crucial function in a democracy.

Another fundamental denial of rights inherent in the new anti-terror laws is the prevention of proper representation by lawyers. The lawyers in these cases are not having an easy time. It is the duty of lawyers to assert their clients' rights without fear or favour, challenging infringements of rights through the courts. A detainee can appeal against the Secretary of State's certificate that he or she is a threat to security to SIAC (the Special Immigration Appeals Commission), which can confirm the detention or nullify it, but detainees and their legal representatives are excluded from any part of the hearing which deals with the intelligence on which the detention order has been made. If they are denied sight of the reasons for the Secretary of State's decision and cannot test whether the decision is reasonable, the process cannot be just. Nor can there be real legal representation if lawyers are not given access to the evidence against their clients.

In 1984 Michael Mansfield and I represented a member of MI6 called Michael Bettany on charges of attempting to give secret information to the Soviets. There was material which the security services did not want defence lawyers to see: we were tempted to take it personally but we were assured by the then Attorney-General that he too was being denied access because it was so hyper-sensitive; a claim that seems untenable now. The original charges had to be dropped because Mike and I went to the Bar Council and indicated that we felt professionally compromised because our ability to properly defend was being undermined. In truth our stance had not mattered a jot, because even with the reduced charges Bettany got 23 years, which is probably precisely what the Lord Chief Justice Lord Lane had in mind from the outset.

Under the current anti-terrorist arrangements a state-approved counsel is appointed to represent the interests of detainees. This is someone who has been security-vetted and is deemed trustworthy with classified information. The government saw two routes to the fulfilment of their duty to allow counsel of choice. Either they would mount a challenge to individual lawyers they did not trust, or they could allow detainees to have their lawyers of choice but with no access to the sensitive evidence. Behind closed doors concerns were voiced that Muslim accused might choose Muslim lawyers whose loyalty to Islam might override any loyalty to the British state, but it was recognised that it would be highly inflammatory if the government was forced to voice such fears publicly.

One of the vetted special advocates just happens to be someone who in our youth took me to a Socialist Workers' Party meeting. At the meeting, when the book came round for attendees to give their names and contact numbers, I innocently entered my details and then noticed that my companion had put down a name that was completely fictitious. I was amazed when he explained that he never used his real name for anything political, 'just in case'. Now I think, 'just as well'.

The moment the specially appointed advocate sees 'closed' material which has come from the intelligence services and is secret, she is forbidden by statute to speak to the person whose interests she represents, who is the one person who may be able to shed some light on the information, showing it is bogus. This means that the special advocate is put in an absurd position. Ben Emmerson QC, [illegible] that the judges and the professional bodies like the Bar Council should be taking up with government.

As of May 2003, 16 non-UK nationals have been arrested and detained under Anti-Terrorism Crime and Security Act 2002. The names of all the non-UK nationals are covered by a UK contempt of court ban and cannot be published. Two volunteered to be deported. Another has been released. One of the remaining detainees, Mahmoud abu Rideh, a Palestinian refugee and torture victim, has been removed from Belmarsh to Broadmoor Psychiatric Hospital as he is suffering from post-traumatic stress disorder and is seriously unwell. Psychiatric authorities at Broadmoor recommended against

Rideh's transfer to them because in their considered opinion detention in a high security mental hospital is not conducive to his recovery. This revival of internment creates a hierarchy of human rights, where a proper trial and humane conditions are reserved for the citizenry but are not available for non-UK nationals.

All those arrested appealed against their detention and the hearings were held in May 2003. None of the detainees – save Abu Qatada, a Muslim cleric accused in the media of inciting anti-West sentiment and Islamic jihad against the US and whose public arrest made secrecy redundant – could be named. Not only were the press excluded from chunks of the process when intelligence officers gave evidence but so too were the defence lawyers. Abu Qatada's case was outlined by government lawyers as showing that he supports the overthrow of Arab governments by violent means and the establishment of Islamic states in their place. Apparently there is video evidence of him giving sermons to this effect as well as evidence of links with terrorist groups. Under the Terrorism Act 2002 it is an offence to incite or plot the overthrow of foreign governments so it is hard to understand why he has not been charged and put on trial.

A judgment upholding the decision to detain without trial or charge was given by Special Immigration Appeals Commission C on 30 October 2003. The judgment acknowledged that 'the standard of proof is below a balance of probabilities' and would not stand up in an ordinary court of law but explained that Parliament had passed this legislation because of the nature of the risk being alleged by the state. The three judges criticised two MI5 terrorism experts, saying that they were too quick to draw conclusions or inferences in assessments and that they did not have detailed knowledge of the political background in Algeria or Egypt or of various terror groups. An MI5 officer claimed to be unaware of common and public allegations about ill-treatment in Guantanamo Bay. Yet the judges said that the questionable aspects of the intelligence did not diminish the evidence!

In 2001 Lord Steyn, one of our most distinguished Law Lords, was clear in his view that the suspension of Article 5 'so that people can be locked up without trial when there is no evidence on which they could be prosecuted is not in present circumstances justified'. There's a hero.

How can the detention of suspected terrorists under broadly drafted powers, seriously restricted procedural protections and very limited recourse to the courts be regarded as consistent with the rule of law? This is arbitrary preventive detention and the very antithesis of legality. It is interesting that the Australian High Court declared a similar preventive detention measure invalid because it turned the court into an appendage of the Executive.

In December 2003 Amnesty International published a damning report on the UK detention of non-nationals without trial, calling it the British 'Guantanamo Bay'. The report highlighted that the Home Secretary refused to rule out relying on intelligence material obtained by torture around the world in his decisions about who is detained. Amnesty was supported by a battalion of Bishops, other religious leaders as well as Mathias Kelly, Chairman of the Bar Council, all of whom pointed out that this internment offends every notion of justice, equal treatment of people and the rule of law, and called for the detained men to be put on trial or released without delay.

Ever since the events of 11 September 2001, the question has been posed as to whether a new legal regime needs to be invented to engage with phenomenon of international terrorism. Indeed it was claimed by the American Deputy Assistant Attorney-General, John Yoo, that the administration was seeking to do precisely that – create a [illegible] whether [illegible] upon [illegible] appropri[illegible] identifiable [illegible] Prof[illegible] article in [illegible] between a [illegible] group [illegible] constitutional lawyer, Phillip Bobbitt, in his book *The Shield of Achilles* published in 2002, argues that Al-Qaida is tantamount to a virtual state, which is why it should be treated as such in the war against terrorism.

> The multinational terror network that Osima bin Laden and others have assembled is a malignant and mutated version of the market state. Like other states, this network has a standing army; it has a treasury and consistent source of revenue; it has an intelligence collection and analysis cadre; it even runs a rudimentary welfare programme for its fighters, and their relatives and associates. It has a

> recognisable hierarchy of officials; it makes alliances with other states; it declares wars.

It sounds to me more like a multinational corporation.

Whether or not Al-Qaida operates like a virtual state, I remain to be convinced that a completely new legal regime for international terrorism is required. However, I do acknowledge that new procedures are necessary. Any state confronted with terrorism must decide what existing legal regime it is applying: the laws of war or the laws of the criminal justice system of its own nation. What cannot be acceptable is the creation of *ad hoc* legal regimes, pieced together in the face of events (as we have seen in Guantanamo Bay), or the passing of anti-terrorist legislation against no backdrop of principle. Severely criticised after the Bali atrocity for its failure to act against extremists, Indonesia quickly passed new anti-terrorist laws; what do we think that will mean in a place like Indonesia, where the rule of law is a fragile concept? After the UK and the USA passed their recent legislation curtailing civil liberties and violating human rights Australia, Belarus, China, Egypt, India, Israel, Jordan, Kyrgyzstan, Macedonia, Malaysia, Russia, Syria, Uzbekistan and Zimbabwe all followed suit. In many of those countries the word 'terrorism' will be interpreted very liberally.

Can terrorism be defined? Different legislation in different jurisdictions has attempted the task but finding an acceptable definition is very difficult. Until there is an internationally recognised and sufficiently restrictive definition, it will be hard to have confidence that struggles for self-determination and other political activities will not be wrapped up in accusations of 'terrorism'. Of course, even where there is a legitimate struggle against oppression or movement for self-determination, there are always means which are impermissible: the necklacing of informers in South Africa, where petrol-filled car tyres were placed around their necks and set alight, or the suicide bombings in Israel, where young Palestinians join a civilian gathering and cause mayhem as well as their own death – these are never the legitimate conduct of struggle.

Terrorism is not and never has been in itself a criminal offence. However, those who commit terrorist acts are committing acts which fall within the definitions of crime. They commit murder, attempted murder, criminal damage – the list is endless. But, unless we accept the thesis of Phillip Bobbitt, as non-state actors they are not waging wars in the sense acknowledged by present international law. That body of international law should only be changed with the consent of the whole of the international community. To develop some hybrid process in which the best of both legal regimes is surrendered is to undermine the values for which civilised nations stand. What I do accept is that the sacrosanct nature of national sovereignty must be revisited in light of border-crossing terrorism. If a nation like Afghanistan is providing sanctuary for terrorists and refuses to take steps to extradite or deal with their presence then the international community is entitled to take action but only where there is international consensus, not in the form of unilateral assaults on a neighbour.

Many liberal democracies have faced the dilemma of how to deal effectively with political violence and most have sought to stigmatise such actions by using the criminal label. That was an option open to the United States. If this is the adopted course, we have to establish the extent to which a state confronted with terrorism can and should depart from normal legal safeguards, without jeopardising the essence of the rule of law.

In dealing with terrorism the police and intelligence services need to be em[illegible]d. [illegible] would resist the creation of tougher laws coupled with [illegible] surveillance. Controlling the flow of money [illegible] individual. The same is [illegible] organised crime. But getting [illegible] to work together on this is not [illegible] Security Council Resolution [illegible]73 [illegible] September, which [illegible]ed that all [illegible] money laundering for terrorist purposes, it is still proving a real challenge to translate that into reality. While most banks will no longer accept briefcases full of unexplained notes over the counter, unmasking phoney companies or charities set up to provide cover for money transfers requires the sort of transparency which sometimes meets opposition even from democratic countries. Governments are often loath to turn on a spotlight which may illuminate their own arms trade, or the financing of covert activities abroad by intelligence agencies, or the tax avoidance activities of their largest financial donors. The super-rich with their offshore accounts, tax havens and sophisticated methods of tax avoidance are unhappy about greater scrutiny of money transfers, trust funds and companies in Liechtenstein. They want guarantees that intelligence-gathering and anti-terrorist initiatives should be 'outcome specific' so that any uncovering of fiscal irregularity will not be used against them.

Eighty-four countries have still failed to legislate against the financial support of terrorism. There is a particular sensitivity in many countries about investigating charitable-giving which is intrinsic to Islamic religious observance but could be used as a cover for illegality. Another problem relates to Hawala, an informal banking system, which enables the transfer of money without leaving a trail of paper or the 'footprints' left by electronic transfer. The system which is centuries old in the Arab world is based on trust so that money can be paid to a dealer in London and collected from a corresponding dealer in the Gulf or Afghanistan or Pakistan. I have come across the system in international drugs importations but it is also used quite legitimately by immigrants sending money home to family who have no bank accounts.

New technologies, 'smart' money laundering and ease of travel make terrorism hard to combat. Citizens in developed liberal democracies, who have enjoyed growing freedom, have to consider what incursions into their civil liberties they will countenance. Counter-terrorist campaigns inevitably involve some invasion of privacy and surrender of rights formerly enjoyed: searches on entering public buildings, the ever-present eyes of CCTV, proofs of identity, forfeiture of sharp objects before air travel, monitoring of internet sites. In investigating terrorism we would expect greater vigilance at ports of entry, the expansion of police powers to investigate bank accounts and e-mails (with proper oversight by the judiciary), the changing of thresholds for obtaining search warrants, expanded intelligence gathering, electronic eavesdropping and surveillance. I would accept that my passport should carry a fingerprint or iris identifier for the purpose of ensuring that the document is indeed mine. This trade-off by citizens of personal freedom for greater security is understandable.

The only way to counter international crime and terrorism is through working across borders, and law has to develop synergies and systems to meet new demands for collaboration. And we can do it – think of the co-operation necessary to make postal services work worldwide: even at their most estranged, Cuba has delivered letters for America and vice versa.

Nevertheless, we should be aware of some serious issues inherent in this move towards closer international collaboration of intelligence agencies, and of closer links internally between the police and the secret services. Traditionally, law enforcement or policing has focused on the investigation of crime and the collection of evidence for trial. The police are open to public scrutiny and can be kept effectively within the strict parameters of the law. In contrast, intelligence agencies operate in secret, they at times act outside the law and they give the highest priority to protecting their sources. Our own domestic experience in Northern Ireland, and the domestic experience in the United States in the late 1960s and early '70s, vividly illustrates that when law enforcement agencies and intelligence are allowed to work in tandem, innocent activity is monitored, catalogued and the information retained for future use against individuals who find themselves at odds with the prevailing authority. Even more alarming is the recognition that the evidentiary value of material passed by, for example, MI5 or MI6 to the police may be tainted because it was received from foreign secret police and not obtained under the standards necessary for any process involving removal of liberty.

The commingling of information sometimes makes it very difficult to evaluate its quality and origins. Information from foreign i[illegible]ig[illegible] s[illegible]ces [illegible]es [illegible] h[illegible] th[illegible]ame [illegible]ssurance o[illegible] re[illegible] a[illegible]cc[illegible]cy[illegible]ort[illegible] is [illegible]d, [illegible]rsa[illegible]nd [illegible]ossip are in[illegible]clu[illegible] t[illegible]'r[illegible]so[illegible] Ir[illegible]na[illegible]al [illegible]w, [illegible]herif Bassiouni, [illegible]f [illegible] U[illegible]er[illegible] [illegible]ag[illegible]has [illegible]in [illegible]ou[illegible]n h[illegible]s contribut[illegible]on [illegible] I[illegible]na[illegible]a[illegible]r [illegible]oci[illegible]n' [illegible]po[illegible]on *[illegible]nternational T[illegible]* [illegible] ([illegible]3), [illegible]ar[illegible]is [illegible]e c[illegible]e [illegible]egr[illegible]com[illegible]onents of the [illegible] i[illegible]ig[illegible]e [illegible]am [illegible]in[illegible]an[illegible]ati[illegible]s'. [illegible]aving disc[illegible]ve[illegible] wealth of hearsay evidence out there, this is probably the rationale for our own government's enthusiasm to abandon the rule against hearsay in the British court system. Information is often obtained illegally by such covert means that foreign agencies do not even want to discuss their methods, and UK agencies sometimes think it is better not to ask. This is one of the reasons why the security services never want to go into the witness box and subject themselves to cross-examination. So although the nature of international terrorism may require us to increase co-ordination between policing and intelligence, the potential for the rapid and substantial erosion of civil liberties and fundamental human rights is great. During the

Scott Arms to Iraq inquiry in 1996 Lord Howe, who had been Foreign Secretary, said of intelligence reports: 'Many look at first sight to be important and interesting and significant and then when we check them they are not even straws in the wind. They are cornflakes in the wind.' Lord Hurd, his successor, made the same point: 'There is nothing particularly truthful about a report simply because it is a secret one. People sometimes get excited because a report is secret and they think that therefore it has some particular validity. It is not always so in my experience.'

Sir Peter Heap, a former ambassador, suggested in an article in the *Guardian* on 2 October 2003 that 'the whole system of intelligence gathering is all too often prone to producing inadequate, unreliable and distorted assessments, often at considerable cost . . . Very rarely is intelligence material subject to the same scrutiny, verification and testing as information governments receive from other sources.' He explained that it was common to see MI6 reports that were little more than gossip and tittle-tattle that an embassy's political and economic sections would not have thought worth reporting. 'Intelligence facts' were often at variance with the known facts and sometimes drew on dodgy newspaper reports. Sources claimed to be reliable were often being paid substantially and had incentives to lie. The value of telephone intercepts was often questionable because identifying the source accurately was so difficult. In Peter Heap's view the methodology of the intelligence agencies had to be reviewed and their information used sparingly and selectively. Yet this is the kind of material upon which men are currently being detained without trial.

We should also make a clear distinction between actions that involve incursions into our liberty to investigate or prevent acts of terrorism, and the actions that are taken once persons are detained. No change should be countenanced which involves detaining people without charge and without the right to judicial review, or the lowering of standards when seeking to establish guilt.

The principles of equality before the law and of fairness demand that we extend the same rights to everyone. Whenever we deny to one class of suspects rights that we treat as essential for others, we act unfairly, especially when that class is politically vulnerable, or identifiable racially or by religious or ethnic distinction. In a state of emergency the principle of equality before the law should require at the very least a strong case that there is no alternative but the reliance on special powers or procedures.

There are important questions for the legal community to ask about what departures from legal norms are acceptable. Would a state be justified in lowering the burden of proof so that conviction might be based on the balance of probabilities? (Professor Lawrence Tribe, the American constitutional expert at Harvard, tentatively argued before the United States Committee on the Judiciary on 4 December 2001 that while it may be right in more normal times to allow 100 guilty defendants to go free rather than convict one innocent one, the arithmetic should be reconsidered when one of the guilty might blow up the whole of Manhattan.) Would it be acceptable to remove the right to silence? Is it ever acceptable to deny access to the lawyer of one's choice? Is it right to eavesdrop on what are normally privileged client–lawyer consultations? Is it fair to subject suspected terrorists to a higher risk of unjust conviction? Would a state be justified in lowering evidential standards by admitting hearsay, ignoring the need for corroboration, accepting confessions obtained in oppressive circumstances?

The answer to all those questions must surely be no.

Yet there are problems for the state where they have intelligence reports that cannot be revealed because the life of their informant may be endangered but which indicate that the detainee is an active terrorist, or conspirator. The accused may be the best person to [illegible] the [illegible] information, ha[illegible] wh[illegible] the [illegible] exposes [illegible]'s [illegible] sources of information [illegible] people with [illegible] people who perceive [illegible] in the [illegible] they [illegible] or [illegible] criminal activities [illegible] forgotten [illegible]. But should the state [illegible] its [illegible] intelligence [illegible] by [illegible] to make such evidence available to the accused, yet allow it to go before the court in camera? Does such a step undermine the concept of fairness and, if so, is such unfairness justifiable in the interests of safety and security? The argument made by governments is that a trade-off is necessary between civil liberties and security. However, the language of trade-off or balance is misleading since most citizens will not be required to make the trade. It is the rights of the 'other', the alien, that are being traded.

In all the deliberations of legal change or modification, it should be acknowledged that short-term security victories purchased at the cost of long-term political estrangement are not successes at all, as they threaten to act like a spark in the dry tinder of existing grievances. Over 500 people of Muslim background have been arrested in the UK since 11 September 2001; yet only four have been charged with criminal offences. This has led to protests from the Muslim leadership and the mosques. There are rarely law and order solutions to political problems. Steps taken to counter terrorism tend to creep insidiously into the general fabric of a nation's law, creating new paradigms of state power. As I have said, we have seen this in Northern Ireland. So the notion that such changes relate to 'others' should not provide too much comfort. In the summer of 2003 peaceful protesters at an arms fair at the ExCel Exhibition Centre in London were stopped and searched under section 44 of the Terrorist Act 2000; the power is supposed to be used only if officers consider it 'expedient for the prevention of acts of terrorism' and in parliament at the time of enactment the Home Secretary claimed that it would be used only in the context of 'high risk' terrorist attack or emergency.

So how do we proceed if we are not going to give in to terrorism? Any legal modifications should be tested against the concept of proportionality. Do the new laws reflect pressing social need? Are the reasons necessary and sufficient? Could alternative methods be used which are less abusive of civil liberties and require fewer departures from the ordinary legal arrangements? Is the deleterious effect proportionate to the value to the security forces? In Northern Ireland sectarianism was so great that a schedule of offences was created and jury trial was withdrawn from cases which had terrorist links or where justice could be undermined because of the social divisions. Although there was great concern about the removal of a fundamental right, fears that pressure would be applied to jurors provided persuasive. Even now with the peace process in Northern Ireland under way, it is not felt that jury trial can yet be reinstated despite pressure from the Northern Ireland Human Rights Commission.

In the UK we have a raft of legislation to deal with terrorism. In 2000 legislation was introduced which made it an offence to incite, plan or support terrorism elsewhere. In January 2004 a new Civil Contingency Bill was introduced into Parliament to give the state exceptional powers to deal with the real emergency of a large scale terrorist attack. This is perfectly reasonable so long as the powers are not available on a lesser excuse and the time frame is strictly limited.

Some extension of detention prior to charge may well be permissible in dealing with alleged terrorists but safeguards must exist to ensure that it is consistent with human rights and habeas corpus must be available after a stated number of days. Fourteen days, as we now have as a result of the Criminal Justice Act 2003, is too long. And detention without trial is not acceptable. Legislation which departs from the normal rules of law must be highly specific and targeted. It should also have inbuilt 'sunset clauses', declaring the lifespan of such law, so that it does not sit permanently on the statute book. Targeting the wrong people is worse than futile. It does nothing to protect the public, damages innocent people and destroys confidence in the government in the end.

But what do we do about suspect foreign nationals whom we cannot deport back to their country of origin because they would be executed and such an act by the UK would contravene our commitment to human rights? If they are here and there is sensitive intelligence that they are members of Al-Qaida how do we proceed? It may be that the evidence falls short of anything that would stand up in a court of law. It may be that we have good intelligence but we cannot place it in the public domain or let it be seen by the suspect or his lawyer – who is obliged under professional rules to let her client see evidence – because it is too sensitive. It may be that the intelligence comes [illegible] telephone taps or [illegible]bile [illegible] satellite interception [illegible] evidence from ele[illegible]ne [illegible] cannot be placed before a court [illegible] but even the former Director of Public Prosecutions, Sir David Calvert Smith, called [illegible] a change [illegible] the law to make such evidence admissible, a change which [illegible] resisted by the intelligence community). However, [illegible] the [illegible] is not good enough for a successful prosecution [illegible] is too sensitive for disclosure there should be no detention.

In Sweden the authorities were presented with precisely this dilemma: do we detain without a proper trial or do we maintain our high evidential standards and the probity of our legal system? They decided that their legal system was too precious for them to depart from principle. They arrested suspects and sought to question them; when met with silence, they released them but have kept them under constant surveillance ever since. The suspects know they are being watched and having their calls intercepted 24 hours a day. The Swedes see this as legally preferable and probably no more expensive than the route chosen by Britain.

The Council of Europe's Commissioner of Human Rights published a report in 2002 which criticises the UK derogation, pointing out that no other European country sought to introduce such changes in law, and advocating precisely the course taken by Sweden. A review body comprising privy counsellors from all parties has also now criticised detention without trial, calling for the release of prisoners or for them to be charged and tried in the traditional way.

It is also right that we should look at ways of improving extradition procedures. This should not mean an abrogation of standards. When there is talk of 'creating better synergies and common modalities' it almost invariably means a levelling down rather than up. We are frequently regaled with stories of French fury at the failure of British courts to hand over a suspected Métro bomber for trial when our judges were rightly concerned that testimony on the basis of which he was sought was improperly obtained. In the last two years efforts have been made to strengthen transatlantic co-operation to catch terrorists and serious criminals. An extradition agreement with the United States was signed by David Blunkett, the Home Secretary and John Ashcroft, the US Attorney-General on 31 March 2003 which in effect removes the need for a prima facie case before removal of suspects to the US. There was no consultation or warning. There had been lobbying by human rights groups over American use of the death penalty, which offends European standards on human rights, and to get round the issue the US has given a pledge to Britain that if a death penalty is imposed on an extradited person it will not be carried out. However, there is concern that US law enforcement procedures have serious weaknesses of competence and integrity, as we saw with the arrest of a British pensioner, Derek Bond, in South Africa on 6 February 2003 at the behest of the FBI. Despite clear evidence that he was innocent he was left in prison for three weeks. In the same month, a British citizen Jackie Elliot was executed in Texas after a judge refused an application for delay to secure new DNA evidence which might have exonerated him. British intercessions were ignored, which raises questions about how watertight the pledge not to execute will be, given that each individual American state has its own jurisdiction.

The case of Lofti Raissi showed very powerfully the need to keep to stringent standards. Here was a young British man arrested in London on 21 September 2001 in the afterheat of the events of 11

September. The US authorities sought his extradition on the basis of suspicions that he may have been involved in the attacks upon the US. It was initially claimed that he was a flight instructor of some of the hijackers and a co-conspirator in the Al-Qaida network. On 24 April 2002 the case against Raissi was halted, with the magistrate saying: 'I would like to make it clear I have received no evidence whatsoever to support the contention that you are involved in terrorism.' He had spent seven months in custody. Under the new treaty the magistrate would not have the power to examine the quality of the evidence and Raissi would probably have been surrendered. The new extradition process brokered by Blunkett will simply involve determining identity and procedural compliance. Raissi's lawyers are now concerned that the new treaty could mean another attempt will be made by the US authorities to secure his handover.

Lawyers and politicians concerned with human rights have pointed out that there is no reciprocity in the treaty. American citizens will not be handed over to Britain without a prima facie case being established because to do so would contravene a citizen's constitutional rights. The very least that might be expected before such a treaty is signed is that it is done so on a fully reciprocal basis [illegible] from our special partner. The difference is that Turkey has agreed on reciprocity and has at least signed up to the European Convention of Extradition, which requires that significant safeguards on human rights are met, whereas in the United States there are very real differences between states with regard to legal representation, legal aid, prison conditions and other human rights considerations. We wait to be convinced that Turkey will meet those standards but no such thresholds are being set for the US. We are entitled to ask whether we would extradite without inquiry people to be interned in the legal limbo that exists in Guantanamo Bay or hand people over to be tried before a military commission on dubious evidence.

*

Political expediency always finds its place in decisions on law. The arguments for swifter, easier extradition have been around for years but have been given a boost by the alarm about terrorism. It is crucial that fugitives from justice should be caught. But the new Eurowarrant, which streamlines extradition throughout Europe, will not be confined to terrorism. It is a prime example of levelling down to reach agreed standards rather than the raising of all to a place in which justice is the likeliest outcome. This European-wide arrest warrant makes no habeas corpus provisions, which means that a British citizen can be arrested in Wigan for actions which are not criminal in the UK on an arrest warrant issued in another European country. After a British court has ensured that there is 'propriety with the process' (that the documentation is correct), the person can be taken and held in a foreign prison awaiting trial. This process can take many months. Italy, for example, has incredibly long delays before trial and regularly comes before the European Court of Human Rights for breaches, but now it will only have to whistle and the handover of British citizens will take place even for trivial offences. We have failed to insist on a handing back if there is unacceptable delay.

In Britain, up to now, a court would first decide on whether there was a case to answer before any extradition proceedings could commence and those who were accused by foreign governments could use the opportunity to obstruct and delay for years on end. It is obvious that procedures had to be found to prevent such abuse of the system, but the new streamlined process could mean real injustice to innocent people. If someone is able to show that they were not in the requesting country at the time of the offence and a mistake has been made, our courts would have no role in assessing the alibi and refusing extradition. The organisation Fair Trials Abroad gives horrifying examples of British citizens being refused bail in another country simply because they are foreigners, having inadequate access to legal advice and interpreting facilities. Before adopting the Eurowarrant, which is in principle a good idea, the British government should have insisted that legal aid be at an adequate level. They should also have insisted upon a system of Eurobail so that if a national in a country would have received bail in the same circumstances then so would the British citizen. Many European countries like Spain and Greece still provide little or no legal aid.

In 1998, a system was set up by the Council of Europe to monitor compliance by signatory countries with the European Charter of Fundamental Rights. It examined the justice system in all European states. Some of the findings were unexpected: they showed the existence of political interference, especially concerning judges; cases of corruption – largely due to the poor salaries and status of judges; a shortage of resources; frequent delays and an alarming proximity of prosecution and judiciary. If these are problems even in advanced democracies, we can reasonably anticipate worse failings in nations which are candidates for eventual membership of the Union and which until recently did not have independent legal systems. An arrest warrant issued in Bulgaria may raise worrying questions.

We are also being told that Europol and Eurojust – the new European body to strengthen collaboration between justice ministries and prosecution services – will only act on 'specific intelligence'. This is to rely on the integrity of the state and its officials, something that we in Britain are rightly sceptical about. But it also means relying on the intelligence of other countries and, as I have said before, we have no idea about how this might be collected and by what standards. Justice does not permit shortcuts, but [illegible] around the civil law model. Surrendering a citizen was seen as a state's failure to provide protection. France, Germany, Holland, Denmark and Greece, amongst others, have all at times refused to extradite their own nationals, much to British annoyance. In some cases they would put them on trial themselves but the difficulties that presented for victims and witnesses was very real. The advance in the creation of the Eurowarrant is that the interpretation of a state's obligations to its citizens is being changed, with a recognition that combating serious crime requires collaboration.

Sometimes, however, this can be abused. Russia's attempts in 2003 to extradite from Britain Akhmed Zakayev, the Chechen leader who is a renowned actor, were wholly without merit. The allegations included terrorism, armed rebellion and assorted crimes, which had been examined meticulously by the Danish authorities and deemed to be unfounded. Much of the evidence Russia offered was based on hearsay and the central allegations came from a former colleague of Zakayev, who appeared at Bow Street Magistrates' Court and testified that he had given false information only because he was tortured. It was manifest to the court that the prosecution was political because Mr Zakayev once fought against the Russian federal forces in Chechnya. Extradition was refused. Zakayev's real offence was being a persuasive champion of non-violent Chechen self-determination. This kind of example shows how worrying international agreements for slick handover are when there are terrorism allegations.

The nation state is in the process of redefinition. In *The Shield of Achilles,* Phillip Bobbitt maintains that the old nation state is evolving into a market state, with Britain being seen as the prime example. In the new state, national sovereignty recedes where economic benefit requires it and the state reduces its delivery of services to its population. Whatever the advantages accruing to states in this deregulated world of exchange and mart, the downside is becoming daily more apparent.

As multinational corporations have gone in pursuit of international markets, insisting upon a junking of inhibitory rules or any laws which might get in the way, so international criminals have swum in their wake, taking advantage of the same freedoms. Terror networks like Al-Qaida and other international criminal organisations greatly resemble multinational corporations, making use of all the same advances in communications, swift transport and rapid money transfer.

Law is seen as an encumbrance to liberal free marketeers, save in the ways it protects commercial transactions, provides remedies for default and makes the world safe for global capitalism. The minimalist state wants minimalist law. In this vista it is important to protect human rights against the ugly consequences of untrammelled markets, which encourage the exploitation of people, the growth in poverty and alienation and the flourishing of crime and terrorism.

The principle of 'human dignity' is directly protective of the basic rights of the individual. What is involved in respecting human dignity is to be found in various international human rights charters, including the Universal Declaration of Human Rights. Given the status of such international agreements it is entirely appropriate that anti-terrorist laws should be subjected to scrutiny by reference to them. Respect for human dignity is a thread running through them all. Of particular relevance is the prohibition on the use of torture or inhuman or degrading treatment. This is why even a true confession should not be admissible in a court of law if it has been procured by torture or oppression. One of the concerns about detaining people in Guantanamo Bay is that it is an intelligence-gathering project, falling outside the normal legal protections. Even the renowned civil liberties lawyer and Harvard professor, Alan Dershowitz, seemed to lose his moral compass after 11 September. In his new book, *Why Terrorism Works* (2002), he posited the hypothesis of an arrested person who might have knowledge of the location of a ticking bomb. In such circumstances he suggests it should be possible for a judge's order to sanction a little bit of torture. That sort of thinking is precisely what brought the UK before the European Court of Human Rights in the 1980s for its treatment of detainees in Northern Ireland. Recently I was asked by a young Israeli lawyer what I would do if I [illegible] tion in oppressive conditions without access to lawyers is an affront to the values which underpin Anglo-American jurisprudence. The US does not deny that it is using sensory deprivation and 'interrogation in depth' techniques, banned in 1972 by the British government. Used intensively and together, such techniques can amount to torture.

Legally, Guantanamo is being treated as a no man's land. It is not in US territory, even though it is leased from Cuba by the American government, and the American government argues that neither the constitution nor any other US law applies there. Applications made by the Centre for Constitutional Rights before the District Court of

Columbia for habeas corpus for a number of those detained failed on the basis that a US court had no jurisdiction. The appeal to the circuit court upheld that decision and the case is at the time of writing heading for the Supreme Court. The Cuban courts have no jurisdiction. The Americans also argue that the Geneva Convention does not apply because this is not conventional war and the detainees are not entitled to the status and protections afforded prisoners of war. America's own Fifth Amendment rights guarantee the right to silence and the right to the presence of an attorney but quite intentionally that writ does not run in Camp X-Ray and Camp Delta.

The men in the camp are held in solitary confinement in cells which are 6 feet by 8 feet; they are only allowed to exercise twice a week for fifteen minutes; letters from home are stockpiled for months and handed over in a bundle, undermining their potential to sustain emotional well-being. None of this fulfils human rights standards. Some detainees were 'rendered' to Pakistan's security force in the knowledge that they would be tortured outside any legal boundaries whatsoever.

At least three juveniles – aged between 13 and 16 – have also been detained in the camp, contrary to the Convention on the Rights of the Child, never mind the Geneva Convention. The US response was that these were not children and they presented a lethal danger, which justified their detention. Every country in the world has signed up to the International Convention on the Rights of the Child except the US and Somalia. The children are still to be released, despite prolonged international pressure.

For over two years, hundreds of men have been detained in this legal limbo with no access to the writ of habeas corpus to determine whether their detention is legally justified. Links with Al-Qaida have been made in very few cases – it is believed that the majority were men in the wrong place at the wrong time or low level members of the Taliban. After incarceration in these unlawful circumstances, releases are slowly taking place but without apology. The Red Cross has described the camps as principally centres of interrogation rather than detention. Officials have been reported as saying that the techniques of interrogation are 'not quite torture but as close as you can get'. Some of the prisoners have attempted suicide and psychiatrists have expressed concerns about the damaging effect of indefinite incarceration, when it means being essentially incommunicado from family and lawyers, with no sense of what the future holds. The uncertainty, they say, is a recipe for mental instability.

Detainees who are eventually tried will appear before military commissions. The judges will be members of the armed forces appointed by an American politician, Paul Wolfowitz, and he will also appoint defence lawyers from a vetted military panel. The procedural rules allow for the admissibility of statements made by prisoners even if they were under physical or mental duress at the time 'if the evidence would have value to a reasonable person'. Delivering the F.A. Mann lecture in Lincoln's Inn in November 2003, Lord Steyn, one of the most senior judges in Britain's highest court, described these commissions as 'a mockery of justice'.

There was not a squeak of disapproval by the British government publicly about the nature of these camps and the disregard for international law by the United States, despite there being British citizens detained in them. That failure amounted to a collusion in the process. It was only when it was announced that two of the British men would be put on trial before the military commissions that the Prime Minister was pressed into action by a public outcry. The Attorney-General was sent to Washington to seek the return of British prisoners or if that failed to dicker over how the military [illegible] Guantanamo Bay and in the corridors of power on both sides of the Atlantic.' It is yet another example of creating a hierarchy of human rights, when the principle is supposed to be that all human beings are born free and equal in dignity and human rights.

The *Washington Post* has also claimed that Al-Qaida prisoners are now being held on Diego Garcia, a British-owned island leased to the Americans. The journalist Barton Gelman claims they are being held for 'rendering' before being transferred to Camp X-Ray but the British government has denied that any permission has been granted for such a use of the facility (Mark Seddon, *Independent*, 13 December 2003).

*

Far from being confined to Al-Qaida suspects, this retreat from legal principle is spreading. There is now concern about the detention of prisoners in Iraq, especially senior members of the Iraqi regime, with regard to their status in international law and the means of interrogation. If there is evidence, Saddam Hussein and his henchmen should be charged with war crimes or crimes against humanity and tried before an independent tribunal in Iraq or an international tribunal set up under UN auspices, not before some questionable legal body which would not have broad confidence. Ordinary soldiers should be treated as prisoners of war and freed. According to the conventions, any doubts as to the status of prisoners should be resolved by a competent tribunal.

Adherence to the rule of law and human rights does not prevent the passing of counter-terrorist legislation. However, the principles of fairness, equality before the law and human dignity must remain the touchstones. Finding and punishing those who commit terrorist outrages is vital and prosecution of those who commit crimes against humanity is entirely appropriate for state authorities seeking to enforce the criminal law, even where the crimes have taken place outside their territory. That is why it is so important for countries to give their domestic courts jurisdiction over crimes against humanity as the UK has now done. It is also the reason why it has been essential that we establish an international criminal court.

The nature of a government's response to terrorism within its borders will depend on the type of violence, its history and roots, its seriousness, the extent to which it has community support and the effect on the international community's respect for human rights. Sensitive political judgements have to be made. The way in which mature legal systems deal with subversion or attack has global implications: toleration of infringements of civil liberties gives poor signals to those nations which are struggling to establish democracies. It also gives succour to tyrants who have little interest in the rule of law or the pursuit of justice.

The débâcle in the Security Council of the United Nations over the war in Iraq, with international law being flouted, made a mockery of the rule of law. There are only two possible situations in which one country can take military action against another, according to the UN Charter. The first is for individual or collective self-defence, which is a long-standing right under customary international law. The second is where the Security Council decides that force is necessary to 'maintain or restore international peace and security' when a nation has failed to comply with Security Council decisions. A pre-emptive strike would be justified in self-defence but only if a nation was in imminent danger, and any force used would have to be proportionate. (The whole issue is mirrored in the domestic case of Tony Martin who believed he was entitled to shoot a 16-year-old burglar in the back with a pump action shotgun because he would not heed warnings and came back to burgle. Alternative strategies like getting a burglar alarm or a pair of Rottweilers might have been a less drastic solution.) The mere fact that Iraq might build the capacity to attack someone at some unspecified time in the future was an insufficient basis in law to wage war. In any event no one believed Iraq was about to attack America or the UK.

In the weeks before the war the British government conveyed to Washington its concerns about the law, explaining that the preponderance of its legal opinion was that war would be unlawful without a second resolution from the Security Council. The response was that they should find themselves some different lawyers. A very senior woman lawyer in the Foreign Office resigned over the decision to go to war without a second resolution because [illegible] personal kite in the courts. Clever lawyers never find it impossible to conjure up an argument with a veneer of plausibility but the real question is whether it will win the day. Nothing as crude as a phone-around took place. The United Kingdom has a vibrant and significant international law community; a wide range of international lawyers were frequently debating the legal aspects of the war and their opinions were well known. The majority were firmly of the view that the law was not on Blair's side. Only two signed up to the proposition that the use of force would be lawful and one of them was Christopher Greenwood, Professor of International Law at London School of Economics. Unsurprisingly, it was his opinion that was eventually sought by the Attorney-General, who is not an international lawyer, and it was used to formulate the government view. As has been pointed out by the Member of Parliament, Brian Sedgemore, this will provide a defence against any accusations of illegality mounted against the Prime Minister.

The real court for Tony Blair has been that of public opinion. For the public's ears, the British government argued that it had the law on its side because Resolution 1441 passed by the Security Council at the end of 2002 authorised the use of force against Iraq. It had warned Iraq that it would face 'serious consequences' if it continued to violate obligations spelled out in the resolution. However, the magic words 'by all necessary means' were not included in the text of the resolution and those are the formulaic terms in UN-speak indicating that the international community may meet any flouting of the resolution with military intervention. Syria would never have signed up to a resolution putting the right to wage war automatically in the hands of the United States. Nor would Switzerland, which had only recently joined the UN but still relished its neutrality stance and was worried about being sucked into the use of force. A new resolution was necessary but the progress the inspections were making did not encourage such a resolution. The UK government also sought to argue that breaches of past resolutions gave authority for war but again no resolution, apart from Resolution 678 which was passed just before the first Gulf war in 1991, sanctioned the use of force and then it was only to restore Kuwait's sovereignty. As Keir Starmer QC pointed out in his legal opinion for the *Guardian*, which was supported by the widest range of legal luminaries including the former head of the Bar Council, Lord Alexander of Weedon: 'It is true that the cease-fire resolution 678 (after the first Gulf War) requires Iraq to destroy all weapons of mass destruction but under Article 42 it is for the security council and not the US or the UK to decide how it is to be enforced.' The unreality of the reliance on Resolution 678 was summed up by Michael P. Scharf, the former Attorney Advisor for United Nations Affairs at the US Department of State: 'It is significant that the administration of Bush the elder did not view Resolution 678 as a broad enough grant of authority to invade Baghdad and topple Saddam Hussein. It is ironic . . . that the current Bush administration would now argue that this resolution could be used ten years later to justify a forcible regime change.' It is also ironic that Donald Rumsfeld, the Defence Secretary, had himself sold arms to Saddam.

The war on Iraq was not conducted in accordance with international law and I know that many senior judges privately took the same view.

Downing Street argued that the invasion and bombing of Iraq were rooted in the same principles as the intervention in Kosovo, an action with which most human rights lawyers in Britain agreed. However, the differences are marked. Many of us had campaigned about Saddam Hussein's reign of terror and abuses of human rights for years without much succour from government. There was nothing new in his behaviour to suggest the need for action now as distinct from any other time in the past. It was a source of puzzlement to Tony Blair that human rights activists did not applaud his stance. In his diary of the run-up to war, *30 Days*, Peter Stothard recounts the Prime Minister saying, 'What amazes me is how many people are happy for Saddam to stay. They ask why we don't get rid of [the Zimbabwean leader Robert] Mugabe, why not the Burmese lot. Yes, let's get rid of them all. I don't because I can't, but when we can, we should.' No one was happy for Saddam to stay. What alarmed his opponents was the disregard for the rule of law, the creation of alarming [illegible] and the cost of the war in human suffering.

In Kosovo the urgency of the situation and the ethnic cleansing of a people brought to th[illegible] a multilateral consensus that intervention was justified even without a UN resolution, because international law allows not only for self-defence when in imminent danger but also for the defence of others facing direct threat. Necessity can justify that which would otherwise be illegal. But Iraq was very different. Tony Blair needed to persuade the British public that he was taking them to war because of Saddam's threat to Britain, not because of George Bush's obsession with Saddam. A war of choice had to be sold as a war of necessity. The administration led the country into an unprovoked war against a sovereign foreign state for reasons that were certainly overstated, claiming that there was danger of weapon attack which could be mounted within 45 minutes. The legal opinion which was used is treated with disdain across the world and Britain – which has a reputation for playing it straight and being committed to the rule of law – is now held in contempt. The Attorney-General should be required to disclose the legal opinion he gave to the Prime Minister because if it was based on the dossier of intelligence constructed for public consumption then he too constructed a legal argument upon a false prospectus.

We have seen an erosion of international law, the undermining of the UN, damage to British relations with many countries around the world, the impairment of our position in Europe and a galloping distrust of the political processes at home. Most of us could have written the script for the disastrous events now playing out in Iraq. For a man so committed to the Third Way, what escaped the Prime Minister was that a middle route did exist. He could have expressed the strength of British goodwill towards America, offering every support in the aftermath of any war if the US insisted on that course, but he should have explained that law matters.

Those who supported the war on the grounds that we should forget legal niceties when an opportunity comes to oust a human rights abuser like Saddam Hussein should consider the precedent set and the implications for the rule of law in such a course. There is undoubtedly a need to reform the UN Security Council and its byzantine, undemocratic workings but it is worth remembering the impulse which created the UN after the Second World War, which was located in a desire to avoid wars and at every turn to wage peace.

As the international tribunals and courts at the Hague have begun to demonstrate, it is possible for processes to be brought into being by the UN which can be accountable under international law. The UN should be empowered to demand that the same pressure currently applied to individual regimes on weapons control be applied as strenuously to securing freedom, human rights and democracy. Hans Blix's team of weapons inspectors in Iraq should have been joined by human rights inspectors and there should have been UN resolutions demanding freedom for opposition parties, a return of exiles and democratic reforms. Scilla Elsworthy of the Oxford Research Group, which specialises in conflict resolution, had recommended the lifting of sanctions and permission for Iraq to sell oil on condition that a percentage of the revenues went into a UN account to be released as and when democratic reforms took place.

The UN should be looking at ways of making international law more instrumental in protecting human rights. Global courts must exist to prosecute not just Osama bin Laden and Saddam Hussein for their crimes against humanity but also global companies for corrupt behaviour and rapacity in the developing world. It is essential that we secure the engagement of the United States in such a powerful vision because a workable democratic structure of international law will be a far better guarantor of peace and security than displays of power and might. Law is one of the keys to that new order. Otherwise, in our rush to win the war against terrorism we may unleash an even greater terror.

3

THE LAW AND ORDER AUCTION

NEW LABOUR WANTS to position itself as the national party, reaching into former Conservative heartlands while keeping its traditional vote. With this aim in mind, it is alert to public opinion on law and order, which it constantly evaluates through polling and focus groups. There is such a desperation about not letting the Conservatives steal the agenda that it is now impossible for them to find a set of sustainable policies to the right of Tony Blair. In every election, crime now emerges as a crucial political issue. Party leaders all vow to get tough on crime and to make our streets safe; their style of argument is growing more confrontational. The public have always wanted action taken against those who rob, steal, damage and kill: what is new is the increased politicisation of criminal justice, with the government vowing to take on lawyers and judges who they claim 'have a vested interest' in maintaining the status quo. This is yet another way of harnessing public fear to whittle away at rights. The auction started with Michael Howard, now the Conservative leader, back in 1992 when he was Home Secretary facing the young Tony Blair as his Shadow. Each tried to outdo the other in their ferocity about crime.

Politics demands slogans, which is why we get 'The war on crime', 'The war on drugs', 'Zero tolerance on street crime', 'Putting the sense into sentencing' and 'Prison works'. It is why we get instant solutions like on-the-spot fines. It is why we get the ludicrous invention of 'Drug Tsars' and 'Homelessness Tsars'.

But unless a discussion of crime sensitively addresses questions about the causes, about whether prison does reduce criminal behaviour and what the alternatives might be, about what might happen to your child or your teenager if arrested, and unless it considers issues concerning potential victimisation of minorities, loss of social cohesion and risks of wrongful conviction, the general public can lose sight of what the removal of safeguards will mean.

Pollsters' questions tend to distil issues down to very general propositions, and answers recording a natural anger against crime then get interpreted as an informed rejection of complex policy arguments. Good leadership involves having the courage to face down the uglier demands created by misinformation and wrong perceptions. However, the government often finds it easier to confirm the prejudices of voters than to challenge them.

We can see the way policies are tailored to winning votes if we relate public perception of crime to policies like 'zero tolerance', or to the mass of minor headline-grabbing legislation, the blaming of the court system instead of failures of policing for the poor detection of crime, and dangerous initiatives like the abolition of the principle of double jeopardy.

The British Crime Survey in January 2003 showed that more and more people believe that crime is rising despite the fact that overall there has actually been a 28% fall since 1997. The Survey also shows that violent offending has fallen by 27% over the same period: this [illegible] in England and Wales in the previous five years. However, the mass media have remained largely impervious to these developments: only increases in crime are newsworthy.

The false belief that crime is on the increase is matched by falling confidence in the police. Under half those surveyed (47% in 2003) say the police do a good or excellent job. This is a marked drop since the 1996 census when the police approval rating was 64%. Instead of correcting misperceptions on crime levels and talking to the public about ways to improve policing, government becomes defensive and responds as though the perceptions are true – and their response in turn feeds back into people's fears.

It is absurd that the public are still so deeply concerned about crime yet so misinformed about it. One of the areas of greatest distortion is reflected in public attitudes towards sentencing. The public are completely deluded about the way courts dispose of certain crimes. In 2001, 74% of convicted adult burglars were sent to prison but the public believes that the figure is less than 45%. Similarly 98% of adult rapists go to prison but more than half the public think that fewer than 60% are jailed. They seem to think judges send the rest off with a pat on the back and some money from the poor-box.

Phillip Gould, the Prime Minister's pollster, discovered that voters did not believe that crime had dropped because it did not echo their own experience. Although less likely to be burgled or to have their cars stolen, they felt they were encountering just as much vandalism, graffiti, drunkenness and juvenile delinquency.

Mr Gould was right in his conclusion that there is an unfocused and widespread feeling of insecurity. This was reiterated by David Blunkett, the Home Secretary, when he launched his White Paper, *Winning Back Our Communities*, 2002, with the words: 'Britain has never been at a more insecure moment. I think my job is to provide some stability and order. Anti-social behaviour is actually at the foundation and root of insecurity.' But alarmist rhetoric by government ministers also fuels it.

People feel apprehensive in a world where job security has disappeared in the name of flexible workforces, where employers can downsize and outsource or move the company elsewhere tomorrow. The economy is more vulnerable and susceptible to international vagaries over which there is little control. There is war, and rumour of wars. And with those global disturbances come the wretched of the earth seeking new homes. It is understandable that people feel the sands shifting under them and are fearful. Against that unnerving backdrop, crime and anti-social behaviour become the focus of anger and anguish.

Citizens should, of course, be intolerant of crime and yobbishness. Our individual liberty is greatly inhibited by anti-social conduct and it is right that governments should tackle crime and the ways in which the quality of people's lives is diminished by vile behaviour. Many of us have sympathy with the former Mayor of New York, Rudolph Giuliani's theory of 'broken windows', which advocates swift action to mend windows or clean off graffiti because degradation of the environment suffuses the community with a sense of hopelessness. Why bother to clean your windows or care for your garden if trash will be thrown in or paint sprayed everywhere? There is nothing new in that philosophy of care. Ten years ago, when involved in an education commission, I learned from head-teachers in deprived schools that effort had to go into collectively caring for the school environment: clutter should be put away, debris picked up from the playground by the kids, broken toys mended or disposed of, posters which became torn had to be fixed or replaced, chalked walls had to be washed. The rationale that poor children deserved a decent space and could learn to appreciate the beauty of surroundings that are cared for and the self-discipline of playing a part in maintaining it was self-evident. Believing they deserved a good learning environment meant there was more likelihood of better behaviour and achievement. Translating that into a policy for our living environment in communities and housing estates makes perfect sense. Most people accept that the police should have powers to close down 'crack houses' on estates and seal them, to shut down pubs and clubs which are magnets for crime and drug abuse and dementing noise, to prohibit shops selling spray paint to under-18s, to ban the ownership of airguns by [illegible] laws can be used to close pubs and clubs. But the government likes announcing new legislation: indeed, as I have mentioned, it has created almost 700 new criminal offences since coming to office. It is often said that the number of laws in a country is an indicator of how tight a government wants its grip to be.

Where Giuliani got it wrong was in turning that philosophy of neighbourhood care into 'zero tolerance', which meant having no sensible response to the reality that many of the people who commit nuisance offences are themselves suffering from a myriad of problems – alcoholism, other addictions and mental health difficulties chief among them. If you move such people on, out of sight, they take their problems with them and visit them on somebody else. Giuliani liked to claim that his policy led to great reductions in crime, even serious crime such as murder and robbery. In fact other research shows that much more influential were the demographics of New York, i.e. a reduction in the number of young men – the people who in the main commit crime.

The problem with New Labour and crime so far is that the government is so afraid of appearing in any way liberal or soft that it goes for measures which appear tough but are ineffective. The attraction to naming and shaming, the removal of benefits and frogmarching to cashpoints has created scepticism amongst the very people who are supposed to make the system work. In addition, the vast quantity of legislation is drowning their enthusiasm for change. Rather than introducing more unnecessary measures, the Home Secretary should be ensuring that the existing provisions are adequately resourced and appropriately implemented. Politicians ask in a bewildered fashion why the police and courts are not using parenting orders, reparation orders, tagging for juveniles on bail, pagers to alert the parents of truants, or curfew orders. There is so much of this stuff coming out of the sausage machine that half the time no one knows what is hype and what is real. As for the other half, court and probation teams are aware that the resources do not exist on the ground to make the orders work. The Probation Service, starved of finance and low in morale, is drowning in the demands being made of it.

The most effective strategies for tackling crime take time to bed down if they are to bring results; they also need adequate funding. Short-termism and short-changing means the government introduces ever more new projects, so that probation staff have to be taken off programmes that are gradually bearing fruit. Sometimes money is put into only one section of the drug rehabilitation services so that when an addict moves on to the next stage there are no resources and what has gone before is wasted. This problem was revealed in all its sorry glory in the excellent investigation by Nick Davies in the *Guardian*, 22 May 2003.

The government likes to blame the courts for lack of convictions. That an increased conviction rate means better justice is by no means self-evident. The Home Office sees criminal justice as a process leading to an output – convictions and sentences – and to outcomes such as public confidence and victim satisfaction. Managerialism is everywhere. Justice, which has to be achieved by a fair trial whether someone is innocent or guilty, is not seen as an outcome in itself. In fact, the shocking truth, which is too often obscured in hawkish claims by police commissioners that the court system is all to blame for failures to address crime, is that police investigation is disastrous. Seventy-six per cent of crime goes unsolved. According to the eminent historian Conrad Russell, any analysis of crime will show that for centuries the severity of sentences has been in inverse proportion to the likelihood of detection and conviction. The lower the detection rate, the more savage the penalties used to deter the unlucky few who are caught. Currently we are seeing low detection and conviction rates, with ever more strident cries for severity in sentencing. The detection rate of 24% is almost certainly an overestimate as many crimes go unreported because the public have come to accept the low attrition rate for theft of wallets and break-ins to cars and do not even contact the police. Young people under the age of 16 often fail to report theft incidents for fear of reprisals. The inability of police to provide adequate staff for their phone lines also leads to under-reporting and it is further understood that police concern with performance indicators leaves many reported crimes unrecorded.

We should be examining better ways of investigating crime and [illegible] to get witnesses. Everyone was in the lavatory.

The government is able to boast that it has increased the numbers of police but the pressures upon the police are greater than ever before. This is not only because the nature of crime has altered but because public expectations have changed; there are greater requirements for record-keeping and procedures in police stations are more complex. In the effort to be more sensitive to the needs of victims police necessarily spend much more time maintaining contact, explaining developments in investigations and retaining their confidence. While we want to ensure that witnesses have this support, greater thought has to go into how this can be achieved amongst all the other pressures on a depleted force. Quite simply, we need more police. The police are still under-staffed and, although there are doubts as to the effectiveness of 'bobbies on the beat' in reducing crime, the public are reassured by a visible police presence and want to see more police on the streets. The increasing demands on the police mean that cases which do come to court are often unsupported by reliable evidence: the solid footwork and slog has not been done.

Police chiefs and court administrators repeat the accepted wisdom about reforming the systems but they do increasingly resent the micro-management that comes from the Home Office. The ever expanding lists of performance indicators and targets are seen as bureaucratic burdens that offer little benefit to society. The police argue that the targets and performance indicators skew priorities; they require the collection of information already known, they take up too much time, and fail to take into account local conditions or causes of crime outside the police's control. In the loudhailer promise of 'Safer Streets' the Prime Minister insisted that street crime would be greatly reduced within a tight time limit. Ten police forces with serious mugging problems were given a deadline. Chief constables were forced to divert £67 million and dozens of staff to tackle the problem, which meant other initiatives such as cutting road deaths were abandoned and crimes like burglary had to be sidelined. It cost an estimated £14,500 for each reported mugging incident.

In Nottingham, street robbery had accounted for just 2,700 out of 150,000 recorded offences over the 12 months between 2001–2002 – less than 2% of the area's total crime. Yet 13,000 burglaries and other offences were put on the back burner to fulfil the political imperative.

The on-the-spot fines to curb yobbish behaviour descended into farce when it became clear that many of those issued with the fixed penalty notices just gave false names and addresses. The parking-ticket-style fines of up to £80 were mainly given to people for drunkenness: 40% of the 3,040 have gone unpaid in the first six months and it is the least problematic souls who pay up. The Home Secretary sees the fixed penalties as a crucial way of bearing down on all sorts of low-level crime and is now considering giving security guards, neighbourhood wardens and community support officers the power to hand them out. The failure to give proper names and addresses will strengthen his arguments for identity cards. Every encroachment leads to another.

The stock response when the issues of more effective policing and ill-considered initiatives are raised is that there are no resource problems, only management problems. In some instances that is true but not always. While it is essential to drive up standards and improve efficiency, this is only done successfully by fully understanding how something works, recognising the potential repercussions of a given course and listening to people at the coal face who have experience rather than to management consultants. John Birt, the former Director-General of the BBC, offered his services to government and was asked to look at law and order. It is hard to know what happened to his wisdom on the subject as we never heard another word but when he explained to me that it was going to be 'a paper exercise' I already had misgivings.

In the police inquiry into the Damilola Taylor case in 2002, where four teenagers were acquitted of killing a black child, Sir John Stevens, the Metropolitan Police Commissioner said that lack of police manpower meant officers were diverted from the inquiry to other murder cases. This led to the case being poorly prepared for [illegible] put it out of their considerations.

There are many similar cases. A recent review of the Suzi Lamplugh case, where a young woman estate agent was murdered, showed that staggering ineptitude on the part of the police had probably allowed her killer to escape justice. They had never made the link between the name 'Kipper' in her appointments diary for the day of her disappearance and the fact that a suspect was known by that same name amongst his close friends. In the investigation of the Paul Burrell case – where Princess Diana's former butler was accused of stealing her belongings – the police had become so intoxicated with the celebrity and exalted nature of the personalities involved that their judgement went to sea. The individual police officers may have been exonerated but it was acknowledged that mistakes were made. Many feel that it was a prosecution that should never have been brought, and it cost the taxpayer millions of pounds. The police investigation into the Soham murders of two children, Holly Wells and Jessica Chapman, was also shown to be inept, with the police ignoring clear pointers that the school caretaker, Ian Huntley, was responsible.

The problem of inadequate or flawed investigation is not confined to the police. The largest fraud case launched by UK Customs and Excise collapsed in January 2003 when it became clear that material evidence had not been disclosed to the defence and that the credibility of a customs officer was in question because of his relationship with an informant. Seven men had their convictions overturned as a result and it is anticipated that up to 90 other people convicted in a series of linked prosecutions could now bring successful appeals. The cost is likely to be over £2 billion in lost revenue to the Treasury, because the fraud was allowed to run long after it was discovered, as well as £200 million in costs. There are also possible claims of millions in compensation. Lord Justice Longmore, who presided in the Court of Appeal, was very down in the mouth about the case. 'This is a melancholy result. The court is compelled to allow these appeals even in the case of a man who pleaded guilty. The vitiation of these proceedings is to be greatly deplored.' The bill will be footed by you and me in our taxes, of course.

While the record of the Crown Prosecution Service has greatly improved, there are still shortcomings. Research conducted in two London crown courts showed that many cases have to be delayed or abandoned because of failures on the prosecution side. In 2003 we had the shameful saga of the Victoria Beckham kidnap conspiracy, where the trial of five men collapsed spectacularly when it came to light that the source for the conspiracy was a car park attendant with previous convictions for dishonesty. He had been paid £10,000 for his information by the *News of the World*. Yet despite this knowledge the police and the CPS pressed on with the case for seven months, abandoning it only when forced to disclose the payment to the defence. They had to acknowledge that there was no other evidence of any plan. Meanwhile the accused had languished in jail and one has to question the judgement of the Crown lawyers and police for letting it go so far. In the view of one of the defence lawyers, Penny Muir, the CPS was 'dazzled by the case's high profile', as in the Burrell case.

The remedy for prosecuting failures has been to assign CPS

lawyers to work more closely with the police, even locating them in police administrative units, which may help but it raises worrying issues about prosecutorial independence and the blurring of boundaries.

The murder of Stephen Lawrence, a young black student, sent shock waves through the criminal justice system when he was stabbed to death by a group of white thugs on 22 April 1993. The case has become a key indicator of the law's failures, replacing the Irish miscarriages of justice as the gauge of police and legal ineptitude. The manner of the investigation left the Lawrence family with no trust in the system, even parts of the system which were doing their job properly. The Crown Prosecution Service, examining all the evidence before them at the time, decided that there was insufficient evidence initially to secure a conviction against the young men suspected of the offence. They were right. There was only one eyewitness, Stephen's friend, who had been deeply traumatised by the incident and whose account was, not surprisingly, shaky on some aspects of what took place. He now feels riddled with guilt.

Had everyone waited, the chances are that further evidence would have come to light. Groups of people who swear allegiance to each other *in* [illegible] have [illegible] difficulty remaining silent in the [illegible] term. [illegible] religion, people abandon old lo[illegible] people [illegible] together with others in whi[illegible] accus[illegible] wield the knif[illegible] chan[illegible] eventually break was in my view [illegible] high. [illegible] who had not actually wielded the [illegible] would have [illegible] something else and would have [illegible] a deal with the police on the basis that he would testify against the killer. A continuing rigorous investigation was what was needed: that, and a waiting game. A family carefully supported and kept abreast of each development by the prosecuting authorities would not have felt so marginalised.

The Lawrence family had no trust in what they were hearing because of the way they had been treated. The system's failure derived from stereotypical assumptions about race, and the family's anger and distress was wholly justified, as the report of the Macpherson Inquiry published on 24 February 1999 showed. The police had been crudely insensitive in its dealings with Mr and Mrs Lawrence, making assumptions that Stephen must have been up to no good, perhaps involved with drugs, in some way authoring his own fate. Nothing could have been further from the truth. However, the legal advice to the Lawrence family to bring a private prosecution showed a serious lack of judgement. The private route to criminal justice taken in default is always hamstrung because the rules are set for a contest between the might of the state and the individual. The legal advice given to the Lawrence family was utter folly. No one says so aloud because as lawyers we are all capable of making mistakes and analyses of a strategy are always much easier in retrospect. The judge ended up having to enter verdicts of not guilty because of insufficient and unsatisfactory evidence and the men now walk free but are still suspected of having committed the crime.

Correcting the terrible wrong that took place because of a disastrous investigation is virtually impossible. There is currently no new evidence that could justify bringing the suspects back before the court. A documentary film showing the men larking about, simulating a stabbing and speaking in disgusting racist terms, does not prove that they killed Stephen Lawrence. The recent conviction of two of them for a racist assault upon a black policeman does not prove they were murderers of Stephen Lawrence. But the more important question is: how could any jury be found that would be impartial after the saturation coverage the case has received? Justice is now impossible.

There are lessons to be learned from this about improving police investigation and eradicating racism from the system. They are about giving proper support to victims and their families, establishing trust and giving clear explanations for decisions. Interestingly, the family of Jill Dando, the famous television presenter who was murdered in 1999, had only admiration and gratitude for the way the police supported them, so it can be done. The answer to a failure of justice such as that experienced by the Lawrence family is not to start dismantling the legal protections and principles which underpin the system but to make sure that all the victims and their families get the treatment they deserve with their human rights properly respected.

The cases of Stephen Lawrence and Damilola Taylor have been used to justify retrial of those who are acquitted. This step means an end to the principle of finality. The rule against 'double jeopardy' – that the state cannot prosecute a person again once he or she has been acquitted – existed for centuries. It recognised the anguish of being put on trial, with the prospect of losing your liberty, and acknowledged potential abuse if the police pursued vendettas or if prosecutions were repeated for political purposes.

Everyone acquitted of serious crimes now faces the possibility of being brought back to trial if new evidence is put before the court. It does not even have to be evidence that has only come to light after the original trial. Any evidence that was not placed before the court at the original trial could be deemed 'new'. Evidence the police failed to gather or use or which was at the time inadmissible could be presented to justify retrial.

To do away with the double jeopardy rule, even in serious cases, lets the prosecuting authorities off the hook of conducting proper investigations the first time round and allows them a second go where they can try to fill the gaps. It also opens the gates to media abuse. Imagine the response of the media when there is an acquittal which upsets a victim or a victim's family. On the steps of the court there will frequently be a declaration by family members that they will never rest until there is another trial and the accused is behind bars. The police will be under pressure never to close the books on a case. And the press will take up the cudgels, determined to have their pound of flesh, particularly in high-profile cases. We are seeing the creation of a new verdict, a 'provisional' acquittal, with no one [illegible]

[illegible] impact of coverage up to that point. Though many lawyers complain about the quality of press coverage of crime and the willingness of some papers to act as judge and jury, the media are vital to the system. Justice must be seen to be done. It keeps the trial process and the judge under public scrutiny and the general public informed about what is going on in the courts. Since few people have the time to actually attend court and sit in public galleries, the media provide open justice. Public trust in the system would evaporate if justice was conducted behind closed doors.

There are many reasons why the Court of Appeal hearing for a retrial should not be closed. An accused may want to complain about the oppressive nature of the prosecution and the behaviour of the police. Openness brings forward witnesses. In any event the damage of saturation publicity will have happened long before any hearing in the Court of Appeal. Unjust restrictions impinge on open justice and are not the way to repair a flawed reform.

The reform contained in the Criminal Justice Bill, 2003, means that the retrial of an acquitted person only takes place after judges in the Court of Appeal consider the new evidence so compelling that a retrial is justified. It has been suggested that there may be cases where DNA might be discovered after someone is acquitted – yet they produce no evidence of such a thing ever having happened nor have they confined the ambit of the reform to the emergence of new scientific evidence. The cases of clear miscarriage to which they can point are few. Two of them concerned professional gangsters who boasted of their criminal activities and made money out of their notoriety. Ronnie Knight wrote that, although he was acquitted in 1980, he had hired a hitman to kill Alfredo Zomparelli; Freddie Foreman told a TV crew he killed 'Mad Axeman' Frank Mitchell and Tommy 'Ginger' Marks, despite being acquitted. Both men were making money out of bragging about their criminal activities and would hardly be credible witnesses even against themselves.

A case of a different order which does test our notions of justice is that of Billy Dunlop who was acquitted of murdering Julie Hogg in 1989. He was tried and the first jury could not agree on their verdict. At a second trial he was acquitted. The police had again been inept in their investigation. They searched Julie's flat when she went missing and failed to look behind the bath panel. As a result three months passed before her body was found, which affected the evidence-gathering.

In 1998 when he was serving a sentence for another offence, Dunlop confessed to a female warder that he had killed Julie and was haunted by her death. To the horror of Ann Ming, Julie's mother, he could not be retried because of the legal rules. As a result he was prosecuted for perjury, admitted the killing and was found guilty. The judge gave him six years, explaining that he could not sentence him for murder and that the maximum penalty for perjury is seven years. It is hard to imagine a more serious instance of a person lying on oath to subvert justice, avoiding responsibility for a terrible crime, and it provides an argument for the government legislating to increase the maximum sentence for perjury so that some justice could be secured in such a singular case. Of course, it does not meet the profound pain and loss of Ann Ming or her feelings that injustice has taken place but it would have gone some way towards preventing guilty people escaping justice completely.

The answer was not to take peace away from all those who have been acquitted rightly. Society functions better when there is closure and people get on with life. The idea of finality has been entrenched in our system because the risk that certain people may be hounded relentlessly is very real. The removal of the double jeopardy rule takes no account of how terrible it is to stand trial and it means that after an acquittal an accused will not leave court believing the nightmare is over, that they can put the allegations behind them for ever and get on with life. To pretend to a person who has been found not guilty that they will never go through the trauma again would not be true. To leave a man or woman with the fear that at any time their security could be shattered by a knock on the door or a hand on the shoulder undermines all that freedom stands for.

Justifying this reform, the Prime Minister explained that some other countries had no double jeopardy rule, citing the first three he could rustle up: Finland, Sweden and Germany. The double jeopardy rule is still cherished in the United States, Canada, [illegible] corruption. This is precisely where we go so badly wrong. Systems create their own rules to deal with their own situations. In systems which are judge-based and where there is no jury comparative to our own, the preoccupations are different and the main worry is that judges might be paid off to produce a wrong verdict. If such a thing were to happen, a retrial would take place. Because we have a jury of 12 individuals and we accept majority verdicts from at least 10 it is hard to imagine the situation of a jury being bribed to produce a verdict. At least three would have to be corrupted.

In any event if a jury were found to have been paid off in this country and there was a tainted acquittal there is already legislation in place to deal with such an occurrence. The Criminal Procedure and Investigations Act passed in 1996 provides for an acquittal to be overturned and a retrial ordered where a person is convicted of tampering with the jury that returned the 'not guilty' verdict. The law in Sweden does allow for retrial if some extraordinary evidence comes to light showing guilt. However, they have a system where persons going on trial remain anonymous until after conviction. So concerns about adverse publicity are greatly reduced. According to their Chief of Police, the law is never used because of concerns about oppression. In Germany and the Netherlands, the possibility of retrial exists but again it is only ever used if new evidence comes to light which was not available at the first trial. Filling the holes in poor prosecutions is not supposed to be permitted.

The main point is that verdicts in these jurisdictions are not produced by ordinary members of the public – a jury – who are likely to be more vulnerable to outside influences such as saturation media coverage. All our checks and balances are there because we have a system of jury trial for crime and we believe it works.

Lord Falconer, the Lord Chancellor, did not want to confine retrial to murder or rape but produced a list of 34 categories of crime in an appendix to the Criminal Justice Bill where the right to request retrial could be sought. He says cases tendered for retrial would be few and far between; but the fewer the cases, the less credible the argument. In exchange for doing justice in extremely rare cases you have to unsettle the sense of finality for everyone who has ever been acquitted of a serious offence. The campaigns for retrial will inevitably attract huge publicity. How can there be a fair retrial? A second jury might assume that, since our cleverest judges find the new evidence highly persuasive, their role is simply to endorse a conviction. The assumption at a retrial brought about because of new and compelling evidence will be that the defendant must be guilty. How does this square with the presumption of innocence? The legislation is also drafted so loosely that a person who is acquitted of a crime anywhere in the world could be at risk of retrial in Britain. O.J. Simpson had better not accept an invitation to speak at the Oxford Union.

Already there is media speculation that the police want to go after Winston Silcott again. Silcott was jailed in March 1987 for murdering a policeman, Keith Blakelock, who was hacked to a horrible death during a riot, which took place on the Broadwater

Farm estate in Tottenham in 1985. Silcott was acquitted on appeal because the only evidence against him was extracted by the police from vulnerable witnesses. One thousand photographs were taken by police and press photographers at the heart of the mayhem but Silcott appeared in none. However, the police have never been reconciled to the acquittal and have frequently leaked information to the press about Silcott. His friend Delroy Lindo who campaigned on his behalf was picked up 37 times by the police and after complaints an internal police inquiry was undertaken which admitted that Mr Lindo had been subjected to 'unwarranted police harassment'. The fear that Silcott will invite the same oppressive attention is well founded and it will make it very difficult for him to rebuild his life.

The retrospective nature of the intended legislation makes it doubly wrong. It is a fundamental, but unwritten, safeguard of British law that it cannot be changed to criminalise past actions or specific individuals after the event. The defendants in the Stephen Lawrence case, the Damilola Taylor case and the Julie Hogg case were all tried on the basis that if acquitted they could not be tried again. The police and Home Secretary should be concentrating, not on rewriting the past, but on ways of ensuring that similar mistakes [illegible]

reform that is populist the Conservatives did not want to register objections or they would be accused of running up the white flag on crime. What is happening is a strange kind of law reform in response to high-profile cases, with insufficient thought given to the reasons for the rules. Peter Goldsmith, the Attorney-General, explained that if the change did not go through he would not be able to look Ann Ming in the eye and although it is easy to see how hard that must be, it should not be the basis for law reform of this kind.

The French call this kind of policy-making 'Le pragmatisme Anglais', where we change education systems or privatise railways and do the research and thinking afterwards. Our politicians are frequently driven by short-term goals, which makes them oblivious to long-term consequences.

In the hunt for ways to increase convictions – or in government-speak, 'measurable outputs' – criminal justice bills are passed every other year: the latest, in 2003, had 289 sections and 29 schedules, defying proper parliamentary scrutiny. This new way of legislating with voluminous bills of real complexity means the public have little idea what is going on and half the time parliamentarians are also in the dark. I frequently raise justice issues with MPs and find that they do not know the small print of the legislation or how it will play out in real life. The combination of heavy whipping, with pressure applied by party functionaries to get the government business through parliament, simplistic messaging to MPs and huge burdens of work in areas of specific interest means that it is hard for parliamentarians to keep abreast of changes.

Included in the Criminal Justice Act 2003 was the scrapping of significant rules of evidence as they have traditionally applied in criminal cases. Juries and magistrates are not trained judges and it is for this reason that exclusionary rules exist. The judge is supposed to be above the emotional response, trained to compartmentalise material which is more prejudicial rather than probative of guilt. He or she learns how to reduce the weight to be attached to evidence that might excite bias, a skill developed with experience. Even with all this training and practice, judges do not always succeed in abandoning their prejudices either. But the strength of juries is precisely that they are not legally trained. It is for this reason and to avoid prejudice that efforts are strenuously made to exclude material which might seriously interfere with their judgement and which is in any event of questionable evidential value in determining actual guilt.

The doublespeak on the issue of evidence allowed in court is remarkable. According to ministers it is paternalistic to make a whole range of evidence inadmissible because of fears that a jury may misuse the information in a prejudicial way against an accused. Juries are smart, intelligent people and should be given the full facts. Yet when it comes to fraud and complicated matters like money laundering, it is argued that juries are too stupid.

The Criminal Justice Act 2003 has now changed exclusionary rules into inclusionary rules. The presumption will be to include hearsay or bad character evidence. Fortunately after much haggling the government relented and the trial judge will remain the final arbiter but the philosophical shift to include such evidence should sound alarms.

Hearsay – that is second-hand evidence of the 'Charlie Brown told me he saw Jimmy with blood on his shirt' variety – has been traditionally excluded if Charlie Brown is not being called. Charlie could have been mistaken. Charlie could have made it up. Charlie could have been joking. The rationale for the rule is perfectly sensible because if the evidence cannot be tested in cross-examination, we are left guessing as to whether it should count. It is important that rumour does not become fact. We all know the old game of Chinese whispers where subtle changes take place in the course of repetition. The famous example is the order passing down military ranks 'Send reinforcements, we're going to advance' evolving into 'Send three and fourpence, we're going to a dance.' The rule is that statements made in the absence of the accused should not be admitted unless the witness is called. It is sometimes hard for a non-lawyer to realise how powerful cross-examination is in exposing the weakness of evidence.

The rules against hearsay were complex and needed to be [illegible] how the judges interpret the legal changes.

Even more invidious is the government's effort to introduce previous convictions into a trial. The previous convictions of the accused were not disclosed as a matter of course in the English system, although there are often circumstances where it is done. The exclusionary rule is to avoid jurors reaching conclusions on someone's record rather than upon the evidence. Including previous convictions is another very serious erosion of the presumption of innocence, doing precisely what the rules are designed to prevent – showing that someone who has committed a crime before has probably done it again. That is sometimes true. The problem is that people who commit crime are also more likely to come under suspicion again and more likely to be accused of something they did not do. As in the film *Casablanca*, the temptation for the police to round up the 'usual suspects' is great, but even more alarming is the risk that jurors will use the existence of a bad record, and the suspicion it will raise, to fill gaps in the evidence.

I have argued for the sexual history of rape victims to be excluded in most cases for the same reason that I would argue for the exclusion of aspects of an accused person's past – because it is rarely relevant to the central issue and only serves to blacken the character of the person in the eyes of the court.

We can see the kind of effect introducing material of this kind can have if we look at Peter Mandelson's forced resignation, second time around. This was a vivid example of the current political instincts when it comes to due process. The allegation by the press was that he had made intercessions to the Home Office on behalf of the Hinduja brothers about their applications for British citizenship, at a time when they were being courted for financial contributions to the disastrous Millennium Dome project. He denied any impropriety. The trial was summary, quick and dirty, with no opportunity to call evidence from civil servants to support his account. But with the media baying for blood the tribunal, who were all lawyers – the PM, the Lord Chancellor and the then Home Secretary, Jack Straw – rushed to judgment. Mandelson is understandably insistent that a miscarriage of justice took place. He certainly didn't receive a fair hearing. His 'previous conviction' was what really caused his downfall. An undeclared loan from a ministerial colleague, which caused his previous withdrawal from government, was his undoing. There was a presumption of guilt.

Putting previous convictions before the jury has pernicious consequences. Even in apartheid South Africa, where there was no jury but a judge sat alone, the past of an accused was excluded. The potential for adding to the stigmatisation of our black community is particularly real if the rule is substantially changed. As the distinguished black Queen's Counsel, Courtney Griffiths, has put it:

> Which group in British Society has been systematically criminalised over the past three decades? Who in consequence will be disproportionately affected by such a change? Which group within our society already makes up 20% of the prison population in

> England and Wales, when they constitute a mere 5.5 percent of the total population? Whose numbers are therefore likely to increase in our prisons as a result of a measure such as this?

Nowadays jurors are very well informed about the rules in trials. Courtroom dramas and police soaps are beginning to demystify the whole business in positive ways. But this also means that jurors know that, if they have not heard about a person's criminal record, it usually means they have some convictions. For this reason lawyers often decide on balance to disclose a client's previous convictions by agreement with the Crown if the offences are minor, committed a long time ago and of a different nature. It is better to expunge speculation rather than have a jury imagine your client is Jack the Ripper. The problem arises where an accused has a previous conviction, which bears no relation to the charge for which he is before the court but which is for the sort of offence which could inflame a jury against him, perhaps the beating of a woman or something of a sexual nature, or where the accused has a list of convictions as long as a day of fasting but is adamant that he is wrongly in the frame this time. That happens more often than is realised. If the police are looking for a young black robber, they often [illegible] made is to deny reality.

Introducing previous convictions also presents time-consuming diversions that ministers have not even countenanced. Those who are accused will want to explain how previous convictions seem more serious than they were; they will want to recast how the conviction came into being and will sometimes insist that the previous conviction was unjust.

Professor Sally Lloyd Bostock is a lawyer and psychologist who has been conducting research on the potential impact of previous convictions on juries. She is concerned that insufficient consideration has been given to the effect of any change to the law. 'I think not enough account has been taken of the psychology of how people are going to use this information. A previous similar conviction, especially a recent one, is psychologically a very powerful piece of information.'

In the United States this is known as 'bad man theory', where evidence finds its way into the proceedings which then predisposes jurors to believe evidence of guilt and to disbelieve evidence of innocence. It usually operates at a subconscious level and creates confusion among jurors even if they are warned to handle the information with care. The juror considers the character of the defendant as providing evidence of the question of guilt of the crime before the court. Ambiguous evidence of guilt is fortified because the man on trial is 'a bad man'.

Most people don't know that there are already situations where convictions are revealed because the jury is entitled to hear what kind of accused they are dealing with. This may happen if a prosecution witness is accused of lying by the defence or an attack is mounted on the credibility of a Crown witness, after a warning by the judge.

The Crown can also argue for the inclusion of previous convictions and previous conduct where the manner of execution discloses a pattern of behaviour. This is called 'similar fact' evidence. It used to be that the previous conduct had to be so unusual that it bore the hallmark of the accused. He did not have to commit the crime wearing, as one judge described it, 'the ceremonial head-dress of an Indian Chief' but the common denominator had to be very distinctive or 'strikingly similar'. In sexual cases it is not unusual to find such patterns. Men who rape often use the same threats each time or truss women in the same way or insist on the same indignities. A case in 2002 had an accused who was a serial apologiser. He always phoned the next day to express remorse to his victim.

In the case of *DPP* v. *P* 1991 [2AC447] the definition of similar fact evidence was widened to prevent it being over-restrictive; the test is therefore no longer 'striking similarity' but has become 'relevance and probative force', meaning that it is highly persuasive evidence of guilt. Quite a number of recent cases have loosened the test further so that even past acquittals can be introduced where a course of conduct is disclosed, for example Re Z 2000 [2AC483].

The case which alarmed the Prime Minister so much so that he sees the measure of putting previous convictions before the jury 'as a clear priority', involved a doctor who was alleged to have raped a patient under hypnosis. The jury did not know that the apparently respectable doctor was serving a sentence of six years' imprisonment for sexually assaulting nine other patients. He was cleared by the jury and the woman who had testified against him feels very strongly that her evidence was stilted because she could not explain openly the background to her allegation. It was when she saw publicity connected to his assault charges on other women that her own suspicions were fuelled that she had been raped by the doctor without even knowing it. She feared that her daughter had in fact been fathered by the doctor, not by her husband, and this was subsequently shown to be the case by DNA testing. The assaults on all the other women had also happened under hypnosis, when patients were undergoing 'relaxation therapy' for sexual problems. The woman understandably feels scandalised that her account was made to sound less credible because she could not give it truthfully and coherently, because she had to avoid reference to the previous conviction, which was the very reason for her having concluded that she too was raped. It is true that juries sometimes feel they are not hearing the whole story and could assume a witness is holding something back when she is in fact constrained by the procedure.

[illegible] remarkable [illegible] the similar fact rules could have applied here. If [illegible] crimes in a similar way, disclosing a pattern of conduct, a judge can be asked to allow the evidence into the trial if it is relevant and probative. Repeatedly persuading women patients to undergo therapy under hypnosis and taking advantage of their vulnerability would fulfil the new criteria. Was an application made to include the background? If so, why did the judge refuse it? Are prosecuting counsel being assertive enough in their attempts to get this evidence before the court and are judges willing to recognise patterns of conduct?

One of the examples given by ministers draws on this case. They put the hypothesis of a doctor who is charged with indecent assault. He denies that any indecency took place but in the past five years two separate patients have made similar complaints, although the allegations dealt with separately were dismissed. On the basis that it defies belief that a third allegation could only be an unlucky coincidence, a persuasive argument is made by proponents of change that the previous allegations should go before the jury. But supposing there had only been one previous allegation, should a jury be told of it?

Some professions are particularly vulnerable to accusation because of the intimacy involved in the relationships with their patients and clients. All the caring professions are at risk. Yet these are professions where opportunities for abuse are too often taken up by the unscrupulous. Where should the shield of protection remain and where should it be removed? These are hard decisions that should be made by judges after argument by skilled advocates and will depend on the circumstances of individual cases. They cannot be legislated for, or encapsulated within a rigid rule created by statute. So many of these cases go wrong not because the law needs to be changed but because the lawyers and the judges need to be changed – or at least changed into people who do not come to rape cases already holding reservations about the complaint.

Male judges and lawyers trying sex cases can often suddenly become zealous about fairness in ways that amaze. Fairness must be at the heart of our process but there is a strange disjunction when it comes to sexual offences against women, with a judicial reluctance that is not manifest elsewhere. I see good reason to have patterns of offending in sexual cases admitted but to extend that to boys breaking into cars or stealing mobile phones is quite another circumstance. To assume that because someone stole a car radio before then he must have done it again is of a very different order from that of the distinctive patterns which emerge in sexual behaviour.

The courts have been evolving a more inclusive approach to 'similar fact' evidence and it is perfectly fine for government to give that development statutory form, even if only to reinforce the changes in the minds of lawyers and judges. It would also make it easier for victims and their supporters to insist that prosecutors explore these avenues of probative evidence. However, the Prime Minister and his Home Office ministers want every bad lad to have his convictions spelt out to juries, well beyond the similar fact circumstances which I have described, and they are clinging to the coat-tails of this shift in the area of sexual offences and capitalising on it. Forget similar fact rules, they want something much cruder which will be applied well beyond the examples of rape or domestic violence that are trawled before the public in the radio soundbites. They want the starting point of 'exclusion' of previous convictions to be changed into a starting point of 'inclusion'. The sleight of hand is the argument that complex rules are being made simple. The real purpose is to stack up the weight of prosecution evidence to secure a higher conviction rate, whatever the risk of injustice. The planned changes to the bad character rules were watered down after political horse-trading over the legislation in order to get it through parliament but an alarming erosion has begun.

Many other shifts are taking place which may seem obscure to the general public but which eat away at the fairness of a trial. After the run of serious miscarriages of justice in the 1970s and '80s, many of which arose from forced confessions and failures to disclose exculpatory material to the defence, new rules were brought in to constrain the police. The Police and Criminal Evidence Act (PACE) 1984 forced the police to tape interviews and the Crown to disclose evidence which might help the defence, even if it weakened their own case. The police clawback against the strictures of PACE is behind many of the current shifts. The defence will be expected to disclose a list of their witnesses so that the police can go and interview them in advance of the trial. This can already be done with alibi witnesses but it now extends to every witness. Many witnesses from marginalised communities are reluctant to come to court as it is: it will be impossible to secure the attendance of people who do not want the police arriving on their doorstep. There is also the serious anxiety that pressure will be applied or fear induced by the police. In the Guildford Four appeal in 1989 it came to light that the police had actually contacted a witness who could have cleared Carol Richardson of involvement in the bombings but who had been so intimidated by the police that he made himself scarce and the defence could not trace him.

Even expert witnesses who have been instructed by defence lawyers but whose advice will not be used in the trial will now have to be disclosed. This is so that the prosecution can comment on the failure of the defence to call the particular witness because it will be assumed that the evidence is inculpatory. The outrage of this change is that sometimes an expert is instructed so that the defence lawyer can cross-examine a Crown expert such as a pathologist more effectively. On other occasions an expert will be instructed simply to explore whether there are other defences of which the defending lawyers may be unaware, for example in the mental health category.

In the target-setting world of Whitehall, success in the courts is to be measured not by effecting justice but by securing convictions. Bureaucrats hate what cannot be measured and they find proxies to fill the gap. Justice, like trust and all the other things which have real value, is not susceptible to easy measures. But convictions can be counted. The Home Office now refers to 'the justice gap' which is to be filled with a higher number of convictions. This is like measuring police success by the number of arrests – it is an invitation to injustice.

Why does it matter if it is just another part of the true picture? Because it challenges the starting point. Something like the criminal justice system requires a founding premiss, a foundational norm. The starting point could be that if the police arrest someone they must have done something wrong; from that foundation, it would then be for the accused person to show that they had not done something wrong. That starting point, or norm, is one we associate with totalitarianism because we know how hard it is to prove a negative. We are also conscious of the might of the state.

Our starting point is one of innocence until proven guilty, but once previous convictions are introduced to show propensity we shift to a different premiss where, although we can pretend nothing has changed, the accused is really being required to show that he or she is innocent.

We should have learned by now that when the system fails to deliver justice it is usually not because the legal principles have failed us. It is almost invariably because we have failed to live up to those principles. The answers to the problems are almost always to be found in better policing, lawyering and judging.

We should be finding ways to oil the wheels of justice, avoiding delays, reducing waiting times for witnesses, keeping costs down where possible – but the good management of courts should not be surrendered to a leaden managerialism. Often the blame lies with the creation of unrealistic expectations by governments which are looking for votes. New and much-needed initiatives can take place without sacrificing our carefully constructed checks and balances, which come out of the wisdom born of experience.

A graduate police officer providing protection to one of our cabinet ministers quietly wished me well in my efforts to keep government to its old commitment to civil liberties. He could see very clearly the risks to justice. As we parted he said that he had been involved in some of the Irish terrorist cases as a rookie. He explained that it was when they saw Gareth Peirce, the stalwart and committed solicitor, arrive at the police station that they knew they had to be on their mettle. Civil liberties lawyers were a firm reminder to play by the rules.

In one of the many House of Lords debates about reducing jury trial the late Lord Gareth Williams dismissed concerns about erosion of rights, saying that he too had resisted changes when he was a practitioner, such as giving the prosecution the right of appeal on sentences deemed too short, or limiting the right of silence. In retrospect the changes were sensible, he suggested, and the sky had not fallen on our heads. Of course, he was right up to a point. Taken one at a time, as in a game of pick-up sticks, the system does not collapse with a single reduction, with each thinning down of civil liberties. But slowly the mortar in our democratic architecture is destroyed. The effect is cumulative. As Andrew Napolitano, an American judge wrote in the *New Jersey Law Journal* a month after the assault on the Twin Towers: 'In a democracy, personal liberties are rarely diminished overnight. Rather they are lost gradually, by acts of well-meaning people, with good intentions, amid public approval. But the subtle loss of freedom is never recognised until the crisis is over and we look back in horror. And then it is too late.'

Before any changes are countenanced the policy makers should produce evidence to show that the change is necessary and likely to achieve the desired outcome – reducing crime and bringing those who commit crime to justice. The burden is on the government to prove such a radical departure from principle is necessary. Like evidence-based medicine there should be evidence-based law reform.

Tilting the law in favour of the prosecution and against the defence is dangerous. It is to confuse the principles of justice with the administration of justice. The principles are sound but the administration can always do with a shake-up. Victims, witnesses and jurors are frequently treated with disrespect. Their time is taken for granted and they spend hours waiting around because the highest priority is put on filling court time. This is often interpreted as running the courts for the convenience of the judges but it is really about pressure on court administrators by government to optimise the use of courts for financial reasons. Business imperatives again. By the hour, courts are costly to run: it is not just the salary of the judge, it is all the other people who are required too – shorthand writers, ushers, security officers, clerks – and keeping one empty is like keeping an operating theatre idle in the NHS. It does not make financial sense. However, inviting people to be there 'just in case' creates terrible frustrations. Calling witnesses the night before to tell them they are needed in a case is infuriating, when they have to rearrange their lives. The current reforms of the court structures and the streamlining of court procedures with a more collaborative approach on the part of the police, the Crown Prosecution Service and the Courts Service will make a great difference. The criminal justice system needs a faster, more sensitive, enforcement of existing law, not a raft of new laws.

The government, in fact, has quite a lot to crow about and it should be using the media to tell us, not to intensify our fears. It has introduced many innovative strategies. The reforms on youth offending are already having a real impact. The likelihood of young people re-offending has fallen by nearly a quarter since 1997. The Home Office attributes the 22.5% drop in the reconviction rate to early intervention and the issuing of 'final warnings'. This replaced the heavily criticised practice of repeat cautions and it involved diversion tactics of sending young people to anger management courses and drug rehabilitation courses instead of introducing criminal charges. Effort is being made by government to invent serious and effective alternatives to prison. But such drivers need popular support – they should be talked up rather than engaged in secretly for fear that the *Daily Mail* will find out. There are good arguments, for example, for extending parenting classes on a voluntary basis for the mothers and fathers of children in trouble. Although this is not the kind of programme that grabs headlines it eventually reaps rewards. The results of pilots show that most parents at first resented being asked to attend, with fathers the most reluctant, but in nine out of ten cases families felt they benefited and the children committed half as many offences in the year after classes began. Lord Warner, who was head of the Youth Justice Board, has said this could be 'the most cost effective measure for cutting crime by young people'.

The same applies to drug treatment and to testing orders which give drug addicts the chance of avoiding prison if they undergo weekly urine tests to prove they are drug free. Yet in many areas the courts ran out of the allocated budgets within a few months of the start of the current financial year. That is what happens when you apply misconceived business concepts to something as complex as the criminal justice system – and when you don't fund it properly.

In the years leading up to Labour's 1997 victory it was Tony Blair who said, 'If prison works, America would have proved it beyond doubt.' He also said, 'if you have to lock a kid up you have lost. You have to intervene at a much earlier stage.' This thinking fired the Sure Start programme of childcare, support and education for 'at risk' children under school age, following all the research that good nursery education for our most disadvantaged children is the best social investment of all in preventing crime, mental illness and anti-social behaviour.

Sure Start – like alternatives to prison – needs more resources and higher priority. Polly Toynbee, the political journalist, has been a persistent and passionate voice arguing for investment in pre-school childcare, pointing out the strong effect nurseries have. Among children at risk of social exclusion, their life chances can be turned around by the experience. US long-term studies show that the effect of a two-year nursery programme lasted for ever, with more of those who had gone to nursery having further or higher education, owning their own home, never being unemployed, having less mental illness and less resort to state benefits or to crime. Currently the government plans that 650,000 of the poorest children will have places by 2006. They should multiply the numbers, accelerate the pace and make this their 'big idea' on changing society.

However, despite these areas of progress the government still succumbs to pressure from the punitive brigade. Our masters live in dread of being accused of being soft; no heart is better than a bleeding heart. When the Home Office put a *Daily Mail* journalist, Simon Heffer, on its 'Law and Order Think Tank' it was clear that government had not just lost the plot but was handing over the plotting to their most feared critics.

We all want to see less crime and more guilty people brought to book – and the ambition of getting more convictions is easily fulfilled if we abandon protections. What matters is what we feel about locking up the innocent who could, of course, be you or me. Is that just collateral damage in the war against crime or the winning of votes? Is it really an acceptable price?

4

YOU, THE JURY

> There is always freedom of choice to change or desist from a counter-productive course if the policy maker has the moral courage to exercise it. He is not a fated creature blown by the whims of Homeric gods. Yet to recognise the error, to cut losses, to alter course, is the most repugnant option in government.
>
> Barbara Tuchman, *The March of Folly*

ONE OF THE great weaknesses of this government in its law and order policies, as I have noted before, has been its extraordinary willingness to see greener grass in other systems. It is frequently wrong. This is not because the ways of the Americans or Europeans are necessarily less good but because they are not always right for us. Taking bits of other systems and trying to stitch them on to ours is more often folly than not. The first mistake is a failure to see that law is cultural. It does not come out of nowhere and law's genesis explains the way in which checks and balances develop and the ways in which consent is secured. Consent is essential to effective legal systems.

Unlike the rest of Europe, which has what is called the 'civil law' system with codified laws and a career judiciary, we have a common law system. In the Middle Ages most European societies rediscovered Roman law and, having reworked it, they received it as the basis of their national systems. The English held out and through the creation of the Empire exported the Anglo-Saxon-based common law to all the English-speaking colonies.

The common law therefore became the basis of the legal systems in the US and Canada, Australia, New Zealand, Hong Kong, Singapore, Nigeria and other parts of Africa and remains so. However, as new democracies have emerged around the world and sought to adopt a Western model they have most frequently replicated civil law systems because they are easier to take off the shelf. Their basic rules take the form of codes – huge statutes which set out the laws in detail, number by number, along with the central concepts and doctrines. For the most part the judges have little or no power to add to or subtract from the law, which is entirely contained in the codes. Their function is to interpret these rules.

The common law on the other hand was essentially created by judges as they decided actual cases. Judges in the higher courts dealt with appeals from lower courts and, in pursuit of a real rather than formal justice, took account of the experience of real litigants and real situations. One of the reasons why contemporary markets thrive in common-law-based nations is because Napoleonic, codified systems entrench bureaucracy. The dead hand of the state is heavier where there is little legal flexibility. The discretion vested in judges provides just enough 'give' to prevent rigidity. Even today, when large parts of the law are created by statutes passed in parliament, the judges have a significant role in developing the law. While our judges are drawn from the ranks of practising lawyers with everyday experience of representing clients, judges in the civil law system are civil servants. Judging is a career from the start and the training of judges is separate from that of lawyers.

The civil system is an inquisitorial system whereas our system is adversarial. In the UK's new environment of consensus politics, emotional literacy and victimhood, doing battle in the courts is considered by many to be outmoded. The criticism is that the system is too adversarial: there should be no opposing sides in the pursuit of truth. Yet the Socratic method of debate, seeking to reach truth through testing a position, is rigorous and effective. How that can be done in ways that are not humiliating or bullying of a witness, I shall return to in a later chapter about victims. But being respectful of witnesses should not mean turning the witness box into an analyst's couch or cross-examining ineffectively.

What is also forgotten in the haze of memory is that the adversarial system and inquisitorial system are based on different conceptions about the relationship of the citizen and the state and the protection of civil liberties. The adversarial system is based on a scepticism of state power while the inquisitorial system places more faith in the state as a protector of individual freedoms. Clearly the state does have a duty to protect its citizens and should be encouraged to fulfil that role effectively but that does not mean assuming its better nature. Governments do not like this scepticism of state power and envy systems which do not have this inbuilt challenge. They would like us to shed our doubting.

I was brought up in Scotland where at the heart of the education system was the belief in developing the democratic intellect – it probably explains the number of Scots in politics. We were encouraged to question and look for explanations other than the ones given. We were taught to debate and made to take the side with which we had no sympathy so that we would understand how others might think about a subject. To this day it has helped me cast a critical eye on the bill of goods I am being sold.

Shed scepticism? The answer to that is a resounding NO. Healthy scepticism is what keeps governments on their toes.

One of the great things about juries is that they are constitutionally able to acquit in protest at unjust laws. This stems from the principle that trials are about justice as well as law. The former Lord Chancellor, Derry Irvine, once questioned why a jury should be able to fly in the face of laws passed democratically by parliament. The answer is that even with the best will parliament cannot conceive of every possibility that arises in that extraordinary business called living, and justice matters more than law. That is the magic of the jury. It is a mini-parliament, another democratic forum, making law respond to the realities of people's lives. Technician-lawyers just don't get it, which is why they cannot keep their hands off juries.

No judge could have acquitted Lord Melchett, the Greenpeace activist and his fellow demonstrators as a jury did in September 2000, when they destroyed a field of genetically modified crops, in protest that the public had not been adequately consulted or informed about the possible consequences. No judge would have acquitted Clive Ponting, an assistant secretary in the Ministry of Defence, who leaked documents concerning the sinking of the *Belgrano* during the Falklands war. A jury acquitted him in 1985, clearly believing that government secrecy was unacceptable on certain subjects. There was much gnashing of teeth amongst judges in 1991 about the acquittal of Randall and Pottle. They had on their own admission helped the spy, George Blake, to escape from prison 23 years before and it was clear that the jury was more in tune than the judiciary with the public sense that the events belonged to an era which had passed, and that the conduct of the security services had left something to be desired. The law of infanticide was introduced in 1922 to provide a lesser charge for women indicted for murdering their babies because juries stopped convicting poor women who killed their babies in despair, often having been made pregnant by the master in the places where they worked. Juries now acquit when people with multiple sclerosis are tried for using cannabis to alleviate pain.

Jury equity, where they acquit in the face of the evidence, is not about juries acting on whims but about taking a just approach to the evidence of the case as a whole. The number of cases involving such verdicts is small and in each one some justice can be found in the jury's decision. But many judges hate it. Lord Justice Auld, who produced a report in September 2001 on juries, gave us a glimpse of the judicial underbelly. He wants it declared by statute that juries have no right to acquit defendants in defiance of the law or in disregard of the evidence. He also wants judges to be able to sit on juries, no doubt to keep them on the right track. He also wants a radical reduction in jury trial and has formulated a redesign of the courts to deliver it.

We need to weigh carefully the gains and losses if we abandon this tradition of citizen engagement. In Britain research into the way juries reach their verdicts is not allowed by law. Such research might be valuable so long as it was strictly regulated academic research. The Law Commission in New Zealand conducted such inquiries amidst the very same clamour we have here that juries are not equipped for the job and cannot deal with complicated issues. The results demolished all those claims, showing what trial lawyers already knew. The New Zealand researchers found that juries were perfectly capable of handling complex trials and reached appropriate verdicts.

In a letter to the *Independent* in July 2002, Stephen Wyatt, a university-educated Ph.D., described being on a jury of very mixed age, education and ethnic origin at the Old Bailey. In their ten hours of discussions to reach a verdict, they treated the case in his view with seriousness and commitment. 'Jury deliberations are one of the few genuinely democratic processes left in our society. The more middle class people who are compelled to go through the process and recognise the worth of the views of others who are in their view socially and educationally inferior the better the chances of our society moving on.'

In a recent article in the same paper, the columnist, David Lister, provided a delicious description of his just-completed time with 'all human life' on a jury. After some vivid portraits of barristers, judges and a Dickensian usher, he concluded:

> My experience has not dented my confidence in the essential democracy of the jury room. I found an earnest desire to discuss and analyse the cases, a determination that the Crown must prove its case, however unappealing the defendant; and a willingness to listen and be influenced by opposing views, which is something one seldom finds outside the jury room.

One of the most central and significant differences between European and other civil legal structures and our own is that civil law systems do not have that democratic input. The rationale for juries has always been that the best way of securing public confidence in the law is by engaging the public in the process, bringing the values of the community to the proceedings. The risk in civil law systems is that people can feel that justice has been handed over to the Town Hall and is run by bureaucrats. Whether that criticism is true or not, civil justice systems have as many if not more miscarriages of justice as will ever be found in any common law system. There is certainly a higher level of judicial corruption because in the jury system there is no point in trying to bribe a judge, given that he or she does not decide on the verdict.

Some civil systems do have lay participants sitting with the judge for certain cases but these jurors do not go off, deliberate on their own and reach a verdict independent of the judge. Research in France, Germany, Poland, Hungary and other countries has shown that the role of these members of the public is essentially passive and their influence negligible.

Originally, juries in England were involved in the full range of cases, including civil claims for compensation, disputes over contracts and even divorces, but slowly it was recognised that in most civil cases no overriding public interest was served by having juries, since these cases did not involve allegations of crime and a potential loss of liberty. The power was given for judges to try civil cases alone. However, a number of exceptions were made. In 1981 the Supreme Court Act preserved the right to jury trial for cases of libel and slander, malicious prosecution and false imprisonment. In libel cases a jury could be retained because it was felt that the issue of whether a reputation was damaged was best decided by a representative sample of the public rather than a judge alone but either party could choose whether to have a jury. The other exceptions – malicious prosecutions or false imprisonment – reflected our belief that liberty matters and that representatives of the state like the police should not be given impunity should they abuse their power. Malpractice by those acting on behalf of the state was so egregious that the public should sit in judgment. Here, the plaintiff could apply for a jury trial.

As I have already said, a huge number – over 95% – of all the 1.8 million criminal cases are dealt with in the lowest courts before lay magistrates who are unqualified (but advised on legal issues by a legal adviser) or before a single legally qualified magistrate now called a district judge. The lay magistracy is another unique part of the legal system: upstanding citizens dealing with less serious or uncontested cases. However, magistrates do not command the same confidence as juries in contested cases largely because they do not have the same fresh approach to the facts. People who sit regularly become case-hardened, their antennae dulled by hearing and seeing cases which are deadeningly similar. Victor Mishcon, the very distinguished solicitor who is now a Labour peer, tells a classic story of waiting for his own client's case to come on at Bow Street Magistrates' Court, when he was a young lawyer. A down-and-out came before the magistrate on a charge of pickpocketing. The testimony of a be-suited gentleman was that the tramp had sidled up to him, asked him the time and then hurried off. The man had then felt in his pocket and found his wallet missing. The accused denied the charge vehemently and insisted that he had asked the time quite genuinely because he wanted to get to a hostel by a certain time so that he could sign on for the night. The magistrate did not blink: 'There's too much of this going on. It's always the same story – someone asking the time. You're guilty, go below so that I can have a report.' When Victor Mishcon rose to begin his own case, it was interrupted. The man who had testified against the vagrant explained that he had just gone home and removed a suit from the wardrobe to take it to the cleaners and the wallet was in the pocket.

Every criminal lawyer has witnessed the injustice caused when the justice arteries harden. Whether judge or magistrate, this is the destiny of many who try cases. Juries sitting in the higher courts bring fresh eyes.

In a House of Lords debate on juries Lord Mayhew, a former Attorney-General, presented the scenario of a young mother of four children, who is harassed and has a lot on her plate. She is shopping in a supermarket when she suddenly realises she is running late for collecting children from school and, in a state of distraction, she leaves the store without paying. She is charged with shoplifting. Lord Mayhew expressed the strong belief that she would have a far greater chance of acquittal by a jury than by a magistrates' court, however conscientious the magistrates. He went on to explain that the woman existed and was his wife, who 25 years before had gone through that terrible set of events.

There is nothing like raw experience for strengthening the resolve to protect juries. In a committee stage debate in the House of Lords, the former Commissioner of the Metropolitan Police, Lord Condon, explained that he had recently stood trial as a defendant for five weeks in No. 2 court at the Old Bailey on a health and safety charge and it had confirmed his belief in the jury system. Although his liberty was not at risk, he knew that his reputation and the future of operational policing were on the line. He said:

> I knew within a few days who I wanted to adjudicate on these important issues. I looked across the room at the decent men and women on the jury and I was absolutely content and reassured that it was a jury adjudicating on the issue and not some other form of tribunal. So I find myself, perhaps against the police stereotype, wishing to preserve and protect the role of the jury at the heart of the criminal justice system.

The public's engagement in criminal justice runs through the common law systems. Because the United States has a written constitution which entrenches the right to jury trial, Americans have developed their own common law system in ways which are different to ours. So, even legal transplants from common law systems may not work because the cultural immune system is so different. Juries remain in civil cases so you see extraordinary trials where tobacco manufacturers are sued and huge awards are made by juries. And because of the sacrosanct constitutional right to freedom of speech the media and lawyers can talk about cases so openly that potential jurors have to be quizzed about their prior knowledge and predisposition. They also have to be sequestered in guarded hotels in many cases so that they will not be exposed to television news reports and opinionated commentary about the case they are trying.

Here, we live under very different constraints. Juries, even in the most serious criminal cases, now go home at night even when they are deliberating on their verdicts. The media are not supposed to report matters which could prejudice a fair trial because of strict *sub judice* rules. Very occasionally security requires that jurors are given police protection but they can watch news reports and read newspapers like every other citizen unless specifically advised not to. Lawyers do not go on the *Richard and Judy Show* or *Newsnight* to discuss what is happening in their case or declaim against the other side. So although the differences between the English system and the continental system are more stark, even within the common law family legal cultures can be very distinct.

One of the problems is that policy advisers, like sneak thieves, peruse other systems and burglarise what they think can be transposed with no reference to the larger context. As we saw with night courts, raiding other systems does not often work. I have observed criminal trials in the United States, Russia, France, Portugal, Turkey, India and Italy. I can state with honesty that despite all my criticisms of the English legal system I have seen no system that strikes a better balance between the prosecution and defence, the public interest and, increasingly, the interests of victims. We can still do better on the interests of victims, particularly children, and children accused of serious crime. In any event you cannot move to an inquisitorial system just by taking jury trial away. As the Labour MP Robert Marshall Andrews QC has pointed out, 'You don't make a boat by simply removing the wheels of a car.'

John Rawls, one of the twentieth century's greatest progressive thinkers, created a potent tool for those of us in pursuit of the just society. In *A Theory of Justice* (1971) he invented the idea of 'the original position', in which he asks us to imagine how we would want society arranged if we had no prior knowledge of the characteristics and qualities we would possess or the social position we would be born into in that society. We could be black or white, a Jew or a Muslim, rich or poor, high born or low. Under this 'veil of ignorance' about who we are, what kind of society would we invent?

He suggested that out of sheer self-interest we would choose a society in which all had as much freedom as could be reconciled with the freedoms enjoyed by others and in which there was fair equality of opportunity. If asked what kind of legal system we would invent if still in that state of ignorance it is fairly clear that people in Britain would choose jury trial. I certainly would. Most members of the public see trials in magistrates' courts as less fair. In a 2002 MORI poll, 85% of those surveyed said they trusted juries to come to the right decision; 82% believed they would get a fairer trial from a jury than a judge and 81% believed that the quality of the justice system is better when it includes jury trial as often as possible.

If the polls are right the public believes as passionately as I do that juries are an important element in our justice system. That being so, we must embrace some of the special rules created to sustain them in their function. We have to recognise the reason for the rules in our system about limiting evidence to what is reliable and relevant, which means excluding previous convictions and, in some circumstances, hearsay evidence.

All people – white, black, Asian, Jewish, male, female, gay, heterosexual – view the world through the prism of their own experience. The great strength of jurors is that they bring that diversity to the courtroom. Like most groups of people juries are susceptible to every prejudice imaginable: racism, sexism, homophobia, hostility based on class and age, as well as fear and loathing of particular kinds of crime. But gloriously and reassuringly, finer characteristics usually win the day, the collective product being greater than the sum of its parts. The seriousness of purpose brings out the best in people, who have increasingly rare opportunities to participate in public processes that make a difference to other people's lives or contribute to the well-being of society. As they deliberate and carefully consider the evidence, juries make sense of even very complex issues.

The jury tradition is not only about the right of the citizen to elect trial but also about the juror's duty of citizenship. It gives people a vital role as stakeholders in the criminal justice system. Seeing the courts in action and participating in that process maintains public trust and confidence in the law. And where else do we have such collective endeavours which draw people from across class and race divides?

One of the reasons why the jury trial is under assault is because of the course the British government took in Northern Ireland, where jury trial was suspended in a large number of cases because of conflict and replaced with what became known as the Diplock courts, named after the senior judge who made the recommendation. As I explained when discussing terrorism earlier, this was generally accepted as necessary because of the entrenched divisions: on both sides of the religious divide many believed that a jury could never be impartial. While that may have been true in Northern Ireland, it has had consequences for the rest of the United Kingdom too. When jury trial is removed, we see a move towards greater judicial power and away from democratisation. The Northern Irish judges have become vocal advocates of sitting alone without a jury. They have come to enjoy the shift in power it has meant for them and laud it to their English counterparts.

The creation of the Diplock courts has shown that removing jury trial has consequences for the whole trial process. The dynamic of the trial changes. Removing juries leads to a more inquisitorial approach and there is an 'adversarial deficit'. The court becomes much more like the Court of Appeal where jury-style advocacy is taboo. Sympathy points or a full contextual narrative are sidelined, significantly reducing the scope of the argument. The judge moves centre stage and is more interventionist. As well as being judge of law he is also judge of the facts, which may take him into terrain well beyond his personal exposure. What does a middle-class male judge really know of life on estates or drug use amongst the young? That richness and variety which derives from the collective experience of juries is missing. When a judge sits alone or even with assessors he essentially controls the way in which judgments are arrived at; decisions of law and evidence are less starkly separated from findings of fact. Evidence from Germany and Northern Ireland shows that judges have difficulty putting out of their minds evidence they have ruled inadmissible when it comes to deciding guilt or innocence. In our system juries are the judges of the facts and would have been absent during the legal arguments on admissibility so their judgment would not be contaminated. Judges are much more literal about law and do not create a bulwark against oppressive laws as juries do; they are also much more willing to believe police evidence even when it is highly questionable.

From another viewpoint those judges who favour limiting or scrapping juries often fail to realise the huge protection that juries afford to the judiciary. Because the verdict comes from a group of individuals who disappear back into the anonymity of their daily lives, there is no personal recrimination. The media may complain about the jury collectively but there is no singling out, and identification is forbidden by law. Apart from the Lord Chief Justice, judges in the United Kingdom have a low profile; they do not enjoy celebrity; their lives are rarely opened up to media scrutiny. This means that there are few attempts at corruption and few attempts to assassinate judges and few attempts to destroy their reputation for fairness. Once judges become the verdict-givers they can bid farewell to the comparative anonymity they have enjoyed. That anonymity has benefits not just for them but for the system. The press will take a much greater interest in verdicts which come from judges. In advance of trial, judges will be required by lawyers to disclose their interests. In frauds, they will be expected to show the nature of their stocks and shares and pension investments as well as those of their wives or husbands. They will have to disclose a list of their clients in their years of practice in case of conflicts of interest. If judges sit alone in fraud trials, their acquittals of white-collar criminals will be translated as class justice. This close scrutiny of judges as dispensers of verdicts, once begun, will inevitably spill over into other cases.

Listening to, and being influenced by, opposing views is rarely a virtue of governments and this is particularly true of those who enter the portals of the Home Office. The Home Office is a strange ministry in that once they work there otherwise sane men and women seem to be inducted into a cult in which they all acquire, to appropriate Ann Widdecombe's famous expression, 'something of the night' about them. Their perception of the world becomes askew, maybe as a consequence of the constant barrage of police reports about vile crimes. Perhaps the Home Office should be amalgamated with the Ministry of Culture so that a 'rebalancing' of the political culture takes place!

Getting rid of juries was a potential reform which had been sitting around in the Home Office for decades. Former Conservative ministers claim that during the Thatcher years it was regularly pulled out and presented by officials for consideration but always rejected as a non-starter with parliament and the public. This was almost a challenge to New Labour. Labour came into government determined to strip its approach to policy of any ideological baggage and ever since it has been applying a 'what works' test to many of its public service changes. If reducing jury trials would get more people convicted and speed up the system it sounded good. So the assaults on juries started life not as some radical set of proposals but as recycled Home Office policy bin-ends, connecting up to the shallow pursuit of modernisation on all fronts.

There is no doubt that a group of mandarins, influential lay magistrates and senior judges think the time has come to jettison juries. They think that widening the pool to everyone on the voters' register has reduced the quality of person sitting, especially since so many middle-class people find a way to avoid their service. In the world where Mammon is god and even two or three weeks out of the office threatens chaos, the managerial and professional class can usually work up an excuse, especially if they claim that their absence affects the employment of a large number of other people. This does not seem to be an obstacle to their summer vacations, however.

The former *Sunday Telegraph* editor, Trevor Grove, who after serving on a jury at the Old Bailey wrote a fascinating book called *The Juryman's Tale*, has made commendable proposals for the reform of jury service. He has suggested that professionals and business people should be required to nominate a period in the next calendar year when they would make themselves available, just as they would arrange an operation and period of convalescence.

Currently juries contain a higher proportion of public servants, employees and the lower orders than our masters would like. Instead of immediately resolving this with rules about civic duty and a requirement to participate, they want to ease jury trial out of existence. As well as a disdain for the general public, some of this cabal also believe that as we try to create greater synchronicity with other legal systems juries are a handicap. They require us to have different evidential rules and they are not required to give explanations for their verdicts, which judges must do in civil law jurisdictions. Although few believe in the European *corpus juris* concept, with all-consuming legal harmonisation, across European states some see juries as a block to better synergy and see their abandonment as a crucial step to seamless legal cooperation.

The establishment of international tribunals and the International Criminal Court under the UN has forced us to look at ways of knitting together a legal process which would satisfy the international community as a whole. The problem is the clash of judicial cultures between common law and civil processes. I recently interviewed Carla del Ponte, the Chief Prosecutor and her legal team who are prosecuting the former Yugoslav premier Milošević before the International War Crimes Tribunal at the Hague for a television programme; the tensions are clear. Here is a prosecutor who is used to working so closely with the police, as European prosecutors do, that she wants to have her hands on the investigatory aspect of the court's work. Boundaries are not sharply delineated. She recognises few limitations on what can and should be legitimate evidence. Rules of admissibility do not really exist in the European tradition as they do under British or North American law.

This approach is countered by the common lawyers who think that prosecutors as well as judges should consider the value of certain kinds of evidence and not present to a court that which is questionable.

These debates about how to establish legal regimes for international courts and tribunals feed back into the policy ideas of technocrat lawyers, who then think our domestic system should also be freed from legal rules, which actually have a purpose in our context.

There are also more banal arguments given for change. Some New Labour modernisers seem to think that anything old must be in need of a make-over. They say we once had trial by ordeal and ducking stools but saw the light and moved on. Juries are apparently part of an unfashionable approach to legal decision-making. They even point to human rights instruments like the Universal Declaration of Human Rights and ask where there is any suggestion that there is a right to jury trial. Their folly is in failing to appreciate that within different cultures there are fundamental values which should be respected and that wishing to retain juries is not a constipated compulsion to retain something just because it is old. Citizenship can only ever be understood within the context of the history of the country in which it is exercised. A jury trial exquisitely and democratically combines two aspects of our citizenship – the right to be tried by our fellow citizens for crimes of any serious consequence and the duty to participate in the process when required to do so.

Jack Straw was the first Home Secretary after the 1997 Labour victory. He must have imagined that getting rid of jury trial would be a welcome relief for most of the voters who mattered. He certainly thought the public believed juries were a bad thing in these days of specialist knowledge. He was making a serious misjudgment, dismissive of the role that citizens can play. What the public do not like is crime. What the public want is more criminals brought to book. The way to do that is to give the police the resources to do the job. The public would also like less crime, and the way that is achieved is largely by tackling social problems.

What politicians so often overlook as they try to justify their policy decisions is that the language they use can feed fears and misperceptions: they did this with the descriptions of 'bogus' asylum seekers, creating a belief that genuine refugees hardly exist, and they do it all the time with crime. Straw insisted that juries are duped by clever criminals and smart-ass lawyers, getting away with it time after time. It is true that guilty people are acquitted of crime but while we defence lawyers like to bask in the notion that our advocacy skills played a vital role, very often acquittals happen because the prosecution has not presented a persuasive case, meeting the high standards we are entitled to expect if liberty has any meaning at all. I always remember being embraced by a grateful client, while an elderly nun who had supported him throughout his trial made it very clear that the result was nothing to do with my efforts but was the work of Padre Pio, her link to the Almighty.

It made me laugh that in the ill-fated Millennium Dome was a 'Self Portrait Zone', which extolled the virtues of the British people and our sense of fairness, proudly boasting that we invented 'trial by jury, the best way of determining the guilt or innocence of an alleged offender'. Yet at the same time government was planning to carve a hole in the jury system.

Jack Straw's first attack was presented as a minor adjustment – the removal of the right of accused people to elect trial by jury in the crown courts in a range of cases which were not considered too serious. It was ridiculous, he railed, that the more expensive option – the Rolls-Royce – of jury trial should be used for unimportant cases rather than the serious stuff: it was also estimated that £120 million could be saved. For serious cases, jury trial was extremely important, he emphasised. But it was wrong, he said, that recidivists with loads of convictions for dishonesty should be wasting the courts' time, electing trial by jury, especially when so many pleaded guilty on the first day, when they could be dealt with speedily in the magistrates' courts. Indeed, it was a kindness to save them from themselves, since many ended up getting longer sentences as a result of being in courts with greater sentencing powers. A way had to be found to stop old lags electing trial.

In the film *Enemy of the State* (1998) one of the protagonists puts her finger on the problem: 'They say they will not suspend the civil liberties of good people but who decides who are the good people?' Jack Straw had the answer. Instead of the citizen getting to choose, magistrates would decide who would merit the Rolls-Royce, picking and choosing between accused, deciding who was deserving and who was undeserving. The criteria to be used would include 'reputation' and previous convictions. The whole project was repugnant to many people but it was still the early days of a Labour government and loyalty meant that good folks muttered behind their hands rather than publicly.

Choice, which has been elevated to totemic importance by New Labour in policy on schools and hospitals, suddenly loses its potency when it comes to citizens who fall foul of the law. Giving the choice to magistrates who are largely white and middle class – 94.5% are white – and not legally qualified was a hard pill for many sections of the community. As indicated, magistrates do a great job, handling the bulk of criminal cases, most of which are pleas of guilty. And they come cheap. The cost to the public purse is comparatively small. However, with the best will they do have a propensity to become cynical about the people who appear in the dock and, if I were facing a theft charge or contesting a charge of assault, I would certainly want the fresh eyes and breadth of human experience that comes with the jury, just like Lord Mayhew's wife. Why should it be within the magistrates' gift? And if I was refused my jury trial, were the magistrates who would hear my case going to speculate as to why I was not in a crown court getting jury trial? Would they assume I must have a load of convictions or be a jobless layabout? The black community was entitled to be alarmed at this change because they foresaw how invidious such choosing by the magistrates might be. If reputation was the basis of entitlement what would happen if you were unemployed or homeless, or you were a young black man with a couple of convictions for cannabis but were now charged with assault or burglary? And of course then there would be the usual variables between your chances before the Croydon bench as distinct from the beak in Ipswich.

The potential for discrimination in this new legislation was considerable. It would be socially and racially divisive. It was as though the debates around Stephen Lawrence's death existed inside a box marked 'police' and had no relevance to other parts of the criminal justice system where there is also institutional racism.

Part of the folly in 2000 was that much talk in Whitehall was expended on social inclusion and citizenship. Think tanks were thinking, yet here the most awe-inspiring example of citizen engagement was being eroded by the same people who agonised over the loss of civic responsibility. Since the public has to pay for the incarceration of those who are convicted and live with those who are acquitted, a scheme which allows them to take key decisions is invaluable. The process also provides a high degree of validation for difficult decisions, which is especially important in high-profile cases where the public at large may be concerned about the conviction or acquittal of a particular accused. With a jury the decision has been taken by the mirror image of the public, not by a man in a wig.

Many lawyers do not automatically or naturally function on the basis of right or wrong, preferring the rules and the processes. When a panel of non-lawyers is introduced, both sides are obliged to take notice of moral issues and judgments. As an advocate I am constantly attuning my conduct of a case to the way in which a jury might evaluate evidence. The other crucial factor is that presenting arguments to 12 ordinary citizens demystifies the law. The 'mission to explain', as they say, forces the law to remain comprehensible. Lawyers and judges always end up speaking legal shorthand when the discipline of the jury is taken away. As a result lawyer–judge hearings inevitably lead to public misapprehensions about what goes on within the system – a system which they fund and depend upon for protection.

Criminal trials are almost always about evaluating people and their motivations and particularly assessing what was going on inside the mind of an accused. Juries often have to reach judgments about what someone thought or believed at a certain moment. Did the battered woman genuinely think she was going to be hit again when she stabbed her husband or was she getting her own back? Did the driver know his passenger was carrying a firearm? Twelve of their fellow citizens offer such defendants real insight into their emotions and beliefs because of the range of their experience. Without such empathy – not sympathy – the chances of a just outcome are greatly reduced.

Jack Straw's bill to remove the right to jury trial was a thoroughly illiberal measure that deserved to be voted down. It was roundly defeated in the House of Lords. When he tried to introduce it a second time with a bit of trimming at the edges, again it was defeated. The fury in the Home Office and Downing Street was extraordinary. Wielders of power cannot bear to be opposed. The Home Secretary stubbornly asserted that a third bill would be brought forward but his plan had to be abandoned because an election was called.

The hubris of the Home Office is hard to credit. Having failed to convince the public that lower-level criminals deserved no trial by jury, the battle switched to the other end of the spectrum with the arrival of David Blunkett in the hot seat, as Home Secretary. He proudly boasted that he would make Jack Straw look like a pussycat and he does, taking delight in bating his critics with references to 'airy fairy civil liberties'. On the issue of juries, he waited for the report of Lord Justice Auld who had been commissioned by the Lord Chancellor, the Attorney-General and the Home Secretary to review the criminal justice system. It is claimed by some that Lord Justice Auld was hand-picked for this task because his views were known to chime with those of the powers that be. This is roundly refuted by Lord Justice Auld, who apparently came to his task with his mind a *tabula rasa* and responded judicially to the arguments he heard. I have no doubt that he approached his task with integrity and was thoroughly well intentioned but, even so, his 2001 report was used for political purposes. This is always a risk when judges step outside of their traditional role.

There is a well-worn policy tactic which involves threatening summary execution so that people are relieved when they only have their legs cut off at the knees. To his annoyance, Lord Justice Auld's report was widely trailed as the death knell of juries. It finally advocated a wide-scale redesign of the court structure, which meant radically reducing the right to jury trial, though not total extinction. The government removed its preferred plums from Auld's report, threw out anything too costly or over-complicated, showed how reasonable and Third Way it was by limiting the reduction in jury trial to fraud, other complicated crime and cases where there might be jury-nobbling. In the view of many, Auld was 'hung out to dry'.

In a debate on juries, the Home Secretary revealed that he had been profoundly influenced by that authoritative source on matters legal, the American novelist John Grisham. His thriller, *The*

Runaway Jury, had shown the Secretary of State what happens when a jury case goes on too long. 'It is excellent. It is an excellent, excellent book,' Blunkett told the House of Commons. While he has been less forthcoming on the provenance of some of his other policy shifts, it is very likely that they too have derived from the shelves of airport bookshops. The fact that the above page-turning yarn by Grisham is about a tort action against tobacco manufacturers in the United States – where there are still juries in civil litigation, unlike here, and where no question of liberty of the subject is involved – seems to have been beyond the ken of the Home Secretary.

The jury reforms were trailed as relating to fraud trials but by the time the Bill was drafted the word 'fraud' had disappeared off the radar and been replaced with the legend 'long and complex', which opened the gates for much serious crime being tried by a judge alone. The new plans were rationalised because complex cases were beyond the abilities of the average juror. Yet you only have to ask prosecutors and defence lawyers alike whether that is true and the majority consensus is the opposite. Financial cases which are well presented by the Crown pose no problem for juries. Fraud trials are invariably about whether the defendant was aware of particular transactions and if so whether he or she was dishonest.

The real fraud being perpetrated by government was that of maintaining that the problem lies with the 12 good men and women. As with the famous miscarriages of justice, it is rarely the fault of juries when things go wrong. Lord Irvine insisted he was not being 'in the least patronising about juries' when he suggested that complex fraud cases are really 'beyond their technical competence'. Apparently he was just worried that juries let 'serious fraudsters go free'. However, there is no evidence of this either. In fact, the modern conviction rate is 86%. This is a higher strike rate than that achieved in virtually every other area of crime. But then why should evidence get in the way of anything? It is difficult to find a case in the last 10–15 years where it could even be fairly argued that juries let fraudsters off. What Lord Irvine does not seem to realise is that fraud cases fail because of incompetent preparation by the prosecution and police and poor evidence gathering. His own high IQ seems to make him blind to the obvious.

In the NatWest case in 1996, which involved complex financial matters, the jury took to the issues with great aplomb, learning more about rights issues, stock placings and investment bank trading books than most stockbrokers. They demonstrated their knowledge by asking the judge in writing the most technical and probing questions imaginable. The judge decided the case did not stack up and directed the jury to acquit. A number of the jury members were not the least bit pleased and indicated afterwards that they had been minded to convict some of the accused. The Morgan Grenfell case failed because Peter Young, the main accused, became so mentally disturbed that he cut off one of his own testicles. Just about every insider-dealing case has failed, not because of juries but because of flawed legislation, with judges ruling repeatedly that the prosecution has not made out their case. What really needs attention is the investigation of fraud and other financial crime, not the intelligence ratings of jurors.

The police officers who are assigned to financial cases receive totally inadequate training. The Serious Fraud Office (SFO) is chronically underfunded. Until early 2002 the City of London Police had only one officer dedicated to money laundering. There is now talk of encouraging accountants to volunteer as special constables to help with fraud cases. I hope it works but I suspect it might be more effective to bring some on to the payroll and have them there full time. The DTI company inspectorate seems to have little liaison with the SFO and no one seems to know if the Financial Services Authority has any input. Anecdotal evidence suggests that the level of communication between all these bodies charged with rooting out fraud is close to zilch.

It became clear between publication of the White Paper on Criminal Justice in 2002 and the passage of the Criminal Justice Act in 2003 that elitist talk about dumb juries was not a very attractive argument for New Labour to adopt; it also sat uncomfortably with their argument that juries should hear evidence of previous convictions because they are intelligent enough to evaluate their relevance. The argument therefore shifted: it was claimed that it was the length of such trials that was the real problem as it was asking too much of citizens that they should give up months to sit on long trials. The better question is: how can we make such trials shorter?

In October 1998, the Fraud Advisory Panel submitted proposals to the Lord Chancellor's Department for procedural reform in cases of serious fraud. These reforms would substantially shorten the process, lower the cost and reduce the burden placed on juries. The government has taken no action on these proposals.

The original plan was that fraud cases would be tried by a judge with two expert lay assessors, but this idea was abandoned when it was discovered that securing the services of two accountants does not come cheap and the idea of the special jury presented difficulties once the government resiled from their original claim that the cases were too difficult for ordinary folk. In any event problems arise with delineating the role of the special assessors as fact finders rather than as judges of law; the individual accountants could also be challenged because of their own associations and past client base. Additionally, reasoned judgments would have to be given by a single judge which will take much longer to prepare and be much more likely to be appealed than the concise but clear verdicts of a jury. But more important still is the undemocratic nature of special juries. The public would soon lose confidence in a system where suited men from the City are tried by other suited men from the City.

There are other courses available. If governments are tough up front in regulatory control, there is a dramatic reduction in the number of fraud trials. The problems on insider dealing prosecutions were met by a widening of the goalposts, so that the Financial Services Authority now has the civil power to impose crippling fines at the outset to avoid long trials. This is a remedy which should be employed more extensively, for example with VAT fraud. The answer is not to do away with juries in the 10–15 serious cases dealt with annually, especially since the issue at the heart of all those cases is dishonesty, an issue ideally decided by a jury.

But under the skirts of this proposal on fraud trials was the suggestion that anything involving 'sums' or which is complex should be taken away from juries: that means a significant number of serious trials related to drugs and terrorism where there are financial transactions or involving issues perceived to be difficult could be removed. Creating such a two-tier justice system is likely to engender grievances and suspicion in the general public, who see juries as a bulwark against a bully. The social divisiveness of creating separate processes for certain kinds of serious trial but not others has not been recognised.

It is easy to dismiss concerns about 'slippery slopes' and 'thin ends of wedges' but only three years ago the government repeatedly insisted that serious cases 'required' trial by jury (the words of then

Attorney-General, the late Lord Williams of Mostyn in Hansard on 2 December 1999 and 28 September 2000). However, Lord Justice Auld, uncontrolled by the spin machine, was less secretive about what would happen next. In a lecture to the Royal Society of Medicine on 9 May 2002, he explained that the removal of jury trial in fraud would make 'a good starting point . . . If that reform comes about, and if it is a success, then consideration could be given to extending it.'

The government also wanted to remove trial by jury where there is evidence that a jury has been intimidated or might be intimidated. This measure would apply to every case involving allegations of terrorism and organised crime and would create Diplock courts in mainland Britain on the Northern Irish pattern. It is a change supported by little evidence but riding on the current climate of fear about terrorism.

In fact jury tampering is rare. I have spent a large part of my professional life involved in terrorism cases and it was possible to conduct all those cases with a jury. The Auld Report made no recommendation to remove jury trial on these grounds but relentless police lobbying seems to have held sway. If there is jury tampering it needs to be tackled head on. There are existing common law powers for a judge to intervene, stop a trial and order a retrial before another jury often hundreds of miles away. If jury trial is removed under this threat, the problem will not go away but will be transferred to judges. Instead of providing security for juries we shall see judges and their families under police surveillance around the clock.

Serious police corruption is uncommon in this country but where we find it is invariably in those squads investigating organised crime. The temptation to make a well-timed phone call when a trial does not seem to be going well for the Crown is not unreal. Some police officers would much rather have a police-minded judge try a case than a jury.

In very serious cases where there could be a risk, the courts currently order jury protection. Ministers claim that having this protection can be extremely disruptive and an unreasonable intrusion into the lives of jurors. Yet leading politicians usually have a degree of protection themselves which they manage to live with comfortably. An interesting way to measure whether this is a serious problem with substance or just another diminution of trial rights is to consider the legislation introduced in 1996 which allows retrial where an acquittal is produced by jury tampering. Not a single prosecution has taken place.

Into this mix of jury reduction, the government threw the right of defendants themselves to opt out of jury trial. In the House of Commons debate, Vera Baird QC, MP, raised the spectre of men accused of sexual offences or persons on race charges choosing to be tried by a white, male judge rather than a jury reflecting wider society. Joshua Rozenberg, the legal editor of the *Daily Telegraph*, has also speculated that this reasonable-sounding choice could easily slide into a situation where anyone who failed to opt for judge-alone trial would be regarded as virtually admitting guilt.

A fatal flaw in these bids to reduce jury trial is the failure to recognise the great benefit of separating the roles of 'judge' as judge of law and 'jury' as judges of facts. Because a jury is able to leave the courtroom when matters of law are discussed their judgments are uncontaminated by material the judge rules as irrelevant or hears in camera. Increasingly, judges hear what are called 'public interest immunity applications' in serious cases. The prosecution has an obligation to disclose all its evidence to the defence except where it may involve divulging the identity of informants or revealing matters which would not be in the public interest. In the absence of the defendant or his lawyers the prosecution may see the judge and give reasons for non-disclosure of material or seek guidance on disclosure. The judge will often rule that the Crown need not reveal the evidence at the outset of the trial but she will monitor her own decision as the case proceeds and may have to reconsider it as the trial develops. So what does a judge do when she is sitting alone with material and facts at her disposal which may be highly prejudicial but which she is supposed to put out of her mind? Who will believe that a judge sitting alone is capable of such mental gymnastics when she reaches a verdict on the facts of a case?

This government's distrust of the public's ability to make profound and complex decisions is a recurring theme. Yet it trusts us to do so at election time and, as the Society of Labour Lawyers has pointed out, the public will shortly be asked about entry to the Euro, a choice which will combine some highly technical economics, a prognosis of how other European economies might perform and issues of sovereignty. Governments attack juries because juries are independent and beyond their control.

One of the great fallacies is that juries bring about miscarriages of justice when in fact it is the evidence that fails the test. The recent cases of Sally Clark, Trupti Patel and Angela Cannings involving cot deaths are a perfect example of how justice can be thwarted when we have trial by expert. These were cases which turned on the medical evidence but where some experts became 'hawkish', developing the theory that if there was more than one sudden infant death in the family it had to be murder. The fixed mindset was that they were dealing with guilty mothers, who suffocated their offspring, and it contaminated the cases because the experts were pre-judging the cases. In fact, there are repeated deaths of newborns in some families, the medical science is still underdeveloped and there may be genetic factors at work. It has also become clear that experts can over-interpret the evidence, especially if they were not paediatric pathologists, and if they became too close to the police investigating the events. I am currently chairing a Working Group on behalf of the Royal College of Pathologists and the Royal College of Paediatrics to look at ways of developing national protocols for the investigation of sudden infant deaths and the first premiss has to be that the expert starts from a position of neutrality.

The removal of jury trial in cases of child offenders is a more complicated and sensitive issue. I hold the view strongly that those of 14 and under who commit serious offences should be dealt with outside the criminal justice process; their problems and the issues of offending should be addressed as a matter of child welfare. I have twice acted for children of 11 and 12 accused of murder. One was a boy who had been cutting up comics with his sister and in a fight over scissors she had ended up dead – one fatal wound where a scissor blade penetrated her heart. The other was a boy with a form of autism and other emotional problems who had stabbed his baby brother. Both cases convinced me that the criminal trial process was wholly inappropriate. I also acted in a case of a boy of 13 accused of raping a little girl. The girl showed no signs of penetration and some sexual playacting may have taken place but social workers had believed the allegation of penetrative sex by the child because of her vivid descriptions. It eventually came to light that the children regularly watched explicit pornographic films belonging to an older brother.

The killing of two-year-old James Bulger in 1993 produced a highly polarised debate about child killers and children who commit other serious crime. On the one hand there are people like me, who see child offenders as desperately in need of social work and psychiatric intervention, and on the other those who want punishment of a more traditional kind. The government is allowing this latter group to set their agenda. Many fail to understand that therapeutic processes and treatment that confronts behaviour are very painful and hard and much more difficult to handle than simple detention. Yet the government to its shame has introduced a minimum sentence of 12 years for children who kill.

If government were being brave it would create a Child Welfare Court for children up to the age of 14 and a Youth Court for 14- to 18-year-olds. Whatever the crime, a child should not be facing criminal sanctions in precisely the same way as an adult.

The battle over juries which took place throughout 2003 led to a 'high noon' confrontation between the House of Lords and the House of Commons on 20 November, the day the Prorogation of Parliament was due to take place. All business had to be completed but the Lords was holding out on parts of the Criminal Justice Bill, most especially the importance of preserving jury trial. A game of ping pong was taking place with the Bill passing back and forth between both Houses. It was thought that a compromise had been reached between ministers in the small hours the night before but Downing Street had dug its heels in and refused to sanction it – this gives an indication of the source of the antagonism to juries. Again the Lords voted against the changes to jury trial and the Bill bounced back down to the Commons. Finally, a deal was struck; it was agreed that defendants would not be able to surrender their right to jury trial in serious cases. The option of removing juries from fraud trials would remain in the Bill but there would have to be a further vote from both Houses of Parliament before it came into effect. Judges would try cases alone without a jury where there was evidence that a previous jury had been tampered with. The negotiation was rough and ready and all sides claimed victory.

Assaults on juries will not subside completely; they are here to stay. Already government is proposing to limit juries in inquests, suggesting they should only be used in cases where someone is compulsorily in the care of the state and has died in unclear circumstances. At present a jury is always summoned when someone dies in custody and that should continue to be the case. It is also intended to have a two stage procedure where an accused faces multiple charges – with a jury for the first trial and a judge alone for subsequent cases. There will be frequent recurrences of these attempts to erode the presence of the layperson, the amateur, in the courtroom for a number of reasons. There is an increased belief in the need for the specialist in everything. And, whatever the political statements to the contrary, there is a 'post-democratic' resistance to the value of the ordinary person's contribution.

Additionally, the impulse within a shrinking world is to harmonise legal systems. That is what is happening with commercial law and the law of intellectual property rights and in those fields of law it makes sense. However, there are two ways to go in the field of criminal justice – either common law countries will succumb to pressures to codify their systems of law or they will insist on cultural difference but agree international norms, as we are in the process of doing in relation to human rights. I emphatically believe that law derives from the nature of a given society and should draw upon the reserves of history and democratic customs, which create trust and a sense of national identity. This is one of the reasons why juries strike such a chord with the general public.

Because juries are representative of society as a whole they create a collective wisdom which cannot be matched by a judge sitting alone.

Norman Finkel in his book *Commonsense Justice* describes it beautifully: 'Rooted in a legal history . . . the jury, the conscience of the community speaks. In calling the law to follow the path of the community, we are not urging it to heed majoritarian, transitory, ignorant, or unprincipled sentiment. We are asking it to acknowledge what it may have forgotten or lost sight of: the deeper roots of justice.' Or as Jeffrey Abramson said in *We, The Jury*: 'The direct and raw character of jury democracy makes it our most honest mirror.'

The contradictions in the government's approach are extraordinary. Here is a government wedded to the focus group and the finest example of the focus group at work is the jury. But, when it comes to crime, juries – the citizens – are not to be trusted.

By reducing the number of jury trials we institute an erosion, not only of justice, but of active citizenship. The social contract is about rights and responsibilities and here we have just that. Seeing and participating in the process maintains public trust and confidence in the courts and underlines society's connection with its own laws. It is one of the reasons why our criminal justice system is admired around the world. It is also one of the features of our system of law and governance which produces the real social or civic capital to which I referred in my first chapter. Civic capital is not easily reducible to pounds, shillings and pence, but it forms an unquantifiable yet hugely important base from which trust is created and from which thriving societies grow. Sometimes you only realise its importance when it is spent.

5

THE LAST LORD CHANCELLOR?

THE HEADLINES IN the tabloids said it all: 'What have our judges got against Britain?' 'Dictators in wigs.' 'Bogus asylum and the judges who have it in for Britain.' On 20 February 2003 Mr Justice Collins, a High Court judge, found that a government measure to deprive asylum seekers of benefit was contrary to law and breached three articles of the European Convention on Human Rights, which New Labour itself had introduced into English law. The Home Secretary, David Blunkett, was apoplectic. 'Frankly, I am personally fed up with having to deal with a situation where Parliament debates issues and judges then overturn them.' The Prime Minister, who shares most of Mr Blunkett's views, was reported as 'being prepared for a showdown with the judiciary to stop the courts thwarting the government's attempts to curb the record flow of asylum seekers into Britain'. Spokesmen claimed he was going to look at new legislation to limit the role of judges in the interpretation of international human rights obligations and 're-assert the primacy of parliament'. To the *Telegraph*, Mr Blunkett fumed: 'If public policy can be overridden by individual challenge through the courts, then democracy itself is under threat.'

What, of course, is really under threat is the independence of the judiciary and the rule of law. Individual rights have been the great historical counterweight to governmental authority and control; it falls to the judges to decide when rights are being infringed, which means that an independent judiciary is a crucial element in any democracy. Rights are indispensable because they act as a restraint on the state even when it is enforcing certain majoritarian preferences. The *Daily Mail* is not usually associated with detailed analysis of case law yet for two successive days seven of Mr Justice Collins's cases were analysed in detail, all cases where he had taken the government to task. The question was raised in the House of Lords as to whether this newspaper campaign was a result of Whitehall leaks against the judge, especially since the press reports contained details which would only be found in official records. Spinning against those who are proving troublesome is the stuff of modern politics.

The excoriation of the judiciary gathered momentum in the months that followed when a retiring judge, Sir Oliver Popplewell, described the Home Secretary as a 'whining control freak' who hated the independent judiciary because it overturned his policies. The Home Secretary joined battle, ridiculing the judges before the receptive audience of a police conference. He demanded that judges come and live in the real world, characterising himself as a working-class boy pitted against the remote and comfortable judiciary in their Surrey drawing rooms. It is an easy game of one-upmanship. I can play that game too.

However, the vilification of Andrew Collins and the judiciary at large poses important questions. What does the rule of law mean? Whose rules? Are judges only doing their job well if the government likes their decisions? Judicial desire to please government and to reflect this in their judgments has provided cover for terrible abuses of power the world over. Populist governments can get all manner of laws through parliament; the whole purpose of human rights principles is that in their application they provide standards against which all law must be measured. The Joint Select Committee on Human Rights had warned parliament that the powers sought by the Home Secretary in this asylum legislation could be abused and create breaches of human rights. Mr Justice Collins with great *politesse* said he was sure that it was never parliament's intention to render people destitute.

The Home Secretary is certainly entitled to appeal. What he is not entitled to do is launch a full frontal attack on the judge, fuelling invective in the press and undermining the authority of the judiciary as a whole. As the then Lord Chancellor, Lord Irvine, pointed out to his cost, 'maturity requires that when you get a decision that favours you, you do not clap. And when you get one that goes against you, you do not boo'. As well as feeding into a disdain for the judiciary amongst the public, and discouraging good candidates from considering it as a professional career, it also has the effect of putting the frighteners on people who need to be fearless. Some judges already look over their shoulders, anxious not to displease or rock the boat, forever cautious. But this constant undermining means that judges may be less prepared to make the bold decision, and enfeebled judges are bad for justice. Blunkett railed against the courts getting in the way of his policy. He wanted a rough and ready filtering system to reduce benefits and discourage asylum seekers and was prepared to ignore the fact that such rubber-stamping produces injustice.

This was not the first time the Secretary of State had vented his spleen against the judges. He raged over the Oakington decision in 2001 which condemned his policy of detaining asylum seekers purely for reasons of administrative convenience. He blew a gasket over the decision of Mr Justice Turner about the visitor's permit for Louis Farrakhan, the vocal black American activist, a decision which said that the Home Secretary had not justified his interference with free speech. He launched a tirade at the Labour Party conference in October 2002 against lawyers and judges who dared to question his judgement. He was also infuriated when Mr Justice Collins, in a different case, held that the detention of non-citizens suspected of terrorist links infringed the human rights norm of equality before the law, and he must have been mightily relieved when that particular decision was overturned by the Lord Chief Justice.

On top of all this, his growling about the removal by the judiciary of his power to determine when life prisoners should be released was heard all over Whitehall. In 2002 the House of Lords ruled that the Home Secretary's powers to decide how long criminals stay in prison breached human rights principles. There could be no role for politicians in deciding the sentencing tariff of individual offenders because of the temptation to succumb to external pressures. The cases of Myra Hindley and of the boys who killed Jamie Bulger became the battleground on which these constitutional and justice issues were fought.

In response, the Home Secretary decided to rein in the discretionary powers of the judiciary, starting with sentencing of convicted murderers. Under the slogan 'Life will mean life' he unveiled a set of rigid tariffs for those who killed, spelling out what category of offence should merit remaining in custody for ever:

terrorist murder, child murder following abduction or where there was sexual or sadistic conduct, or where there is a previous conviction for murder. He also indicated which categories should face at least 30 years: murders of police or prison officers, killing for gain, murder involving firearms or explosives, killing a witness, killings motivated by race, religion or sexual orientation, a single sadistic or sexual murder of an adult, any multiple murders, and so on. If the judges were going to rid themselves of the stranglehold of the Executive, they would be caught instead in the vice of the legislature.

The tap was to be tightened on judicial discretion by legislating for what judges could do within strict parameters. This was described by the judiciary as Blunkett's Revenge. The problem with minimum sentences for categories of crime is that it is a very rough form of justice with insufficient flexibility to respond to the infinitely variable circumstances of any crime. Most of those who abduct and kill children stay in prison for ever already, as do serial killers. It is highly unlikely that the Yorkshire Ripper or Dennis Nilsen will ever be released. Announcing that this is to be the rule is to suggest that something very different happens currently. To raise the minimum sentence to 30 years in the categories described is a significant hike in penalties – in many cases a doubling of the length – and amounts to no more than an emotional and irrational response to a handful of high-profile cases. The majority of murders are committed within families or kinship groups. A young man who has never thought much about the risks of his conduct may take part in an armed robbery where a bank guard is shot by his mate. He would be convicted of joint enterprise murder. But after 10 or 12 years in jail he may mature into a very different human being who would not only never re-offend but would contribute to society in positive ways. A belief in the possibility of redemption is at the base of all the work that goes on in prisons. It is hard to imagine what it means to give someone no sense of hope, not even a shard. This is retributive justice not only at its most punitive and inhumane but at its most impractical. How do prisons manage prisoners who have no incentive to seek rehabilitation? It makes prisons less safe and endangers prison staff.

Dangerous paedophiles should be kept in prison for as long as necessary but when people become old and infirm is there any point in keeping them there? In the United States, whole wings of prisons have become the vilest kind of old folks' home. Instead of looking to the penal policies of the rest of Europe, the Home Secretary, like other cabinet ministers, seems to be in thrall to the American Way, with prison as the easy answer to fears about crime. As though the timing was synchronised, exactly at the moment when David Blunkett was jumping on judges here, John Ashworth, the arch-Conservative American Attorney-General, was conducting his own attack upon judicial discretion in the United States, insisting that judges who sentence below his minimum range should be named and shamed. Chief Justice Renquist, the most senior judge on the Supreme Court and a man whom only George Bush would consider a liberal, is having to point out that justice requires discretion and that pressure on judges undermines the system. Discretion is required because judges should pay attention to the special circumstances of one case which distinguishes it from other cases. It is necessary to see whether there is genuine contrition, whether the crime was done professionally for profit or some other reason.

This ratcheting-up of sentences by our own Home Secretary will not be confined to the most serious offences because the whole climate of sentencing is affected by the escalation. Research already shows that judges in the crown courts are sentencing people for significantly longer periods than they did ten years ago for the same offences: the rhetoric of punishment has done its work.

When ending the death penalty was being debated in Britain in the 1950s, we looked at the possibility of creating categories of homicide, with some for which the death penalty remained and others where it could be removed. It became clear that it is impossible to classify murders into crude groupings, so the majority in parliament were persuaded to abolish the death penalty completely. The components in individual cases are what make the difference. Hard and fast rules do not work in sentencing, and this has been accepted by every sensible politician and administrator since. There is very good reason to review the whole law of homicide and this course has been urged by two of our Law Lords, but that would not meet the immediacy and timetables of an ambitious Home Secretary.

Many members of the public do not realise that people are convicted of murder not just because they wickedly intend to kill in a premeditated way but because they intended to cause serious harm and the victim later died of the injuries. In some jurisdictions having a deliberate intent to kill leads to a conviction for culpable homicide, which carries an even heavier sentence than other murders. Many people would feel that this distinction makes sense but there should be considered debate on the subject of classification.

The display of antagonism towards judges is not a personal foible of the present Home Secretary: Tory governments have their own previous convictions for falling out with judges. The last Conservative Home Secretary, Michael Howard, and many before him have railed against challenge to policy and what is described as 'judicial supremacism'. When Howard planned to introduce mandatory sentences for particular crimes the late Lord Chief Justice, Peter Taylor, indicated that penal policy should not be dictated by 'the vagaries of fashion'. Howard's rejoinder was that Taylor was 'soft on crime'. Howard also accused the judges of subverting the democratic doctrine of parliamentary sovereignty and giving themselves a more powerful constitutional role, when in fact their behaviour was quite consistent with the mainstream notion of their constitutional role. Kenneth Baker, when Home Secretary, deported a Zairean political refugee back to Zaire, despite having been ordered not to do so by a judge. The House of Lords concluded that his action amounted to contempt (*M* v. *The Home Office* 1994).

I hope it comforts David Blunkett that Lord Waddington, one of the most right-wing Conservative Home Secretaries of the postwar era, expressed brotherly sympathy with him over his exasperation at the judges. Waddington is still a vocal supporter of capital punishment despite having acted for the innocent Stefan Kiszko who spent 17 years in jail for a murder he did not commit, and is vehemently hostile to human rights legislation and the role it assigns judges to protect those who are vulnerable. His perspective is unsurprising; the shock is that Labour ministers too accuse our judges of excessive liberalism. There seems to be a strange authoritarianism running through this administration like the writing in seaside rock. It is easy to blame Mr Blunkett but we should recall that he has been given a licence by his leader. Mr Blunkett will move on but unless there is a conscious decision to change direction Home Affairs policy will continue to be repressive.

The Labour Party has traditionally been suspicious of judges, suspecting a class bias and hidden Conservative sympathies. Past Labour governments have experienced reactionary judges undermining their progressive policies; it was well documented by

Professor John Griffith in *The Politics of the Judiciary*. Normally it would be very easy for a Labour minister to summon party support against a judgment critical of his policy. Yet now the support for the Minister comes from the most right-wing xenophobic elements of the press. It certainly cannot be claimed that this is an example of the judiciary showing its class bias against the politics of Labour.

A common mistake is that MPs come to equate a party political majority in the Commons with 'parliament'. They say ministers are answerable to parliament and not to the courts and by that they mean that ministers should answer only to the Commons, not just for the desirability of the policy choices they make within legal limits, but also on the question of what those legal limits are. They seem to think that as long as a Commons majority approves of what a minister does, nothing more need be said about the legality of his or her behaviour. But it is not MPs who decide on whether a minister's actions are legal or illegal. Since 1688 our constitution has made it clear that the only way ministers can ultimately be rendered answerable to parliament is through judges in the courts ensuring that they do not deploy powers that parliament has not given them. The judges are in fact asserting the supremacy of parliament rather than their own and they need to do so from a position of independence.

If they fulfil their function properly, judges will at times upset public opinion and governments because they will protect the interests of unpopular minorities – those accused of crime, asylum seekers, paedophiles, prisoners and probably fox-hunters. Correspondingly, it is the duty of politicians to recognise that they too are bound by law and that they have a responsibility to preserve the integrity of the judiciary.

In a political climate generated by fear of terrorism, members of the judiciary may be subject to a host of pressures: to interpret the law so as to prejudice the interests of alleged terrorists or to let legislation of dubious constitutionality go unchallenged. But for judges to do anything other than remain independent, including from the Executive, and to administer justice fairly in accordance with the rule of law is unacceptable. Protecting the judicial space is one of the functions of government ministers connected with justice. We need to maintain a healthy legal culture so that the majority of people value law and legal processes, so that they understand the difference between disapproving of the outcome of one particular case and defending the system as a whole, as a distinctive part of our governance.

Of course, individual judges do not always live up to our high expectations. I have frequently criticised judges for their hidebound attitudes to women or their unwillingness to see how the system discriminates, but I am not a government official. When a minister rails against a decision she sets the tone for the next disappointed litigant. Such criticism is also corrosive of judicial self-confidence. Sometimes judges succumb to harassment by the press or ministers or to public pressure. Like everyone else, they too want to be liked. They do not want to fall out with government. They do not want to be tomorrow's tabloid headline.

Attacks also have an effect on recruitment. I have little sympathy with the claim that unless judges are paid even more, then high-earning commercial silks (QCs) will eschew the Bench. If money has dictated a lawyer's every choice it is unlikely that he or she will make a good public servant. There are many lawyers from other disciplines and areas of expertise who want to play their part in the administration of justice. However, if candidates for the judiciary see judges being vilified it certainly does make the role less attractive. We have seen a significant drop in candidates for other areas of public service, from social work through to general practice in medicine and teaching, because willing people feel undervalued.

In accepting the judicial role, judges can become unclear as to their function and relationship with the state. They see themselves as protectors of good order against anarchy, and this can spill over into joining with the police in the battle against crime. Fighting crime is no bad thing but when judges see themselves as allies of the police, impartiality goes overboard. In my early days of practice judges refused to acknowledge unacceptable police practices, but exposure of police behaviour in high-profile cases has dented that confidence. In the Northern Irish cases of the 1970s and '80s the behaviour of some of our senior judges was execrable, with certain of them colluding in the maintenance of wrongful convictions.

Lord Denning has retained his mythological status as a great force for legal good but it is worth remembering his shocking judgment when in 1980 he dismissed the attempt by the Birmingham Six to commence a civil action against the police. It illustrates an attitude which permeated much of the judges' ranks at the time:

> Just consider the course of events if this action is allowed to proceed to trial. If the six men fail it will mean much time and money will have been extended for no good purpose. If the six men win it will mean the police are guilty of perjury, that they are guilty of violence and threats, that the confessions were invented and improperly admitted in evidence and the convictions were erroneous. That would mean that the Home Secretary would have to recommend that they should be pardoned or remit the case to the Court of Appeal. This is such an appalling vista that every sensible person in the land would say it cannot be right that these actions should go any further. This case shows what a civilised country we are. The state has lavished large sums of money in their defence. On their own evidence they are guilty. It is high time it stopped because this is really an attempt to set aside their convictions. It is a scandal which should not be allowed to continue.

Fifteen years later the Birmingham Six case was referred back to the Court of Appeal. Lord Justice Lane and his co-judges made plain their outrage at the allegations made by the appellants' lawyers against the police. The appeal was dismissed on that occasion only to be revisited two years later, by which time the evidence of police misbehaviour and scientific folly was so overwhelming that even Lord Lane had to swallow it.

Periods of high political fever, whether over asylum or terrorism, require a strong judiciary and politicians with constitutional nous should see why this plank of democracy is so important. Weak but clever judges can be intellectually dishonest, making decisions which will please the powers that be and rock no boats. But in recent years we have seen a visible shift as the judges have enforced individual and constitutional rights against the Executive. The development of international human rights law has had an impact on our own judiciary, sensitising them to the role they should play in restraining ministerial abuse. This is not simply as a result of the Human Rights Act. There is now much greater connection between judges internationally, a collegiality which has encouraged greater debate and a more challenging discourse about law, rights and the role of the judiciary in a democracy. It has given sustenance not only to our judges but, even more crucially, to judges in much more beleaguered circumstances in other parts of the world. Even before the arrival of the Human Rights Act our senior judges were tentatively plumbing the rich seams of the common law in new ways to protect citizens against the power of the state. Much of the legal principle which informs the European Convention draws upon the common law: this should come as no surprise, since common lawyers from Britain were key draftsmen of the Convention back in 1950.

Public law has been transformed over the last 30 years. There has been recognition of the crucial role of the courts, standing between the Executive and the citizen. A process called judicial review has developed which enables citizens to take action against a decision by government, calling the Executive to justify inroads into their rights. In addition, the incorporation of the European Convention created a shift in the way lawyers think and added a new dimension to the responsibilities of courts. In a single positive act – The Human Rights Act 1998 – government was saying to the judges, 'You have the clear power to find against us when we act in ways which interfere with the human rights of people.' To preserve the primacy of parliament, judges in the UK cannot strike down legislation and declare parliamentary statutes unlawful, as they can elsewhere, but by their judgments they can show where ministers have crossed the line. It is then expected that government will take steps to rectify their failures. The passage of the Human Rights Act 1998, which took effect in 2000, was the greatest achievement of this or any recent government in the field of legal reform.

In the five years' run-up to the general election in 1997, I was the chair of Charter 88, which campaigned for constitutional reform. Our platform was drawn up in 1988 at the height of Thatcherism, when Mrs T. seemed to have a stranglehold on power and the shortcomings of British constitutional arrangements were becoming all too clear. The call was for a written constitution, a bill of rights, devolution of Scotland, Wales and Northern Ireland, reform of the judiciary, proportional representation, reform of the House of Lords and a Freedom of Information Act. When John Smith became leader of the Labour Party, he agreed to appear on a Charter 88 platform, arguing not just for devolution but also for a bill of rights. As a Scottish Queen's Counsel, he had come to see how ridiculous it was that Britain had failed to incorporate the European Convention on Human Rights so that those with a legitimate grievance against government had to wait up to six years for their claim to reach the court in Strasburg. He was instinctively in favour of human rights legislation and saw it as a great unifier of global aspiration. He also wanted to see real reform of the House of Lords and had no reservations about ending the culture of secrecy by introducing a Freedom of Information Act. The public embrace by the leader of the Labour Party of a substantial part of the constitutional reform agenda was very exciting.

After John Smith's sudden death, the new leadership was alert to the potency of these ideas. Naturally, there remained argument and disagreement over proportional representation, and whether a written constitution was in fact necessary or even a good thing, but New Labour recognised that a reforming agenda was necessary to renovate the political culture and they wanted to be associated with that energy.

It is interesting to audit what happened after 1997. Devolution came to pass and a parliament was created in Scotland and assemblies in Wales and Northern Ireland. The Human Rights Act was triumphantly introduced, with Derry Irvine, the Lord Chancellor, as principal architect. But as power settled comfortably on shoulders, the will for change was sapped. An emasculated Freedom of Information Act was enacted. Proportional representation was dumped. The commitment to a reformed upper chamber was lukewarm once most of the hereditary peers were ousted and it finally hit the skids with the Prime Minister himself pressing for a fully appointed House to retain his patronage and keep the place weak. This was a conservative decision for which Derry Irvine was largely to blame.

It is hard to decide whether it was the delicious pleasure of power which led to this retreat from well-considered constitutional reform or whether the interest was cosmetic and shallow from the outset. It appears that our current Home Secretary frequently sees the Human Rights Act and the UK's obligations under human rights treaties and conventions as a serious inconvenience; he had no hesitation in derogating from the European Convention to intern aliens after 11 September when no other European country found it necessary to do so. He wants to look again at our Convention obligations to asylum seekers. He wants to hobble judges in their ability to interpret human rights law. Indeed, in his speech to the Labour Party conference in 2003, even the Prime Minister vowed to put an end to 'judicial interference' in asylum issues as though the judges are acting outside of their proper function. The lawyers who now hold government office have, of course, no experience of the legislation in any capacity other than as ministers. They do not know what it is like to sit with a refugee who has slept in a telephone box and had no food and explain the legal process, but instinctively some lawyers in government also have concerns about what is happening to rights and they sigh when cornered about the retreat from civil liberties. Derry Irvine as Lord Chancellor, Gareth Williams as the Lord Privy Seal and Peter Goldsmith, the Attorney-General, have at different times tried to exert a restraining influence but they were unable to rein in Home Office ministers. Even civil servants in the Home Office despair at some of the developments.

Before coming into power, Labour had shown commitment to the creation of a Ministry of Justice as a proper counterweight to the powers and propensities of the Home Office. A Ministry of Justice with a Secretary of State sitting in the Commons, responsible for not only the running of the courts but also criminal justice legislation would act as a balance between the interests of the Executive and the instruments of law and order on the one hand and the interests of justice and the rights of citizens on the other, but this was soon abandoned.

Without naming the Home Secretary, in a speech to MPs the Lord Chancellor Derry Irvine referred to judges giving decisions that the Executive did not like. 'Some ministers have spoken out against some decisions they don't like. I disapprove of that, I think it undermines the rule of law.' He was absolutely right but his battles with David Blunkett over judicial independence and Home Office empire-building brought their price with his sacking in June 2003, when he was reshuffled out of office by the Prime Minister, his former pupil. It was the stuff of tragedy, with the kingmaker being rejected by the protégé whom he nurtured to greatness. Blair had outgrown his mentor and found new stalwarts on whom to rely, men and women who echoed his own sentiments on law and order more precisely. Authoritarianism had won the day. Although Lord Irvine had his foibles he had sought to protect judicial independence and had frequently championed liberal values in the Cabinet.

It was announced with a great blast of hype, also in June 2003, that the outmoded role of Lord Chancellor was now abolished and Derry Irvine would go down in history as the last Lord Chancellor. The Lord Chancellor's Department would from henceforth be known as the Department of Constitutional Affairs, led by a new

Secretary of State, Lord Falconer of Thoroton, an unelected politician. Within hours it became apparent that this was constitutional change of a high order, one that required more than a press release. Hundreds of statutes make reference to the role of the Lord Chancellor or his department, and legislation would be required to effect the changes. The Lord Chancellor is Speaker of the House of Lords and until that role could be reconsidered there had to be a Lord Chancellor. Judges still needed to be appointed. Within days of this death knell for the role of Lord Chancellor, Charlie Falconer, the PM's friend, found himself decked out in knee-breeches and silk stockings in a long wig and tricorn hat, sheepishly playing the Gilbert and Sullivan role on the Woolsack. New Labour, which had for so long been ridiculed for its tendency to place presentation above substance, was now being ridiculed for an initiative which was all substance and disastrous presentation.

However, what the changes did not mean was any limit on the powers of the Home Secretary.

Early on in the life of the Labour government, a group of lawyers and academics, myself included, tried to persuade Derry Irvine that the time had come to shed the ridiculous fiction of the tripartite role of the Lord Chancellor, who was supposed to be superhumanly capable of putting on three different pantomime costumes and to separate out his many roles. We even made submissions to the Royal Commission on Reform of the House of Lords on the Lord Chancellor's role. A particular conundrum was, how could he be in the Cabinet and sit as a judge? When I suggested he might take the lead as the great reforming Lord Chancellor and shed some of the roles, he patted me affectionately and explained that it was all about tradition. What it was all about was power. Derry Irvine should have reformed his own role and his reluctance to do so was a great weakness. Pressure was growing for an independent commission to appoint judges, particularly with Harriet Harman MP, the Solicitor-General, emphasising the still poor representation of women and other minorities in the judicial ranks. But Derry was offering only desultory and cosmetic change, with consultations on wigs and gowns and a bit of tinkering with the method of making appointments and a review of the QC system. He was unwilling to sacrifice his role as appointer-in-chief of judges, nor did he seem willing to surrender his entitlement to sit on the Bench of our highest court.

It is also bizarre and unfitting that in the twenty-first century the highest court in the land is still a committee of the legislature, when the judiciary is supposed to be independent. The sittings of the Appellate Committee take place in a committee room of the House of Lords. Judgments are given in the chamber of the House of Lords when peers are gathering for ministerial questions. When judgments were delivered in the first Pinochet case, the crowded benches of the chambers led foreign television viewers to think that Lady Thatcher was one of the dissenting minority who opposed the extradition of General Pinochet. There are probably citizens in Britain who are just as confused. People were entitled to ask why we do not have a Supreme Court like every other great nation. Why do we have a Lord Chancellor who sits as a judge and is head of the judiciary, is also a very active and powerful member of the Cabinet, chairing several influential committees and is essentially the Speaker in that part of the legislature which is the House of Lords?

As the senior judge the Right Honourable Lord Steyn has said:

> Nowhere outside Britain, even in democracies with the weakest forms of separation of powers, is the independence of the judiciary potentially compromised in the eyes of citizens by relegating the status of the highest court to the position of a subordinate part of the legislature. And nowhere outside Britain is the independence of the judiciary potentially compromised in the eyes of citizens by permitting a serving politician to sit as a judge at any level, let alone in the highest court which fulfils constitutional functions.

Not only did Lord Irvine's participation in judicial business serve no useful purpose: it was also contrary to public interest.

Since the collapse of the Soviet Union, Russia has been reforming its legal system and when the President of the Supreme Court of Russia came to London with a party of judges to visit the courts, the British Council arranged for a meeting with the Lord Chancellor. On the way there the Chief Justice described the problems of creating an independent judiciary in the post-communist era because so few people believed that the judges were really independent. Sometimes Russian people still turned up at the back of the courts with gifts for the 'official' who was to try their case. We discussed the need to come down hard on corruption and the whole concept of the separation of powers. With a smile, he then asked me to explain the business of the British Lord Chancellor 'wearing three hats' when it was British lawyers who had helped with drafting their legislation, establishing the Russian judiciary as independent of the political process. I suggested he ask the Lord Chancellor. The official answer was well rehearsed but it sounded really half-baked. How could we play a role in the development of new democracies around the world when our own practices did not bear scrutiny?

Scotland created a judicial appointments commission for its judiciary in 2002. The Bar Council had endorsed a report produced by the former Court of Appeal judge, Sir Iain Glidewell, calling for an end to the present charade. Even the Council of Europe was calling for the position to be rectified, particularly when the new democracies of Europe are required to have a judiciary independent of political control. A resolution by the Dutch member, a former professor of constitutional law, called for a separation of the Lord Chancellor's roles and it was supported by France, Germany, Belgium, Switzerland, Russia and the Ukraine. It was an anomaly that we had not sorted out the issue for ourselves and government was being forced to act. That was why the screws were being applied to Lord Irvine. The press may have said the reform came out of left field and no one had been expecting a change. It was not so. Reform of the Lord Chancellor's role was on the cards. What was unexpected was the failure to engage Derry Irvine successfully in the process, partly because of his own unwillingness for reform, but also because the Home Secretary was determined to carve out a larger empire in any division of ministerial spoils. Now we have a new ministry, headed by Lord Falconer, who shares the Tony Blair/David Blunkett perspective on criminal justice. However, the Department of Constitutional Affairs has been put on notice that if it does not meet its performance indicators for the criminal courts, that aspect of its function will be removed to the Home Office. Leading lights around the Home Secretary believe there will be greater coherence in the criminal justice system if the criminal courts are also run by the Home Office. However, to have the police and the courts in the same department would diminish their independent functioning. The alarm call for anyone concerned with justice issues is that the process is then dominated by a prosecution perspective with the courts corrupted by an emphasis on securing convictions.

The sad truth is that Lord Irvine failed the test. He could have reformed his own role by simply removing the Lord Chancellor's right to sit as a judge and he should have created an independent judicial appointments commission, so that he no longer appointed judges. But it was largely his alarm at the militant tendencies of the Home Office which made him resist the inevitable.

Since coming into office in 1997 Lord Irvine sat as a judge in only eight cases. To claim that this gave him any real appreciation of the contemporary judicial role, or that it forged a spirit of judicial camaraderie, or that it let him see who were the up-and-coming advocates was a nonsense, although all these arguments were put forward.

But it was not just Derry Irvine who clung to the traditional Lord Chancellor role. There is an old guard who still insist that the system has worked perfectly well for centuries and that the only problem was the failure of the last Lord Chancellor to recognise the boundaries. How else, they insisted, could he have considered it acceptable to send out letters to members of the legal profession enlisting their presence at an expensive dinner with the proceeds going to the Labour Party? This tainted his role as appointer-general of Queen's Counsel and judges: lawyers applying for appointments might think they were required to fork out. However, the traditionalists got it wrong. There are good domestic reasons for reforming the role as well as the perceptions of the outside world.

The legal and political landscape has changed radically. The role of Lord Chancellor has become increasingly politicised. The Human Rights Act formalised a process of change which had been taking place for some time, whereby judges exercise greater control in relation to state abuse. It had already gathered steam with the development of judicial review. It is impossible to retain with any decorum the old crossovers between judiciary and Executive and vice versa. There has also been a vast increase in the nature and extent of a Lord Chancellor's executive responsibilities, partly because the court system has become so much more complex, with civil, criminal, family, chancery and magistrates' courts, with tribunals for mental health, employment, social security and immigration, with training for judges and magistrates, financing of legal aid and legal advice centres. The list is endless. Lord Irvine's annual bill for advisers and consultants had risen from £400,000 to £2.5 million since he took office. A spokesman explained that the rise in expenditure on external consultancies was a reflection of the increase in the Department's responsibilities over the past few years. The Lord Chancellor's Department was a high spending ministry yet it got much less parliamentary attention than it deserved, partly because it was cloaked in the fog of tradition and also because there was no senior minister in the Commons to answer for it, which was scandalous.

As well as his close personal and influential relationship with the Prime Minister, manifest in his formulating the 'non-reform' of a fully appointed House of Lords, Derry Irvine was responsible for devising and implementing policies affecting the administration of justice of a highly political nature. In addition he chaired cabinet committees over a large range of policy areas. He was at the centre of political power. The question that had to be asked was to what extent he was bound by the doctrine of collective responsibility; for example, was he expected to support agreed policy even if it undermined judicial discretion?

It would have been possible to have reform without abolition of the role of Lord Chancellor, which is political but which also transcends politics. Although the Lord Chancellor sits in the Cabinet he is also an office holder under the constitution, as Keeper of the Great Seal. This means that he must provide yet another check on executive power by protecting the judiciary. When the talk in Cabinet is of law and order, the Home Secretary might be the voice of 'order' in the political firmament, but the Lord Chancellor has to speak for 'law' and justice. Tensions are inevitable but that is why the check is needed. The ancient role has developed incrementally – that has always been the genius of the British constitution – and replacing the Lord Chancellorship with yet another Secretary of State who has no eye to the long term, who may not be a lawyer and who functions purely politically could be a travesty of our constitutional needs. One remedy is to stipulate quite clearly in the legislation which will abolish the traditional Lord Chancellor functions that the Secretary of State for Constitutional Affairs has a duty to protect the independence of the judiciary. The fear is that legislation alone will not imbue the degree of gravity that needs to be attached to the principle.

Derry Irvine started out his journey as the man of politics whose primary loyalty rested with 'young Blair', as he insisted on calling the Prime Minister. But with time he saw his role differently. He found himself increasingly telling the Home Secretary to get his tanks off Middle Temple's lawns or pointing out that policy ideas were unworkable in the courts. He did act as a vital conduit between

Executive and judiciary over issues like the management of the justice system. However, when David Blunkett sent his grenades in the direction of the judges, Irvine was presented with the greatest test of fealty. There was no doubt in the end where Derry Irvine saw his loyalty as lying. He was first and foremost Lord Chancellor, whose loyalty was to the constitution and the judges. His choice meant that not only was he dismissed but his job was also abolished.

My postscript on these events is that when I pointed out to one of the Downing Street inner circle that the Lord Chancellorship could have been reformed rather than abolished, he mulled it over and expressed regret – not at the passing of a constitutional function of such history but at the loss of the name. 'It is such a good brand!' he said.

6

JUDGING THE JUDGES

WHEN I FIRST practised at the Old Bailey, the judges terrorised the courts, with tyrannical displays of impatience and intemperance. There are judicial names which can still send shudders down the spines of grown men. Melford Stevenson was a monster. When I represented Myra Hindley in her attempt to escape from prison in the 1970s, his behaviour was so abominable that even Lord Longford who saw good in all creatures was pushed to say unkind things about him.

A few years ago I remarked to one of our judges at the Old Bailey that judges had changed. He laughingly dismissed my rosy optimism, saying that judges had not changed it was just that I had got older. The senior judiciary is as white and public school educated today as it was ten years ago, according to the magazine *Labour Research*. And despite repeated commitment to a more diverse judiciary only 2.5% of judges come from ethnic minorities and they are on the lowest tier, the Circuit Bench. Not one has ever been appointed above this level. Women have done slightly better, rising to 14.6%. Some of those increases can, however, be explained by the name change of stipendiary magistrates to district judges. The United Kingdom at last has a woman Law Lord – a judge in our Supreme Court – and not before time. Lady (Brenda) Hale was appointed in October 2003 by Lord Falconer, the Lord Chancellor and Secretary of State for Constitutional Affairs. Here was a woman who co-wrote the first book on women and the law, who as a law commissioner authored the hugely successful Children Act, and helped reform the law on matrimonial property. How Lord Irvine passed her by remains a mystery. Canada, by contrast, has had women Supreme Court judges for over 20 years and now has a woman chief justice. Of 35 judges in our Court of Appeal only three are women. Scotland has recently appointed a woman for the first time, Lady Cosgrove. Of the 100 judges in the High Court, only eight are women. The signs of change are mainly in the lower courts but it is in the higher courts that law is made. Most senior judges are drawn from the rank of Queen's Counsel and again the statistics are appalling, with only about 10% of those appointed being women and even fewer coming from ethnic minorities.

The one positive change is that, despite perceptions, more judges are in touch with the social mores. Many today live lives different to those of previous generations, with wives who have their own careers, and children living at home rather than at boarding-schools, and at least they watch the television and see slices of human existence which were formerly beyond judges' ken. Their lives are less cushioned and remote from those of the people who come before them. Some of them have even done dangerous things like inhaling dope and reading Marx in their youth. And even if they do not know the state of the *zeitgeist*, they come closer to it.

Even a few solicitors and legal academics are now being appointed as judges, but there is still a long way to go to ensure public confidence. Hazel Genn's research, *Paths to Justice* (1999), showed that the public still feel the judiciary does not mirror society. A typical response was, 'I don't know what the mix of judges is but most of them seem to be, you know, white middle aged men . . .'

As the American law professor Alan Dershowitz has remarked of our senior judiciary, 'the small legal clique who select your wigged Platonic guardians seem to believe there is a white, male gene for intellect, integrity, and professionalism'. David Pannick QC described the system as resembling 'a pre-1965 Conservative leadership contest or a Papal conclave rather than the choice of lawmakers in a modern democracy'.

The senior judiciary in Britain is recognised internationally for its intellectual and legal brilliance. We have some of the finest judicial brains in the world in our highest courts. Some commentators say we owe a particular debt to the last Lord Chancellor, James Mackay, who appointed such a stunning array of judges during his years in office. There are fears that more recent appointments reflect an admiration for the commercial bar at the expense of public lawyers who may know a bit more about the human condition. The problem about appointments resting ultimately with an individual is that this sort of speculation about personal preferences and patronage is inevitable.

The old saw is that appointments are made on merit, as though 'merit' was a purely objective yardstick. 'Merit' is always prayed in aid as soon as a bid is made to be more inclusive, particularly bringing women into anything. It is as though we are going to dilute the port. When John Major put together his first cabinet, the absence of women was drawn to his attention and he too explained that appointments could only be on merit. I always felt that the men were sighing with relief at having ousted Maggie, and like schoolboys wanted to put their feet on the table and smoke in the cabinet room.

The temptation for men of a certain age to appoint in their own image and likeness is considerable and they do not even know that they are doing it. Lord Chancellors, who were in charge of these appointments, would remind us that they took careful soundings from other judges, heads of Bar circuits and leading lights in professional organisations and did not act on their own whims, but since such holders of office were almost all men of a similar hue it is not surprising that the outcomes have been so predictable. Unless the gatekeepers are changed the system will continue to be a self-appointing oligarchy.

Derry Irvine was no doubt sincere in his desire to widen access to the Bench. He published criteria for appointment with which everyone would agree: legal knowledge and experience, intellectual and analytical ability, sound judgment, decisiveness and authority. Personal qualities had to include integrity, fairness, humanity and courtesy. 'Candidates must also respect and have understanding of men, women and children of different backgrounds. They must be sensitive to the influence of different ethnic and cultural backgrounds on the attitudes and behaviour of people whom they encounter in the course of their work.' However, advocacy is also listed as a key qualification which marginalises the experience of solicitors for whom it is a less central preoccupation. The skill of advocacy is not one that is required for the Bench. In fact, those who like the sound of their own voices often make bad judges because they are too interventionist. Positions on the Bench except at Court of Appeal and House of Lords level are now advertised. Lord Irvine rose at dawn and personally reviewed every application.

No one questioned the last Lord Chancellor's beliefs or intentions but they seriously questioned the capability of the current system to achieve them.

The genuine inclusion of women within the legal system would change the law materially. The great advance is that so many wonderful women are now entering the law and that most contemporary legal education also alerts men to the issues. Participation by women in legal discourse at every level will have an enormous impact. However, the undervaluing of women's skills continues to lead to their absence in the highest echelons, whether in the judiciary, law faculties or amongst law partners and Queen's Counsel. The explanation is peddled that women are not present because of the extraordinary nature of achievement necessary for such appointments. This fiction that the tests of excellence are neutral and that merit is an objective assessment is perpetually fostered.

In 1999, concern about the absence of women from the judiciary was so vocal that a joint working party on equal opportunities in judicial appointments and silk was established. This led to a research study published in 2000 which called for a fundamental change to the system of secret consultation and its replacement with 'a fair, open and equal opportunity compliant process'.

A judicial appointments commission should have highly regarded academics, solicitors and other members of the legal profession as members. There should also be some younger lawyers and lay representation. It would diversify the judiciary without jeopardising its quality. Under pressure to reform the judicial appointment system, Derry Irvine tried to avert the inevitable by having Sir Leonard Peach, an ex-civil servant, conduct a review but his terms of reference were stiffly limited to an examination of the appointment processes and did not extend to who should be making the appointments. I have no doubt that some cosmetic tweaking was the most anyone had in mind; considering a judicial appointments commission was off limits. Sir Leonard recommended the creation of a 'judicial oversight commission', with the duty of auditing the procedures as well as carrying out the role of ombudsman, dealing with complaints by practitioners about discrimination in the process. This was the managerial response to demands for reform and the Law Society President at the time, Michael Napier, pointed out that 'solicitors, women and ethnic minorities will remain largely excluded from the ranks of the higher judiciary'. It was in fact wickedly clever because many people were deluded into thinking there would now be a commission when it was no such thing.

Robert Stevens, the eminent lawyer and former Master of Pembroke College, who chaired Justice, the law reform organisation, said, 'however much consultation there is, none of it is in public and none of it is open to any scrutiny'. Even the Director-General of Fair Trading has criticised the silk system. Democratic legitimacy has to be at the heart of the administration of justice.

Sir Colin Campbell, the Vice-Chancellor of Nottingham University, became chair of the oversight commission and was trumpeted as the first Commissioner for Judicial Appointments. He sits with a talented and eclectic group of eight non-lawyers, men and women, currently keeping an eye on the judicial appointment process and acting as ombudsman for complaints.

In 2002 I accompanied a woman who had formally complained about the handling of her application for silk (to become a Queen's Counsel) and I was very impressed with the Commissioner's approach to her grievance. However, the process disclosed that the private 'sounding' system included some very unattractive, élitist comments about her not fitting the silk mould and not being silk material. She is a warm, motherly person who looks too much like her clients for the taste of some judges and senior men in her field of practice. Yet here is an effective advocate who is one of the busiest juniors in her specialism, reflecting her popularity with clients and solicitors. If the beloved market forces applied she would certainly be in silk. Not being in the mould should be seen as an attribute, but the usual cloning problem arises. Ninety-seven per cent of those consulted about suitability are male, white and from a narrow social group. A small number of barristers' chambers has a stranglehold on influence: effectively seen as silk and judge incubators. The result of belonging to these chambers is that judges and practitioners regularly mingle and the grooming for appointments starts early. Close study would show that a hard core of chambers monopolise the appointment process and their idea of what constitutes excellence is immutable. There is hardly a black face in any of these sets.

Colin Campbell's first annual report in 2002 showed the system really to be a scandal, with unsupported and sometimes unattributable tittle-tattle and comment recorded against people to their detriment. 'Too primly spinsterish, although her other qualities are self evident.' 'She's off-puttingly headmistressy.' 'She does not always dress appropriately.' 'Down and out scruffy.' Campbell was appropriately judicious in his tone. The commissioners, who have wide experience in industry, academia and the Civil Service, 'had not in twenty years of experience come across comments like them'. What he revealed was a system which is opaque, unduly slow and with no proper audit trail, which means equal treatment of candidates cannot be demonstrated. It was pointed out that although few people complained formally, they were probably reluctant to do so out of fear that they would damage their careers if they did. The Lord Chancellor's Department interpreted his report as being about process, but far more than bureaucratic niceties were at stake.

It is unsurprising that against such a background there is a call for the abolition of the QC system. Queen's Counsel were invented in Elizabethan times as an élite band to assist the Attorney-General in giving advice to the monarch. When one of my children was asked by a young friend what it meant to be a QC, he said that if the Queen was arrested I would defend her in court. The Bar claims that the rank of QC is a hallmark which lets solicitors and clients know who the best advocates are. It also allows some lucky lawyers to put up their fees. The Office of Fair Trading reported that the QC system was uncompetitive and that it was hard to see the benefits to the consumer. Practitioners build their own reputations and solicitors themselves know who is any good. With governments of all shades so committed to market forces it is hard to see why the legal profession should be allowed to justify any anti-competitive practices and protectionism. However, as the Bar is getting larger and the numbers of its users is growing it does help consumers to have a system to mark excellence. The Bar Council also argues that the system is an important means of promoting excellence in advocacy and reflecting the value of experience. However, deciding on excellence has its challenges.

When it comes to judicial appointments, Sir Colin Campbell's first report and the one which followed in 2003 reinforced for me how criteria like 'authority' and 'decisiveness' need unpacking, because perceptions of authority and decisiveness are likely to be perceptions of the male way of doing things. The ideal of the judge – anonymous, impartial, authoritative – is intrinsically male. So long as women can conform to male expectations, they are more likely to succeed. In the old days this used to be taken literally. When I was young I was once told off by a senior woman in the Old Bailey robing room because I had dispensed with my jacket and was wearing a dark shirt and skirt under my robe. I explained that it was because of the heat wave and she promptly put me in my place by pointing out that the men were stoically wearing jackets so we must too. Nowadays, the demands are not about being exactly like men, but successful women are expected, according to the American judge Patricia Wald, to be 'agreeable, charming, bright, incisive, unthreatening, loyal, not irritatingly individualistic, supportive, attractive, maybe witty – to a point – but not pushy, insistent, aggressive, unyielding or any of the other qualities male judges exhibit every day'.

Appointments to the Bench will only be enriched if the pool is widened to include more solicitors and legal academics, with greater opportunities for promotion up the judicial ladder from lower to higher courts. As for Queen's Counsel, in no other profession does the state decide who is pre-eminent. The question is whether the legal profession can come up with an effective and objective system for the appointment of Queen's Counsel which is not another variant of cronyism. Some Commonwealth jurisdictions have maintained the silk system with appointments made by the Queen on the recommendation of the Chief Justice, on the basis of advice from eminent lawyers and distinguished non-lawyers, applying a fair and open selection process. David Pannick QC suggests that the rank should specify in which areas of the law the appointee is distinguished and that appointments should not carry a lifetime guarantee. According to solicitors, the QC badge is not always a seal of quality: there would have to be a way of 'road-testing' every five or ten years to see if the claim of expertise was still justified.

There is however, another important function of the silk system that should not be downplayed, which relates to ethical standards. In an area like crime, it is hard to talk about the market having the control function, with people paying as much as they think a barrister is worth. Satisfied criminal clients might be very happy to have a lawyer whose behaviour is less than scrupulous and it may increase market share if you sail very close to the wind, inventing defences or telling witnesses in advance what to say. Ethical standards are very high at the Bar in Britain. According to some judges one of the reasons for this probity is that ambitious barristers who want to become QCs are very careful to stay well within professional boundaries: this is why it is relatively uncommon to find barristers being prosecuted for corrupt practice. Of course, professional bodies have a role in maintaining standards but the subtle impact of that desire for the new robe should not be dismissed. What the system certainly needs is thorough reform and a separation from the powers of any party politician like the Lord Chancellor, as currently constituted.

Polling in 2002 shows that, despite worries about their being out of touch, the public by and large do have confidence in the integrity of judges, which is reassuring because popular support helps them weather periodic political storms, like the furore when Lady Justice Elizabeth Butler Sloss, an example of a wise judge with tons of common sense, ordered lifelong anonymity, under their new names, for the boys who killed James Bulger and for the child murderer, Mary Bell.

According to the judge Dame Brenda Hale, we need to forge a new picture of a judge who does 'not fit the traditional model but is still recognisably a judge'.

In autumn 2003 the government produced a White Paper on a judicial appointments commission and is receiving views. Once appointed, judges have security of position – judicial independence depends upon it. So the decision to appoint must be the right one in every case. But one of a commission's central tasks will also be to look at the appointment procedures to see if there are new and better ways of attracting a wider range of people to the judiciary: more women, more minority members, and lawyers from a wider range of practice. Developing a judiciary more broadly reflective of society at large will not be easy and any commission will have to be truly independent. The difficult question of who appoints the appointers is fraught with the concern that a government which is over-controlling might find ways to interfere with the appointment process, especially at senior levels where legal judgments can have more serious implications for policy makers. This could be done by stacking the Commission. The current government proposals allow the Prime Minister the final say in the appointment of judges to the highest courts. Again, this is unacceptable.

Once an appointment panel has chosen a person for a senior

position it should only be left for the Prime Minister (or a Cabinet Minister in appropriate cases) to approve the appointment. This means that refusal to approve is a serious matter. However, a new public appointment system has developed in Whitehall – much beloved by government – which requires appointment panels to proffer two names to the Secretary of State of the given Department, so that he or she has the choice as to who is appointed. This places too much power in the hands of politicians. It is particularly problematic in situations where independence from government is a crucial aspect of the role. This is why the judges are so anxious to clarify the government's intentions in reforming the judicial appointments procedures. Allowing the Prime Minister or Secretary of State for Constitutional Affairs a choice in who becomes Chief Justice or a member of the Supreme Court carries the risk that politicians will appoint in their own interests rather than those of justice.

A serious concern is that far from looking for excellence in unusual places and making interesting appointments, a commission may be tempted to play safe, ticking the criteria boxes, but avoiding the more unusual candidate or someone who has strayed from normal career routes. Another fear is that there may be horse-trading between members of a commission with different priorities and, in the attempt to reach a decision, the mediocre will come up through the middle. The only way to meet these anxieties is by reminding commissioners that we want something better from them.

In the midst of complaints it is sometimes forgotten that British judges are not in the least corrupt. We have the least venal judiciary in the world. Occasionally they are caught committing traffic offences, drunk or in bed with the wrong person and 20 years ago a circuit judge was caught smuggling cigarettes across the Channel in his boat, but our judges are not a dishonourable crowd. The Common Sergeant, Judge Peter Beaumont QC, one of the most senior judges at the Old Bailey, received a letter offering him £50,000 as a bribe in the recent trial of the extremist Muslim cleric, Abdullah el-Faisal. Without blinking, he ordered a police inquiry, saying that there was nothing to suggest Faisal knew anything about it. The police view was that the bribe had come from someone who failed to appreciate that the British judiciary is impervious to such blandishments. That deep ethical strength comes about because our judiciary is drawn from an uncorrupt, independent legal profession.

Whenever I visit countries which are trying to create such a judiciary and I see the mammoth task it is to start afresh, as in places like the former Soviet Union or Bosnia-Herzegovina, I become less cavalier about unpicking the multiple layers of custom and practice which establish professionalism and pride. Yes, get rid of the wigs and the Latin. Definitely stop the fat-catting, but take care with more serious aspects.

Our judges work long hours, have to attend continuous training and have a heavy caseload. Gone are the days of shoving off early to the races. On top of this our friends in government came up with the novel idea that judges should also be eligible to serve on juries. (It is hard to think of a dafter proposition but I am sure one will come.) In a wonderful letter to *The Times*, Judge Tonking of Stoke-on-Trent expressed wild enthusiasm for the idea. He wondered how he should reply to the query of a fellow juror: 'And what do you do?' If his secret got out, would it be all right for him to explain to his fellow jurors what is going on in court when they are all asked to retire because a point of law is being discussed? Could he explain why a damning piece of evidence might have been excluded? And if the judge made an error in law, should he send up a note? And where would he serve as a juror? He is rather well known at his local court, which could mean he would be challenged, thus depriving the public of his services as a juror. It looks as though the idea is being abandoned.

The Old Bailey judge who suggested that age was softening my view of judges was right in that lawyers like myself, now dealing with cases at the most serious end of the spectrum, tend to see the judiciary at its best, just as we are also more likely to see policing at its best. The cases often have a high profile so there is intense media scrutiny and judges under the microscope are less prone to bad behaviour. The old routine of silent communication with the jury by judges rolling their eyes to the heaven and snorting at evidence has been greatly reduced. A few years ago I took a case on appeal where the judge's summing up on paper could hardly be faulted but given the right intonation, raising of eyebrows and 'Well, members of the jury, of course it is a matter for you and far be it from me to say, but you may feel this account tests credulity to breaking point', it was all too clear what he expected the jury to do. Speaking in high dramatic tones, he leaned on the jury to get the outcome he wanted. The leading counsel, Sir John Nutting, the fairest of prosecutors, was asked by the judges at the appeal whether he agreed with my contention that the judge's summing up was so biased that it jeopardised a fair trial. He replied very carefully that the judge was an 'old-fashioned judge and this was an old-fashioned summing up'. The euphemism spoke volumes and no one in the Court of Appeal was in any doubt about what had taken place. As a result a retrial was ordered.

While this conduct has largely disappeared in higher courts it still lurks in crown courts up and down the land. The local press cannot have a reporter in every court and some judges run minor fiefdoms where their writ runs powerfully and they try to get their own way.

These judges also turn a blind eye to unacceptable police conduct. The number of cases where police arrive at a scene and drugs are suddenly dropped, or where people end up with injuries because police had to restrain them, or where persons arrested blurt out incriminating statements in the back of police cars is legion. Police are supposed to have reason before searching someone, which is why drugs are planted. Police are not supposed to beat people, which is why we have claims that the arrestee struck out first. Police are supposed to conduct interviews back at the police station and the suspect is entitled to a solicitor, which is why we have people making unlikely admissions at the scene of the arrest or in the van. The police do not have the accused saying 'It's a fair cop, guv' any more. Now they have them saying 'You know I do a bit of dealing but give us a break this time.' Lawyers try to have this kind of evidence excluded but many judges still prefer police evidence when push comes to shove.

The Police and Criminal Evidence Act 1984 was introduced after the scandal of people being framed by false admissions – and not just in big cases. The police were caught writing up interviews after the event, with skill that could have been used to good effect screen-writing for television soaps. It was for this reason that taped interviews came into being, a practice that revolutionised questioning in police stations. As a result it is only at arrest scenes or in the police car that lawyers are encountering the 'unsolicited admission', which cannot be verified by reference to a tape. The police are ever inventive in finding ways of getting round the rules and exaggerating the evidence.

In some cases, police can argue that they chose to question at the scene of an arrest because they were anxious to locate dangerous objects or to prevent other crimes or to acquire information which was in the interests of public safety. However, there should always be scepticism about admissions made away from corroborative sources. Judges do not always hold the line against such sleight of hand but they should remember that it is out of these small infringements that large ones grow.

We have to accept that the power we give to the police carries very real risks and the oversight of that power has to be constant. Judges must be in touch and alert to the crucial role they play in holding police to account. Judicial training has radically improved over the last decade, with far greater opportunity for gaps in knowledge and experience to be filled. However, there is much more that could be done. Judges are happy to have training on new legislation, as they first had on the Children Act and had more recently on the Human Rights Act, but they have been less willing to be told they have anything to learn on issues of race and gender.

Some of the early training on ethnic minority issues was scorned by judges, who saw it all as political correctness, but as the seminars have become more professional there has been more interest and acceptance. Progress on gender issues has been slower but this pattern is replicated elsewhere. Apparently in the United States and Canada judges made conscious efforts first to rid themselves of stereotypical notions about race and colour but it has been taking longer on gender. Here our judges now have an equal treatment bench book but it is only recently that it has included a chapter on gender, addressing domestic violence myths and issues around rape and sexual abuse. Training on domestic violence is just six hours, which is really just one day.

Judges have constant exposure to the establishment views on law and order, meeting police chiefs and prison governors at seminars and other sessions. But they also need greater opportunity to meet with people at the sharp end – ex-cons, community leaders, drug counsellors, child abuse experts, battered women and rape victims. A system of justice will be the richer for diversity of background and experience. As Lord Steyn put it, 'the first principle of democracy is majority rule; the second principle is respect for fundamental rights; the bedrock of the administration of justice is public confidence but the present system is just not good enough to secure its legitimacy'.

*

The government has declared its intention to create a Supreme Court, which will be a great moment in our transition to a modern constitutional state and would reinvigorate public confidence. The Law Lords, who by self-denying ordinance now rarely speak or vote in the House of Lords, should have their right to do so removed altogether. Just as it is inappropriate for a cabinet minister to sit as a judge, it is not acceptable for judges to sit in the legislature. In fact I believe that Law Lords should not, as of right, be part of a reformed House of Lords. My own preference for a democratically elected second chamber or at least one that is substantially elected is on record, but if there is to be an appointed element then it could include retired judges of the Supreme Court to add to the wealth of wisdom.

The judiciary should also resist requests from government, which befuddle the separation of powers. The Auld Report 2001 – discussed in the chapter on juries – which was undertaken at the request of three cabinet ministers, the Lord Chancellor, the Attorney-General and the Home Secretary, crossed the line. Some areas of law reform are constitutional and highly contentious politically. For this reason a review of the criminal courts which might involve an assault upon the citizen's entitlement to jury trial are different from areas of procedural change. The Auld review was presented as the same exercise as Lord Woolf had performed for civil justice, when he examined ways of expediting the system and produced the Woolf Report on civil courts reform, but Lord Auld did far more than look at procedural changes. Issues of constitutional significance were presented as being essentially bureaucratic. This elision of substantive and process change – a weakness of government on many fronts – drew Robin Auld into an inadvertent co-option by government which, as he was a judge of the Court of Appeal, should not have been allowed to happen. It is perfectly appropriate for a judge to advise on procedural reform and refinements. And it is perfectly proper for judges – preferably those who are retired – to chair inquiries. But practising judges should not become one-man policy think tanks at the service of government, advising changes which mean the removal of substantive 'constitutional' rights. Not because judges are not entitled to their views. As Lord Woolf pointed out in a speech to the Royal Academy in October 2002, he is as entitled as anyone to freedom of expression. In his capacity as Lord Chief Justice, Lord Woolf has been publicly forceful in his opinions on the way in which the current government is dangerously swinging the balance of the criminal justice system in favour of the prosecution, putting justice in danger. Indeed he placed a letter in the House of Lords Library in 2003 detailing his concerns about the Criminal Justice Bill which was then going through parliament. Lord Steyn has also used public lectures to express concerns about constitutional issues and human rights. Judges should be able to write learned papers and give lectures to their hearts' content but we need our judges to remain outside the Whitehall embrace.

Henry Cecil, a humorous writer on the law, said: 'I think that a judge should be looked on rather as a sphinx than a person – you shouldn't be able to imagine a judge having a bath.' In fact, I tell young women lawyers that they should always imagine the judge in the bath as it is a great eliminator of fear and a total demystifier. The only problem is stopping yourself laughing. However, Cecil is right that judges should be sphinxlike in their own interests as well as those of the law.

The Auld Report, stimulated by a call to think the unthinkable, and then cherry-picked by government for the least expensive reforms, means the government can claim judicial approval for profound encroachments on citizens' rights. Co-option of the judiciary by government can be subtle but it is a risk to be avoided at all costs. Now that criminal justice is being politicised more than ever before it is very easy for judicial views to be harnessed for political purposes, and judges who are not politically wily have to be much more circumspect about their views. They cannot afford to be seen to engage in the political fray on any side.

When a judge in the Glasgow Sheriff Court was sentencing a local reprobate he said: 'Although you are a fecund liar, I am going to give you one last chance.' Whereupon the accused said, 'I knew you were a fecund good judge.'

Fecund, good judges are precisely what we need.

7

KILL ALL THE LAWYERS

WHEN DICK THE Butcher in Shakespeare's *Henry VI, Part 2* cries, 'The first thing we do, let's kill all the lawyers', it always raises a laugh. Lawyers get a bad press, usually because in the public imagination they combine high salaries with little visible benefit to society. In popularity stakes they are down there with politicians and estate agents. Yet whatever the broader public's reservations about exactly where the legal profession fits into the human evolutionary scale, in countries experiencing oppression lawyers are in the front line. The killing of lawyers is one of the first acts of tyrants.

My own confrères are hardly at risk of extermination but the recent attacks have been surprising and new.

In autumn 2002, Lord Falconer, then Home Office Minister for Criminal Justice, inveighed against criminal defence lawyers. Apparently crime problems are in large part due to this unscrupulous class of being, who cross-examine witnesses at length, spin out trials and assist the criminal classes to avoid justice. Falconer was echoing the refrain of Sir John Stevens, the Metropolitan Police Commissioner, in March of the same year, that criminals are walking free because of clever lawyers. One reason for these attacks is that lawyers argue the importance of civil liberties and have to point out that safeguards need to exist to protect citizens against mistakes or abuse at the hands of the police. It is never very pleasant to have your shortcomings reiterated and it makes the police understandably upset, especially decent, honest cops. However, that is one of the downsides of the job, just as being compared to the lowest form of life has to be taken on the chin by lawyers.

The new element in lawyer-baiting is that the assault now comes largely from politicians, even lawyers. Lord Falconer is a commercial lawyer, a very rich commercial lawyer – as is the Attorney-General Lord Goldsmith and the former Lord Chancellor, Lord Irvine. All three were up there in the million pounds a year bracket before the call of government. These men may not have had the privilege of knowing the lawyers I have known, both solicitors and barristers, who chose law not for the money but because they believed that they could make a difference in people's lives.

These are lawyers who have chosen to be advocates for the poor, the disadvantaged, those on the margins, those who are least well served by the law. At different times they have been called by different names – poor man's lawyers, radical lawyers, alternative lawyers, civil liberties lawyers. Many today are genuinely human rights lawyers. They have included trade union lawyers who took up personal injuries cases for those who suffered industrial accidents and the law centre lawyers who helped people tirelessly through the mire of welfare benefit entitlements; immigration lawyers working on asylum issues; family lawyers dealing with child protection and domestic violence. Then there is the whole bank of criminal lawyers, most of whose work is not with white-collar fraudsters or professional criminals but with the swathes of other people who face criminal trial, many of whom are frightened, hopeless and downtrodden. These are the lawyers who are prepared to challenge state abuse, who are fearless in fighting their clients' cases and who work relentlessly unravelling miscarriages of justice. They work in offices and chambers up and down the country with long hours and for far less money than the sums bandied around in the press. And I am tired of hearing them traduced.

Of course there are lawyers who choose the richer seams of law and, yes, there are few lawyers who do not earn a comfortable living once they are established, but that is true of all professionals. If one looks carefully, the new attacks by ministers are carefully honed to deal with opposition to deplorable government policies which lawyers can see for what they are.

I have a fancy that deep in the bowels of Whitehall, Alastair Campbell used to hold master-classes in how to combat critics of government policy: the line on those who resist the attacks on civil liberties and on the poor is to be twofold – the reforms are necessary 'in the interests of victims' and the opponents are all lawyers who are in it for the money.

The law depends on honest lawyers. Attacking all lawyers feeds into a general denigration of the profession which undermines public confidence and drives away too many talented, idealistic young men and women who are coming through law schools.

The Home Secretary also turns up the volume when he makes speeches about criminal barristers. He wants barristers to be fined for letting 'clients make late guilty pleas in court', which could mean that he wants barristers to make clients plead guilty early. It is a ludicrous suggestion and directly assaults the idea of the independent barrister, who conducts a case fearlessly in the best interests of his client. It also displays a complete misunderstanding of professional relationships and the workings of the courts. People change their pleas for many reasons. Sometimes they start off insisting on their innocence because they are so ashamed or they cannot bear their family to know the truth, but with the passage of time they realise they have to accept responsibility and the people who love them will not despise them for it. It is often because they have developed a relationship of trust with their lawyers that they can be made to see that fighting a case is fruitless. Sometimes they are wrongly charged, or charged with an offence more serious than what they have actually been doing, and negotiation is necessary. Sometimes it is only seeing the door of the trial court that forces reality on an accused and makes her see sense. Lawyers have to carve a very careful route, not forcing someone to plead guilty who says she is innocent but making clear the advantages of pleading guilty in terms of a reduced sentence.

Blunkett has a distorted view of lawyers urging the guilty to fight trials, when there is nothing more debilitating for an advocate than fighting a hopeless case. Having to keep your face straight in front of a jury when your client has a ludicrous defence is not easy. However, lawyers have a duty to point out to the accused the weaknesses in the prosecution case so that the client can make valid decisions as to plea. Defendants will fight cases where the police or prosecution have not put together a convincing case. A lawyer would point out that if the jury is still convinced and convicts a man he will face a longer sentence. What a lawyer has no duty to say to an accused is, 'There is a huge hole in the prosecution case but I think you should plead guilty because it would be morally better for you.' That is the role of the accused person's priest or vicar. It is not the role of the lawyer. As soon as she does that she is judging the issues.

When I was working as a junior on a murder trial with the late great Bruce Laughland QC, our client asked him at the end of the consultation in Brixton Prison whether he believed he was innocent. Bruce explained very eloquently and with great charm that he never allowed himself to consider the issue of guilt or innocence; his duty was to fight as hard as he could for a client's acquittal if the client said he was innocent. This was clearly not good enough for our client, who wrote the next day sacking Bruce, saying he was an arrogant, supercilious wordsmith who had just tried to talk his way out of a simple question. Bruce's aside was that the client had obviously been in communication with Mrs Laughland, who frequently expressed a similar view.

The professional role of the defence barrister in criminal cases presents difficulties for many people, who see it as amoral and unprincipled, but it is in fact based on the very sound principle that the lawyer should not sit in judgment. Once lawyers do that some defendants may go unrepresented, which affronts a central requirement of due process. We all learn in law school of Lord Erskine, who fiercely defended Thomas Paine in 1793, although he clearly despised everything Paine advocated in *The Rights of Man.*

It is already possible for a judge to issue a costs order against lawyers who have caused delays by neglect or by being wilfully obstructive to the process of justice, but apparently that is not enough to stop wily lawyers winning cases. There is now an additional government proposal that lawyers who cross-examine for too long should be fined. There could be a Monty Python sketch of a trial process that would suit the government and Mr Blunkett, with supplicant judges fining lawyers who come forward with a client pleading not guilty and a meter running up charges for every legal intervention.

The majority of those who end up in the dock have no money or admit to none. Legal aid is essential if justice is to mean anything. Also, for very practical reasons, the courts do not want people to represent themselves. Having lawyers who are constrained by professional rules is crucial to the smooth running of the system. Now, under international norms on human rights, persons whose liberty is in jeopardy require legal representation and if they are not well off the state should provide legal assistance. In Britain legal aid is available to most people charged with an imprisonable offence: the criminal legal aid bill is therefore demand-led and not easy to cap, unlike the bill for civil cases. As a result, until now the only way to constrain rising costs has been to freeze the sums paid to criminal lawyers and radically assault civil legal aid.

Faced with these problems, the Lord Chancellor, Lord Irvine, proved that he was not just a renovator of historic buildings with an expensive taste in wallpaper. In his renovation of legal aid he went for the radical option and started the process of introducing a public defender system. The government will create a body of salaried lawyers to defend accused people who cannot afford to pay privately. This was not a mere cost-cutting exercise, he assured us, but an effort to bring quality representation to that body of people who find themselves before the courts on lesser crimes, as yet undefined. In pursuit of evidence that such a system would work, he set up a pilot scheme in Scotland. I would have thought governments might have learned from the poll tax not to use Scotland as a test bed for anything. Needless to say, it became clear to the organisers of the study that, if given a choice, most people being prosecuted by the state preferred to be represented by lawyers not directly employed by the state. Since public defenders were not going to get many takers – or consumers, as our court-users are now described – an element of compulsion became necessary. In the Scottish pilot scheme all persons born between January and April would be required to have the public defender. My fellow countrymen, vocally exercised at the unfairness of not being able to have their regular brief, designated the scheme 'justice by astrology'.

The pilot scheme has now been extended into England and my own Cassandra qualities tell me they will be soon be paraded as a viable, cost-effective alternative. As lawyers in the United States point out, these schemes do work initially when enthusiastic young lawyers are employed and a lot of money is invested in their success. It is later, when they fall prey to inevitable cost-cutting, that the rot sets in. I do not accept the arguments for a public defender system which, it is claimed, will only deal with the most minor of cases. If a public defender system starts in a small way, it will be the beginning of something much bigger, with all people of slender means being required to have representation by the public defender however serious the offence. Will 'choice', that great byword of our times, be available to the accused? I suspect not.

The Public Defender Service will undoubtedly attract committed young lawyers and many will do a good job for their clients, but there is something unsettling about the salaried state defender, paid, selected and ultimately controlled by the state. As Lord Jeremy Hutchinson QC put it in the House of Lords debate on Access to Justice in 1999:

> That fine warrior is to be sent out to do battle on the field of liberty and human rights with his opposite number, his colleague in arms, the salaried state prosecutor . . . Instead of the interests of justice being paramount the culture of negotiated justice will prevail. There will be plea bargaining behind closed doors, pressure to abort trials, cosy relationships between prosecution and defence to maintain the conviction count and get through the volume of cases and to minimise cost. The cosiness will soon extend to the court itself, which will be anxious to rid itself of the stubborn and determined advocate who wastes the judge's time.

In some towns outside of London that kind of collusion already exists between the Bar and Bench because of cosiness, with cases 'cracked' for the convenience of lawyers and the court and not always in the interests of the client. The Bar should admit such abuse does happen rather than pretend to be totally virtuous. But how much greater the problem will be in the new system. In addition we only have to consider the criticisms of David Blunkett and Charlie Falconer about too much cross-examining by lawyers to imagine the pressure which will be felt by defenders on the payroll. Will promotion be dependent on fulfilling targets and 'throughput', as in every other public service area?

I have watched the public defender system in the United States in action. I have seen the pressure put on young lawyers required to deal with cases with little time for preparation and often beyond their experience. They are quickly beaten down and those who remain for years are too often tired, or are second-raters who would not have survived in the competitive system of the independent Bar or solicitors' profession. The practice drives down standards and creates a two-tier system with an enormous gulf between what is available to the rich and to the poor. The effect is that faith in the law suffers because folk stop believing that ordinary people can get justice.

The Lord Chancellor's Department tells us that an ethical code will be published in an effort to ensure that institutional pressures to get convictions do not intrude on professional independence, but I am not confident that such injunctions can be effective. Already, in relation to prosecutors it is being proposed that they should have the chance for the first time to indicate to judges what range of sentence they think convicted murderers should serve. Until now prosecuting counsel have maintained their independent role, willing to give the court any information it requires for the purpose of sentencing but not arguing for a particular tariff.

The other unpleasant aspect of the public defender proposal is that it will let the Bar off the hook on the question of finding a solution to the problems of maintaining a diverse pool of entrants. There is concern that young lawyers who enter the Public Defender's Office will predominantly be those from less privileged families anxious to start earning so that they can pay back the loans and debt incurred while in training to become a lawyer. Many young entrants without private means come to the Bar with £25,000 debt because of the long years of study and the expense of pupillage. Soon only posh kids will be able to afford such study and training and the Bar will once again become the profession of the cosseted and privileged. An inclusive legal system has to be served by an inclusive legal profession and the idea that we shall lose that diversity is chilling.

In the 1970s and '80s there was an exciting burgeoning of opportunities for young people from non-privileged backgrounds to enter the law and I consider myself one of the lucky ones. However, the removal of grants in higher education and the introduction of fees and loans is proving a serious disincentive to the children of less well-to-do families. The long haul of study for legal practice, usually five to six years for those who have no possibility of family support, is driving out many potential candidates from poorer homes. The professions are themselves trying to make scholarships and financed traineeships available but the cloud of debt frightens off many who are already tentative about entering a world so full of uncertainties.

It is worth noting that when the Bar Council tried to persuade members of the Bar to contribute, by way of a levy, to a scheme to support young, disadvantaged lawyers in their early years, to operate on a sliding scale, it was the rich commercial lawyers who objected, although the sums were piffling by comparison with their earnings. A barrister earning £500,000 would only have paid £2,500: one earning £200,000 would have paid £500. Apparently, it was too much to ask.

What is so extraordinary is that while every other aspect of our lives is being privatised, the one area where nationalisation is taking place is in the legal service for people accused of crime. It is important to ask why this reform is flowing against the prevailing tide. I suggest it is because the whole nature of legal aid is being radically reformed: the Public Defender Service will be an aspect of welfare provision for the poor, no more than a safety net, as in the United States.

When the legal aid scheme was first created in 1950, it was the envy of Europe and liberal America. It extended legal aid and later advice and assistance to the greater part of the population and was the second prong of the welfare state. At a time when civil litigation was not the first thought of those who suffered loss, it cost the state relatively little – particularly in cases where the victim would normally win, notably personal injury. This is still true. The net cost to the public purse of all cases was about £35 million in the 1950s and early '60s, which is small beer in the scheme of things. For all sorts of reasons the legal aid bill spiralled. To beat down costs, eligibility limits have been cut and cut over the years so that now only the really poor can get legal aid for civil litigation. No government is going to roll back those cuts. Not even the Scots Nats or the Lib Dems would advocate a penny on income tax for legal aid. Unlike health and education, it has no obvious constituency pushing for it as a priority within the welfare state.

At least New Labour chose not to take the scythe yet again to the eligibility limits but looked instead for real reform. However, they took too much advice from commercial lawyers, who are not renowned for their intimacy with the legal aid system or the needs of the disadvantaged. Withdrawing all legal aid for accident and personal cases, except medical negligence, relies on conditional fee agreements to fill the gaps. Conditional fees are a sort of watered-down version of the American contingency fee whereby the lawyer gets a cut of the winnings in a case. The government had no idea what the impact of this change would mean in the long term and whether such agreements would work across the board. They are still not tested and proven. Insurers, who provide indemnity against the defendant's costs should a case be lost, have increased premiums already and there is growing evidence that these insurers are setting far too high a merits test on a case before providing cover.

Disbursements have to be paid as the case goes along, for example for medical reports, photographs, plans or drawings, or a barrister's opinion; and while these may not be exorbitant, if the solicitor's firm is not one of the legal hypermarkets, but a small or medium-sized enterprise, those items of expenditure can create serious cash-flow problems, particularly if the firm has a large number of such cases. Other changes, such as the provision of legal services like conveyancing, wills and probate and other advice by non-legal institutions, have meant the viability of the traditional mixed high street practice is now seriously at risk. Small firms, especially those outside London, have been driven into merger so that only one or two litigation firms are left in provincial centres. This is obviously bad for client choice and for competition and it can affect the quality of client–lawyer relations because very large firms may not be as personally engaged in the case.

Most importantly there has been a significant increase in the number of practices abandoning legal aid work altogether because it does not make financial sense. Nearly a quarter of solicitors' offices doing legal aid family work in 2000 had dropped out by 2003 and there is an exodus from other specialisms too. Patrick Allen, senior partner at the solicitors, Hodge Jones and Allen in London, says: 'There has been more or less a freeze on [pay] rates for the last nine years but costs keep going up. This year our rent is nearly double and our indemnity insurance is £150,000. Retaining staff is difficult. We have seen a steady drift of people leaving to go to the private sector where they are going to earn substantially more.' Finding a firm of solicitors that does legal aid work will soon become as difficult as finding a National Health dentist.

In order to drive legal aid costs down, solicitors' firms have to win the government contract for areas of service. However, the provision is very fragmented. It is claimed that there is only one housing law franchise for the whole area between Luton and London. For actions against the police, which are so crucial in keeping the police honest, there is no contract holder in the whole of south-east London, which includes Eltham, the area where Stephen Lawrence was killed and where police competence was seriously called into question. If this is access to justice, it is pretty thin.

The other problem about allocating contracts is that too much government emphasis goes on box-ticking exercises. How do you measure whether a firm fights hard for a client, leaves no stone unturned in preparing a case, does legal research, seeks out the hard to find witness, secures the best expert? The government desire for measurement is such an unsatisfactory way of improving public services because what matters is never measurable and what is measurable rarely really matters in the end.

The Law Society has already amassed evidence that legal aid is becoming inaccessible to people living in some suburban and rural areas. Recruiting and retaining staff to undertake publicly funded work is reaching crisis point, a situation which is projected to become worse. Lawyers doing bread and butter legal work are finding it is just not worth the stress, the long hours and the poor remuneration. The average pay of a GP is £65,000 per annum with a pension, while the average publicly funded solicitor earns £35–40,000 per annum. This phoney market-based approach is leaving members of society in many parts of the country with unacceptable levels of access. The crisis is so great that the Law Society is now trying to persuade the government to create GP-style contracts for legal aid solicitors.

A start has also been made on block contracting for chambers. The system of block contracts or franchising started with solicitors; two or three firms would contract with the Legal Services Commission to do all the work arising, for example, at a particular magistrates' court. They would be paid up front for the block of work and it is the luck of the draw whether the cases are straightforward or complex and time consuming. There is no billing based on work done so the savings are considerable. The risk of law firms cutting corners because they have an eye to their profit margins is the downside. Already sets of chambers have contracted to provide advice to front line providers of legal services like Law Centres or Citizen's Advice Bureaux at a fixed hourly rate on an area where the chambers has expertise. For example, my own chambers does this in relation to human rights. What is now on the horizon is block contracts for advocacy.

But again there are questions about how you ensure that the right barrister is briefed. Clerks in chambers have always insisted there were horses for courses, and there are. Will there be space in block contracting to brief the well-known barrister who is a leader in the field of prisoners' rights if he is not on the solicitor's normal block list? Will the solicitor be able to brief the silk who has done so many of the miscarriage of justice trials? Or are we heading for a system which in the end will take choice out of the picture? Barristers' fees have been cut and legal aid applications are closely scrutinised to see if the likely benefit justifies the expenditure.

In July 2002 the Law Society published a report, *Access Denied*, highlighting the emergence of the legally excluded, the poor and the disadvantaged who live in areas with little or no access to legal aid. The report indicated that while the government has placed the fight against social exclusion high on its agenda, there is clear evidence of social exclusion from legal advice.

The Legal Services Commission (LSC), which took over from the legal aid boards, has also set out its concerns in its annual report for 2001/2002. Its own regional offices are reporting that up to 50% of firms are seriously considering giving up or significantly reducing publicly funded work. The LSC believes this is overwhelmingly because of concern at the high levels of bureaucracy, remuneration and profitability. Its own studies showed that at the current rates of legal aid, many firms are at best only marginally profitable. The best immigration and asylum practices are closing down because such work is no longer financially profitable on the legal aid fees available in this field of work, which is complex and highly political. The Prime Minister railed against the 'legal aid gravy train' in asylum in his 2003 Labour conference speech, making a specious, generalised criticism when it is a minority who abuse the system. This means that highly ethical lawyers who have been so persistent and successful in drawing the courts' attention to human rights abuses will leave the field open to the unscrupulous and useless. By 28 November 2003 the government was planning to take an axe to legal aid for asylum completely for the initial stages of many cases. As Maeve Sherlock, the Refugee Council's Chief Executive noted: 'We require lawyers to help us move house and get divorced yet the government suggests we do not need them when we have fled tyranny and are frightened for our lives. Good legal representation may be all that stops a refugee being sent home to torture or worse.'

It is right that expenditure on asylum cases has soared, squeezing the ability of the system to deliver justice to the rest of the poor and vulnerable. This is a direct result of poor initial decision-making by the Home Office. In 2002 there were 14,000 wrong initial decisions which were reversed on appeal.

Law graduates burdened with debt are reluctant to take poorly paid training contracts with legal aid firms. By contrast, if they manage to get into one of the top City law firms they have money thrown at them.

Sonia Behr, a local community practitioner in Gwent, dealing with the whole gamut from divorce, domestic violence and abused children to debt, housing crisis, immigration and crime, finds that legal aid practitioners are overburdened with mountains of unpaid paperwork and fixed contracts, with the result that needy clients are turned away. 'Our basic overheads are £50 per hour and legal aid pay is £50 an hour. The result is nil profit. Our private practice fees subsidise legal aid work but we struggle on because we believe in legal aid.' Most firms do not make that choice. One in ten solicitors' practices has abandoned legal aid altogether, and the numbers are rising.

Young trainee solicitors working on criminal cases, manning the 'on call' roster, are frequently called out to police stations in the middle of the night when someone is arrested. The hourly rate for 'call-out' is less than they would be paid in McDonald's. They work long hours, earn a pittance and only the most committed are able to persist. The same goes for young barristers doing crime. They do not earn enough to live on. These are the lawyers who will tomorrow fight the unpopular cases, unravel the terrible miscarriages of justice and give voice to those who are least powerful in our society. Unless we nurture and value them, find ways to support them financially in their training and reward them fairly in practice, the justice system itself will be impoverished.

The Bar is the end of the profession which is particularly susceptible to the party joke, with earnings a great source of speculation. The average earnings of QCs or 'silks' are always presented as between £200,000 and £300,000 but that average is inflated by the earnings of the commercial high-flyers. We are told that silks like Lord Grabiner and Gordon Pollock earn £2 million per annum but we only have the tabloids as our source. The average criminal silk earns £170–180,000. Out of that they pay chambers overheads of about 20%. They are not paid for holidays and they have no pension. The salary is the equivalent of someone earning £90,000 a year, which is a lot less than a successful accountant or consultant with a private practice and a great deal less than QCs doing other kinds of work. However, it is also a lot more than the vast majority of workers and since I have always felt lucky to be paid at all for doing something I love, I am making no case for raising my fees. What I am concerned about is what kind of service we are creating for the future. The conduct of heavy criminal cases has serious consequences, like the conduct of difficult surgery. There has to be esteem and reward associated with it if it is to attract skilled people. And you are only able to do the murder trials well if you have spent years learning and acquiring judgement on less serious cases.

The government has deliberately stopped the market operating in criminal work at the Bar. Until four years ago there was means-testing and the rich defendant in criminal cases had to pay for his or her barrister, or if granted legal aid had to make a substantial contribution to their legal representation. Not now. Now everyone gets legal aid, rich and poor alike. Even the multi-millionaire property developer Nicholas van Hoogstraten was on legal aid for his trial of being an accessory to murder. Imagine that for one moment. Welfare for all. How can it be that such a universal benefit is being introduced when we are cutting back on welfare? The wealthy fraudster with a long, expensive trial is now just as much a burden on the taxpayer as the poor shoplifter. It was said that the change was made because it was costly to administer a means-testing scheme, though it could have been outsourced, as they say. The real purpose of giving legal aid to everyone was to destroy the market at the criminal Bar. If there is no way of judging what your value is in the marketplace there is no way of driving a bargain on what you should be paid out of public funds. Without a benchmark, there is no basis for negotiation, whether it should be a half or two-thirds of the private fee.

All criminal lawyers are now on a fixed fee scale which means that barristers aged around 34 on average earn around £28–£30,000 gross before tax, which is less than some quite junior civil servants or police constables. Lawyers at the family Bar doing child protection work and domestic violence earn even less.

It is public service lawyers who are having their fees cut away and the effect on young lawyers is considerable. It also means there is a huge reward gradient between the party who is legally aided and the one who is privately funded. This is particularly noticeable when legally aided wives are up against privately funded husbands trying to hide away their wealth and assets, and it is invariably the privately funded male barrister up against the publicly funded female barrister.

This is one of the interesting features of the assault on legal aid. Two women are now applying for every one place in the sets of chambers doing publicly funded work. The same is happening with traineeships in legal aid solicitors' practices. The men make career choices much more related to money and prestige and head for the high-rewarding areas of practice, but women find their place doing poor folks' law. Women invariably do the ill-rewarded work in any field and what follows is a lowering of the esteem of that professional activity.

In every other area of public service the government is interested in consumer satisfaction. However, in the area of crime, the state funder is not interested in client contentment because that usually means getting people off, which is precisely what the government does not want. Looking for ways of creating mixed funding, a public–private mix, would logically mean the creation of the top-up fee where market forces come into play and the sought-after barrister gets something from the client in addition to the legal aid base. It would make lawyers faster, more efficient and ambitious to do a good job so that they get more challenging and interesting cases. However, in the area of crime, the lawyer might often be in receipt of the proceeds of crime, which is why it is untenable.

The retreat from legal aid was the crisis scripted for the Lord Chancellor, Derry Irvine, when the great review of legal aid took place before the Access to Justice Act 1999, but his concern was to lead the way in welfare reform, ahead of health and education reform, in an area where the public was hardly going to get excited and where for once the press would be on his side. The Lord Chancellor's berating of legal aid lawyers as 'fat cats', when the real 'fat cats' were commercial lawyers, was mother's milk to the tabloids and helped smooth the road to reform, which was his priority.

Derry Irvine rightly exposed the abuses of legal aid that were taking place, but there were ways to put an end to both the abuse and the feather-bedding without the risk of losing decent advice and representation for the poor, for example by prosecution of corrupt practice and rigorous auditing. The old civil legal aid system involved a merits test which was so limp that an opinion from counsel could secure funding for very weak cases. It meant lawyers were paid from public funds in cases where the victim eventually got nothing because the case was unwinnable. It was no wonder the Lord Chancellor got the bit between his teeth and it is to their shame that the Bar and Law Society did not put their own houses in order sooner.

In the rush to reform, few people consider the important role legal aid plays in developing our society's values. The whole field of judicial review, holding government to account, has developed from cases which drew down legal aid. The law itself could suffer if sufficient support is not available for cases at the cutting edge.

The government has set up the Community Legal Service to fill the gaps for the poor but in many areas it cannot provide for local needs because there are insufficient skilled practitioners available to do the work. Instead the Lord Chancellor should have used the opportunity to expand and support the community law centres which had concentrated since the 1970s on local provision.

At the time of the Access to Justice debate I made the suggestion that the interest on money kept in solicitors' client accounts should be paid into a collective fund to support law centres or the training of less well off young lawyers. This is money which has to be paid by clients in advance to meet costs at the end of a case or for other purposes, and the sums involved for the big City law firms are huge. There are arguments as to whom the interest belongs but it certainly is not the rich law firms. It could easily be put to useful purposes. At the time the idea was ignored but it is now being taken up by the Attorney-General, who suggests that it is given to charity. However, there are purposes directly related to the current failures in legal provision which should be considered first. Jeffrey Bindman, another Labour lawyer, has suggested that the big firms contribute to legal aid as a gesture of professional commitment but I suspect that will be laughed out of court.

When the Access to Justice Bill was going through, one of the arguments made by Geoff Hoon, who was then the Lord Chancellor's attack dog, was that the government had a duty to the public purse. It certainly has, but no one examines the extent to which the taxpayer foots the bill for the many expensive private sector lawyers who are instructed either directly by government at commercial rates or by National Health Trusts or other public bodies. These are not lawyers restrained by legal aid levels of pay: they are free to charge what the market can bear. The spotlight of the Lord Chancellor's Department has strangely never been cast on them. What we do know is that the Lord Chancellor has paid £2.5 million to lawyers, accountants and business consultants. The bill for external advisers to the Court Service, the agency for which the Lord Chancellor is responsible, jumped from £690,000 to £4 million in 2002. Richard Miller, Director of the Legal Aid Practitioners Group, said, 'I wish he would pay legal aid solicitors at the same rate he pays his consultant lawyers, who get ten times the legal aid rate.'

In the summer of 2003, when government figures faced the Hutton inquiry into the death of Dr David Kelly, which I referred to in the chapter on terrorism, they decided to add Jonathan Sumption QC to their legal team. Mr Sumption is one of the 'million-a-year-club' – the small group of barristers earning more than £1 million a year. According to the *Guardian* legal correspondent, Clare Dyer, he confessed in 2001 to earning, in his own words, 'a puny £1.6 million'. In a letter to the newspaper that year he wrote: 'I earn what I do because that is what my services are worth to the people who pay for them, all of whom are hard nosed professionals spending their own money.' On this occasion they were spending our money.

It would be interesting to know if there is any competitive tender for lucrative work which is 'outsourced' or whether it is left to the personal choice of ministers and others concerned. Are there firms or individuals who benefit disproportionately? Just as high-earning chief executive 'fat cats' end up being a cost to us all as consumers, so do hugely paid commercial lawyers and others who charge inflated fees which in the end either come out of taxation or inflate the cost of living. The outrageous fees of commercial lawyers have had a corrosive effect on the profession as a whole and have played a shameful role in driving up fees across the board. The independence of the legal profession is under threat. The people who sue police, take actions against the state for abuses of power, who judicially review bad government decisions, who expose miscarriages of justice, who point up the failings of our institutions – the awkward squad – they are going to have the life blood drained out of them. So when the government tells you it is after the fat cats, do not believe them. They like fat cats. They have a much more frightening beast in their sights.

8

THE ALCHEMY OF SEX AND VIOLENCE

WHEN I GAVE talks on women and the law in the early 1980s, I would often start with the query, 'Is the law male?' The question invariably divided the audience: some thought it a statement of the obvious and others were mystified by the very premiss.

The idea that the law reflected a male world view and did not include a female perspective was not a conspiracy theory about bewigged men in smoke-filled rooms plotting the subservience of women. However, in those days any of us who questioned the orthodoxy that the law was an objective set of rules was considered iconoclastic, to say the least. I, like others, thought I was stating a simple reality about the nature of law. Since our system is based on precedents passed down by male judges, it was not surprising that it should be made in their own image. Where I was over-optimistic was that although I thought the law's claim to neutrality was bogus, for a long time I believed that if we reformed the law and the judges, we could make the system genuinely fair and equal.

I was one of that generation of women who came to adulthood during the second wave of feminism. I qualified at the Bar in 1972. Women were enjoying greater educational opportunities and greater sexual freedom. Our hopes and aspirations were radically changing and we began to turn our attention to the ways in which social and political institutions maintained inequality. We wanted to change the law and on the whole struggled to do so within the parameters already set. We did not take sufficient account of the fact that our legal cultures are premised on notions which are themselves excluding rather than including.

Women had been implicitly or explicitly excluded from the

community of legal subjects: everything was postulated on the basis that the litigant or the accused was male. While explicit discrimination, such as exclusion of women from political suffrage, the universities, the professions and from rights of ownership, had been successfully challenged by previous generations, we pointed out the subtler, more indirect ways in which legal rules and categories excluded or discriminated against our sex.

Earlier discrimination had always been justified by the claim that the different characteristics of women made them inherently unsuited to a career in medicine or the law say, or to fulfil the onerous responsibilities of voting. The 'persons' cases around the end of the nineteenth century taught women a lot about legal neutrality. The judges at that time, intellectually honest to a man, maintained that the word 'person' did not include women. Understandably, in the wake of that sort of thinking, my generation saw the pitfalls in admitting to any form of difference. Of course, there were biological differences such as women's birth-giving properties which would require exceptional treatment like statutory maternity leave, but otherwise we argued that sex difference was unimportant and socially constructed. Gender ought to be no barrier to a neutral conception of citizenship and legal subjecthood.

Female lawyers began to show how the law disadvantaged women, particularly in relation to part-time work; how women's work within and outside the home was undervalued in pay disputes and in the distribution of assets on the breakdown of marriage; how the defining of sexual offences denied or distorted female sexuality. One of our most senior women judges, Lady Justice Brenda Hale, was at the fore in many of these struggles.

We imagined that positing the ideal of gender neutrality would engender sexual equality but, of course, treating as equal those who are in fact unequal does not produce equality, especially if there is no acknowledgement of the world beyond the courtroom door.

However, in the beginning, we were true to our belief in law's reforming power and whenever any deficit for women was identified, we sought law reform. It was not always wholly successful because, of course, law itself was part of the problem.

Male violence is one of the areas to which women have directed particular attention. People began to see that violence is the ultimate denial of equality and also to become concerned about the sexual double standard which operated in the courtroom so that women were measured by very different criteria from those which assessed male conduct. Rape cases became the central battleground. The guiding principles of rape trials seemed to be that men were victims of their own libido and that women led men on.

Many jurisdictions introduced law reform to limit cross-examination about a woman's sexual history. In the UK too the law was changed but the judiciary was left with the discretion as to when such questioning should be allowed. Sentencing guidelines were issued to prevent courts from dealing with rape as they would theft of a bicycle or minor assault.

More recent legislation has removed the traditional requirement of corroboration by an independent witness and has changed the language of the direction to the jury, which used to be informed that it was well known that women brought such charges falsely and juries had, therefore, to exercise caution about the complainant's testimony. Yet despite such changes, the conviction rate for rape in Britain is still the lowest for all serious crime, and despite increased reporting of rape the convictions are falling. Over the past decade the numbers of reported rapes have doubled but only 7% of complaints ever lead to a conviction. Very few of the remaining 93% proceed to court, because a huge number are withdrawn. This is often because women just cannot face the legal process. Despite all the efforts to improve the system the stumbling block is that the woman knows the cross-examination is tough: it will be her word against the accused. Women know too that it is difficult to secure a conviction; they make their own calculations as to whether they are prepared to go through with it.

Of the cases which proceed to trial the conviction rate is 41%. The generalised conviction rate for crime across the board is 73%. So why is the conviction rate so low for rape?

In her 1996 book on rape *Carnal Knowledge*, Sue Lees showed from her academic research that British judges, who were supposed to prevent invasive, irrelevant cross-examination of sexual history, interpreted their discretion widely and admitted irrelevant and prejudicial questioning. This scandal led to the government introducing new statutory law in the Youth and Criminal Evidence Act 1999 to further restrict cross-examination in rape cases. In the legislation the government made a brave attempt to steer a path away from the demand for a blanket ban, which many women's groups had sought, but greatly restricted judicial discretion, laying down only four sets of circumstances where leave may be given to allow such questioning. Even so, in an appeal to the House of Lords an inroad was created: where an accused man honestly believes a woman has consented she can be questioned about her sexual past, if it explains why he thought she was consenting.

The law's failure in these cases has challenged our optimistic belief that legal reform would relegate injustice to the past.

Domestic violence is another area which exposed how blunt the law can be as an instrument for social change. Fortunately the law no longer recognises a private realm or 'no go' area in which a man is free to beat his wife. Domestic violence is now recognised as a social evil which may eventually have fatal results. (In the vast majority of homicides involving women as victims, the woman was the spouse, cohabitee or former partner and every week two women die as a result of domestic violence.) Figures from the recent British Crime Survey 2003 show that domestic violence forms the largest single category of violent crime – 20%. Home Office figures suggest 25%. When domestic violence came to be dealt with in the courts, the gender-neutral rule, that no prosecutor should proceed with a case unless there is a real chance of securing a conviction, meant the dropping of significant numbers of prosecutions where the female complainant expressed unwillingness to testify. Again, government has acted on women's concerns and many of these failures are being addressed. Legislation is now going through parliament to allow the police to arrest persons accused of domestic violence for common assault without a warrant. Normally low level assaults require one and by the time it is sought the woman has been persuaded to withdraw her complaint. Police will also be equipped with polaroid cameras to photograph injuries and the mayhem they find at the home. This may enable prosecutions even where the woman herself is too frightened to testify. The new law will also give greater powers to the courts to make restraining orders, even where a man has been acquitted of the particular assault, but there is sufficient evidence that physical abuse is taking place on a regular basis. This section of the legislation has understandably caused controversy because the idea that an acquitted person has any infringement on his liberty is usually unacceptable, particularly if breach of the order carries up to five years' imprisonment. Clearly the courts would have to be satisfied that the situation involved ongoing domestic violence and an opportunity to appeal would have to be available to the person receiving the order. There would also have to be evidence reaching the usual criminal standard of proof before any imprisonment.

This is an example of the way civil libertarians have to be more willing to examine some of the law's orthodoxies if they want to see real justice. For many the fear of giving any leeway at all leads them into intransigence, which can entrench inequity. Sometimes the victim is so disadvantaged in the system that we will have to try to refocus the lens of the courtroom process. In some situations a serious tension exists between human rights and civil liberties which means that reforms must be made cautiously. The government does use victim's arguments about the law's failings to justify wholesale restrictions on liberties and it is right to combat such erosions but this is not to say there can be no adjustment at all. It is always necessary to examine the powerful undertows that exist in the law, which if unacknowledged can create injustice.

At the same time, the supposedly gender-neutral law in relation to provocation based upon a sudden and temporary loss of self-control in the face of provoking words or actions, seemed to fail women who reacted not to one provoking act but the slow burn of cumulative abuse. Only after a whole series of miscarriages of justice did the judges begin to interpret the word 'sudden' more generously, with positive outcomes for many women.

The Solicitor-General, Harriet Harman, has called for an end to the defence of provocation because she believes it provides men with an unreasonable excuse for killing their wives. Although the intention had been to include the reform in new legislation, the issue has instead been referred to the Law Commission. There is no doubt that the defence has become weighed down by a complicated set of directions which the judge must now give to the jury but people do kill in the heat of a terrible discovery, men and women. I have acted for a woman who killed a partner when she discovered him sexually abusing her daughter. I have acted for many women as well as men who have been driven to crazed despair. I have also acted for a girl who killed the man who battered her mother to a pulp. None of these people acted with deliberation or pre-meditation. All were provoked beyond endurance and the right verdict was manslaughter not murder. But it was a long haul getting the law on provocation to a position where it was as responsive to the position of women as men.

The hard struggle has forced reformers like myself to ask whether the process of assimilation really works. Equalisation has almost invariably been towards a male norm. The public standards already in place were assumed to be valid, so instead of our all attempting to order the world differently, women have been expected to shape up, whether as lawyers or as women using or experiencing the law. We have tried to secure better outcomes but always within the same parameters.

In characterising the law's shortcomings, I am aware that powerful cultural forces are at work. It is claimed that the law only reflects public attitudes which are prejudicial to women. However, we are entitled to expect more. The law transmits powerful messages about men and women, which construct and underpin our social relations. It is important that those messages do not reinforce stereotypical images of womanhood and femininity, or endorse notions of masculinity that are detrimental to women and indeed negative for men. Ideally the law should be capable of transcending difference by first acknowledging it.

In the areas where straightforward gender neutrality has not worked, new strategies have been adopted in pursuit of justice for women. But these have involved a return by women lawyers and academics to that worrying zone, which we had struggled so hard to avoid: namely a recognition of sexual or gender difference. Those of us defending in the cases of battered women who kill have sought to bring the reality of the battered woman's life into the courtroom, to contextualise her act of killing. In cases of self-defence and provocation we have called expert testimony to answer the currently familiar question, 'If it was so bad, why didn't she leave?' This move towards context has meant the development of ameliorative or substantive rights for women rather than formal rights, as has already started to happen in other jurisdictions like Canada. So, for example, when assets are being distributed after divorce, account is increasingly taken of the career sacrifices women have made and their reduced chances of finding decent employment.

What has become clear since the 1980s is that notions of gender difference, so long feared as a cul-de-sac for women, have to be understood if we are going to secure justice for them, whether as victims or as defendants. It is crucial if we are to change the attrition rate in rape cases that gender difference is accepted. Our judges hate the idea of gender difference, claiming it as an example of creeping political correctness. Allegations of political correctness are often a sign that an area of hallowed and privileged ground is about to be seized from those who have enjoyed it exclusively.

The gender of an accused or victim may not make any difference when the courts are dealing with property offences like theft but will make a huge difference when assessing evidence in offences of a sexual nature because women and men frequently read sexual interactions in different ways. I do not want to pursue the 'men are from Mars, women are from Venus' theory as the basis for law but the idea that the law should be blind to difference simply does not work. This takes us into notoriously treacherous waters about men's and women's minds. Professor Simon Baron-Cohen, author of *The Essential Difference: Men, Women and the Extreme Male Brain* (2003) and Director of the Autism Centre at Cambridge, claims that the female brain is predominantly hard-wired for empathy whereas the male brain is hard-wired for building and understanding systems. (This was also said in the eighteenth century!) Whether these things are inherent or whether they are culturally constructed will continue to be debated *ad nauseam*, and this is probably an unnecessary distraction. What we do know is that women's *experience* is different and men and women approach sex very often with different perspectives. The rules and systems on the conduct of rape trials formulated by men in the law do not acknowledge the ways in which women, even in our contemporary liberated world, may behave differently from men. Just as women tend not to respond like the provoked man in the homicide context by snapping in rage, women in sexually charged situations do not always do what men would do or expect.

The ultimate entitlement of a woman to maintain the integrity of her own body, to choose how it is used and shared, should be sacrosanct. Few women invent allegations of rape. Many more women than those who go to the police feel forced to take part in sexual acts which are non-consensual. All the discussions about rape concentrate on the issue of consent but in reality, when a woman is confronted with a man who is forcing sex upon her she will often silently permit intercourse or perform oral sex rather than face the possibility of a serious assault or greater internal harm. The feelings of humiliation, disempowerment and degradation are much the same.

The desire to win acceptance for the view that most women do not invent such allegations drives some campaigners into the corner of dismissing the fact that there need to be safeguards for the occasions when people do make false allegations. Again the argument turns on whether it is better that ten guilty persons walk free than that we convict a person who is innocent.

People who commit sexual crimes are almost invariably advantaged because their offences are committed one to one. There are rarely independent witnesses to the act; therefore the issue is always one of credibility. Who is to be believed – the complainant or the accused? The acquittal rate in rape cases is so high because in such circumstances the accuser has to be very compelling as a witness or there has to be some other supporting evidence to meet the high standard of proof.

Securing a conviction in stranger rape is not difficult once identity is established. Juries are not inclined to accept that many women consent to sex with a stranger in an alley on the way home from the parent–teacher meeting at their children's school. Instead, the problems arise where the parties come together consensually for some reason but the meeting ends up with sexual acts taking place which are not mutually agreed upon. This can extend from accepting a lift from someone at a club because the buses have stopped running, to offering a coffee to the carpet layer, to going into a hotel room to have a drink from the minibar because the hotel bar has closed.

I remember a particularly inflamed argument with the husband of a friend over the boxer Mike Tyson's rape of a young woman in a hotel room. His view was that a woman who goes to a man's hotel room, whatever the man's pretext, knows that it is really about having sex. It is a view that many men share. The woman's behaviour may be naïve and reckless but what happens next is what counts. No one should forfeit their right to say 'I am sorry but I do not want to have sex.'

A recent furore over another alleged rape related to a girl going back with a famous snooker player and another couple to the Savoy after meeting at a club. Her account was that she had thought it was merely to carry on talking and drinking, but her friend and the other man peeled away and she was left with a man with whom she did not want to have any intimacy. He unzipped his penis and pulled her on top of him. She tried to finesse the situation, explaining that she was in a relationship, but on her account he pushed her into intercourse against her will. The young woman's undoing was that as they parted they exchanged telephone numbers. She said she did this to get away unharmed; the defence said it showed she was at the time not the least traumatised or in fear but had a rethink afterwards and cried rape. Most lawyers would have taken money on the outcome. The jury acquitted. The press rushed to print, demanding anonymity for men accused of rape because a decent chap could be ruined by such a wicked minx. A few days later it was claimed that the man had faced a similar accusation in Australia.

Because of the nature of the allegation the questioning in rape cases is always intimate and invasive, but as I pointed out the law has been changed to put stringent limits on cross-examination as well as discarding the need for corroboration. The accused's right to cross-examine a complainant in person has been withdrawn in recognition of the anguish and terror it can evoke. However, there remain a number of serious problems.

We have to ask ourselves why it is that despite removing the need for supporting evidence like torn knickers or bruises, despite putting a heavy constraint on the discretion of judges, despite removing the right to silence, more than half the men who stand trial are acquitted. The reason is that when a case depends almost exclusively upon the conflicting testimony of two people it is very difficult for a jury to resolve the issue. Whom do you believe? If the complainant is a very persuasive, compelling witness and the accused is not there will be no contest, but often the jury will be left uncertain.

The extent to which myths and stereotypes enter at this point is considerable. Even though we live in a society dominated by sexual imagery, where women live independent lives, free to make choices about sexual partners, no longer stigmatised for loss of virginity or participation in premarital sex, the double standard is still alive and well. Women are still expected to conform to sexual standards which are very different from those which apply to men. As a young woman barrister said to me recently on the subject of rape, 'If you can show a woman is a slapper, the guy always gets off.' The former Director of Public Prosecutions, Sir David Calvert-Smith QC, has publicly acknowledged that rape cases are hampered by the hardened cultural attitude that victims of sexual assault lead men on. He urged the Crown Prosecution Service and the government to tackle the mistaken belief that women 'ask for it', so that more rapists could be brought to trial. He recounted how 30 years ago at the Bar he heard practitioners say that no woman need be raped if she did not really want to be. 'There are still residues of that in the British consciousness. That's one of the things we are looking to break down.'

It goes beyond that. The campaigning about invasive cross-examination has dealt exclusively with sexual history and behaviour, but attacks on a woman's character are much more nuanced and complicated. If the woman who is making an allegation of rape can be shown to have abused alcohol or drugs, or if it can be shown that she has had any psychiatric treatment at all, such as psychotherapy for depression or eating disorders or family relationships, she will be vulnerable to suggestions that she is unreliable as a witness.

A close friend who is a judge has been monitoring the way juries respond in the rape cases when she presides. She feels that juries are very anxious to deal with cases justly and if properly directed will resist the temptation to take extraneous matters like drug use into account, but if a woman has behaved in ways that could be considered reckless – going back to a man's flat after a heavy drinking session where a certain amount of intimacy has taken place even before entering the room – a jury is unlikely to convict. This is not because jurors any longer think a woman is not entitled to say 'no' but because in seeking to reconcile two different accounts they will put the lead-up behaviour into the scales.

As I was waiting to start a murder trial at the Old Bailey recently I sat in on the barristers' speeches and judge's summing up in a rape trial. It is always much more difficult to evaluate a trial when you yourself are involved on one side or the other and it was interesting to hear the end of the case as a bystander.

A young bank clerk and her friends from work used to adjourn to a local pub every Friday after work. She had become friendly with the barman, who would chat her up. There would be a lot of jovial banter and flirtation and it was clear to everyone that she liked him. It then became a habit for her to stay on after the others left and wait while the barman finished his duties. They would then leave together and go back to her bedsit, where he would spend the night. Her account was that after a couple of months she wanted to end it. She found him insensitive and overpowering as a lover, forcing himself into her aggressively and painfully, and she was sometimes afraid of him. She did not want to say outright why she wanted to end the relationship so she simply absented herself from the group outing to the pub.

One night as she was getting ready for bed he arrived at her door with a bottle of wine. She described being embarrassed and tongue-tied when he asked why she had not been in touch with him. He asked to come in for a coffee and she agreed because he was rather drunk and she was worried about her neighbours complaining. As she put on the kettle he opened the wine and poured two glasses although she insisted she wanted him to go quickly. She told the court she felt uncomfortable because she was in her nightdress and a dressing gown, having showered and washed her hair. He started kissing her and she resisted and said she was doing an audit the next day so had to go to bed. On her account he would not listen to her protestations and forced her to have sex, pinning her to the sofa using his full weight and pulling up her clothes. His behaviour was so frightening, she thought he would beat her if she put up much resistance. When she tried to scream no sound came, she was in such terror. She had bruises on her upper arms and a small round bruise on the inside of her upper thigh. A clear case of rape, said the Crown.

The defence case was very similar but very different. The barman was working at the pub to save money because he wanted to go to university but his elderly mother was a lone parent with no resources to help him. He met the complainant when she came with friends to the pub on Fridays. In fact he had not intended starting any relationships at this time but he felt she had made quite a play for him and he really liked her. He called two witnesses who described seeing her flirting with him and getting him to dance with her, even when he insisted he had to serve customers. A witness described seeing her get upset when he paid a bit of attention to another girl in the bar. If anything, said one, she made all the running.

On the night in question, he said that someone from the bank had been in the pub and he mentioned that he had seen nothing of the complainant. Her colleague said the young woman was working a lot of overtime for the bank as they had a big audit coming up. He assumed that this must be why she had not been in touch and decided to call round. He agreed he had had quite a bit to drink but said he was not drunk. He was clear that she had invited him in, despite being scantily dressed. She offered him coffee and had been glad of the wine. They had started caressing and one thing led to another. He denied rape and said that any bruising was as a result of boisterous sexual play. When asked why she would make such a claim he said that he thought she was a very tense person sexually and had some hang-ups. He claimed that after they had sex, they had talked about their relationship and rowed about his flirtation with one of the other girls in the pub. They parted on bad terms, having agreed not to see each other again. He thought that she might have minded that he had been the one to end it.

The jury acquitted him.

What the law does not accommodate is that male and female perceptions of the same interactions are different. Sex is so much about reading signals. And everyone brings their own baggage to the courtroom in evaluating the messages. In the debate on rape, one of the retired judges in the House of Lords described how sex was considered the best of indoor sports in his day. By that he meant that the challenge for a man was to use all his powers to persuade a young woman to succumb to his charms. For that older generation the game plan was all about seduction and it was to be expected that women would say no. Even today when women more readily say yes, a woman may still be deciding whether she really wants sex while a man who is impatient and aroused may read her behaviour as ambiguous.

It may seem that we have moved on from the notion that 'only bad girls' have sex but in a jury there will be a spread of views, reflecting society's complex attitudes. They will include the abiding belief that men are less capable of self-restraint, poor things, and that women should not behave in ways that give men to understand sex will be available. 'Laddish' behaviour by women – heavy drinking, sexy clothing, explicit sexual talk – will all forfeit sympathy. These are views held by men and women both.

One of the remaining hurdles in rape cases has been what is called the Morgan defence. The case involved the rape of a woman by a number of men who were told by her husband that she always screamed and resisted when having intercourse because that was how she liked it. At appeal in the House of Lords in 1974, the judges decided that if a man acted in the honest but mistaken belief that the woman was consenting he had a defence.

Few men run the defence in the Morgan way – she was saying no but I thought she meant yes – but many accused men use it as a backstop. She did consent but even if I am wrong about that, I honestly believed she was consenting. Even if an accused does not say he was honestly mistaken judges tell juries that if they think he might have been honestly mistaken they can acquit.

For juries who believe the woman did not want to have sex but worry about the effect of a conviction on the life of the man, or feel the woman may have given mixed signals by her own behaviour, the judge's direction is a let-out. In the foregoing case we can speculate on their discussions. She did not have to open the door late at night; she did invite him in for coffee; she was very close to undressed; she did not make it clear that the relationship was over; she did not show him the door; she did not scream. Is it any wonder women feel they are the people on trial?

As long ago as 1991 I advocated that when a man claimed that he honestly thought a woman was consenting even if she was not, there should be an objective test: would a reasonable person have thought she was consenting (if she was saying 'no' or was asleep or was drugged)? In homicide cases murder can be reduced to manslaughter if the accused was provoked, but there is an objective test: would a reasonable person have been provoked? The reason for this element of objectivity was to prevent people who flew off the handle at the slightest affront invoking the defence. It seems right to me that the same air of reality is introduced into rape cases. The case would still have to be proved by the Crown in the normal way, beyond reasonable doubt, with the presumption of innocence intact.

In the Sexual Offences Act 2003 the government has now changed the law to embrace this suggestion. The jury have to decide whether it was reasonable for the accused to think the woman was consenting. The change is very controversial and raises the question as to whether such a divergence from the normal criminal rules is justifiable.

In the second reading debate of that legislation in the House of Lords, Viscount Bledisloe chose an unfortunate but telling example from which to draw the principle: 'If I am accused of stealing your property, it is a defence if I show an honest belief that I had a claim of right to that property. That is the general test of the criminal law.'

The question is whether the protection of human beings, not property, from a profoundly damaging experience might justify higher expectations in human behaviour, a greater care and respect for the humanity of others. Is the principle drawing on the experience of women as well as men? In the same debate one of our retired judges, Lord Lloyd, speaking about rape, very sensitively enunciated its kernel: 'the forcible penetration of the vagina is a corruption of the deepest and tenderest of emotions of which human beings are capable'. Homosexuals do not feel any differently, even if the form of intimacy is different. Forcing intercourse upon someone, securing their engagement in sexual activity through fear, is a corruption of lovemaking. The fact that sometimes people do it casually and without any reference to love does not take away from the fact that it is the way we have found to express that profound emotion. That is why sexual offences are so lasting in the damage they do to lives, contaminating what is precious. It is why sexual offences are different, involving an 'abuse of intimacy', and it is why we may deal with them differently.

That does not mean reversing the burden of proof and forcing the accused to prove their innocence but it does mean prohibiting negligent disregard for the other. If human rights mean anything we are here walking on human rights terrain.

The problem for civil libertarians is that this encroaches upon the general argument that there should be no interference with defendants' rights, that we should create seamless principle across all areas of crime. We have to accept that occasionally there will be tensions between human rights and civil liberties, especially when factors such as the historic inequality between men and women and gender differences come into play. We then have to decide how to proceed, looking for ways to improve the chances of securing justice for complainants with a rightful case but without putting defendants at risk of wrongful conviction.

If we are not careful, government can take over the legitimate concerns of women, children's agencies or victims' groups and use them for a generalised assault on liberty. For example, women's groups lobbied for a man accused of rape to have his previous convictions for sexual offences disclosed to the jury if he had cross-examined the rape complainant about her sexual history. But this has now evolved into the government seeking to place everyone's convictions before the jury, whatever the charge. Women campaigned to have 'stalking' criminalised only to find that the offence is now used against political activists who regularly picket commercial enterprises. The motives for policy change can often be disguised in a spin about victims that is so sophisticated that it brooks no opposition or dissent. Caution is dismissed as hostile to the interests of the vulnerable when in fact the vulnerable may be most at risk.

I do think that securing justice for women in rape cases will continue to be fraught with difficulties because of the singular nature of the crime and because attitudes in society about sexuality have changed insufficiently. We keep looking for the magic law reform which will fix what may be resistant to change until social attitudes move on.

9

RACE – THE ILLUSION OF INCLUSION

LABOUR IN GOVERNMENT has been more vigilant about racism than any other administration. Soon after coming into office, it established an inquiry led by Sir William Macpherson into the bungled investigation of the racist murder of Stephen Lawrence, which had taken place in 1993. The 1999 Macpherson Report found that the police were institutionally racist and the government pledged to stamp out racism in the criminal justice system. Yet despite this genuine commitment the government often loses a sense of what the implications of new policy agendas will be for racial minorities and race relations.

We are seeing a serious retreat from civil liberties, mimicking what is taking place in the United States, and experience has taught us that whenever there is such a backlash against civil liberties, minorities are disproportionately affected. And while the government seems blind to the ways in which their policies work on the ground, leaders of the black community know that changes in the legal protections and the lowering of standards will have greatest impact on the most vulnerable; invariably the black community and other minorities will take the biggest hit. The whole menu of illiberal reform, including target-setting, taking into account previous convictions, mandatory and minimum sentences, will lead to still more ethnic minority defendants in the prison population, in which they are already over-represented.

When I started practice at the Bar I spent a large part of my time in courts representing young black men charged with being a 'suspected person'. The accused did not have to commit an offence; it was enough that the police saw him behaving in a way that led them to believe that he was up to no good. There was no right to jury trial. In court, the standard case involved two white police officers corroborating each other, using identical notes made back at the police station. They would describe seeing the suspect behaving suspiciously, looking around him to see if there were observers and then trying a car door handle or pushing against a gate or reaching into a shoulder bag. There were never any fingerprints or independent witnesses or stolen items. Large numbers of young black men acquired criminal convictions on this kind of evidence, with magistrates nodding the cases through.

The leading human rights counsel in Trinidad, Desmond Allum, tells a hair-raising story of his days as a law student in London in the 1960s when he and a friend had just been to visit the great West Indian cricketer, Sir Learie Constantine, in Hampstead. They were walking down to Swiss Cottage when they were stopped by the police and aggressively asked what they were doing in the area. Before they knew it they were bundled into a police van and arrested as suspected persons. They were convicted at the magistrates' court on the lies of the officers and it was only when their case was taken up by members of the Bar like Dingle Foot QC, who knew them, that an appeal to the higher court was successful. Desmond, one of the most admired and eminent senior counsel in the West Indies, always claims that his career hung by a thread but the experience kept him alert to the abuses perpetrated on the immigrant community in Britain.

Although the legislation allowing such arrests was repealed, the distrust created was lasting. The law in itself was not racist but it became racist in its application and the same is true now of stop and search procedures, where people can be stopped if the police have reasonable suspicion that they may be in possession of a weapon, drugs or stolen property. Home Office figures released in March 2003 show a leap in stop and search by 16% against Asian people and 6% against black people in the year 2001–2002. Those of white people fell by 2%. In London over the same period the Metropolitan Police stopped 40% more Asians and 30% more blacks but 8% fewer white people than they had done in the previous year. The disproportionate use of stop and search against the black community is the direct descendant of the use of the 'sus laws' as the most alienating policing tool in contemporary use. The Macpherson Report agreed that stop and search was an important operational tool but said over-use against ethnic minorities had to be stamped out. Darcus Howe, the broadcaster and journalist, describes being stopped and searched ten times in the last 20 years. Once in the West End of London, an officer lied through his teeth and claimed he had seen him dipping into women's handbags with intent to steal.

Garth Crooks, the BBC sports broadcaster and former Tottenham Hotspur striker was first stopped and searched at the age of 18, when an officer subjected him to a torrent of racial abuse. The officer was called off by a colleague who recognised Crooks as a rising star at Stoke City football club. But as Crooks has since pointed out, 'Just wearing a baseball cap and driving a Mercedes are not good enough reasons for stopping someone.' Even the black Anglican Bishop of Birmingham, John Sentamu, has had his own run-ins with the police. He has been stopped and searched eight times when wearing mufti, only to find that the police suddenly become very deferential when they discover who he is. The experience no doubt informed his considerations when he sat as part of the inquiry team with Sir William Macpherson after the death of Stephen Lawrence. Trevor Hall, a senior civil servant, has been stopped and searched by police on 44 occasions in the last 17 years. He retired last year as a member of the Home Office's Community Relations Unit where he advised ministers on race relations policy.

Senior policemen hate any open discussion of bad behaviour by policemen. In the scheme of things, police deviance is minimal by comparison with the huge wrongs committed by criminals, but the difference is that policemen are an arm of the state. One of the problems is that in discussions about legal reform, politicians and pundits always pretend that the police are paragons of virtue and these things do not happen or that if they do they are isolated events. A cordon sanitaire is placed around discussion of the police for fear that even talking about their misbehaviour will undermine confidence in them. It is as though saying it will make malfeasance real. But if you want to know what really happens, ask any black man.

Many a professional black person will tell you that at the weekend, when they put on their anorak and a baseball cap, they are immediately deemed unsuitable to be driving a smart car. Leonard Woodley, the first black Queen's Counsel, was sitting as a judge at Wood Green Crown Court when he slid out at lunchtime to go to the bank. He wrapped a scarf around the neck of his overcoat to cover his judicial collar and white bands. When he presented his plastic bank card and chequebook at the bank counter, the teller was immediately suspicious, signalled to some male colleagues and he was detained. The court sitting had to wait because the bank could not believe that a black man bore the letters QC after his name. Stereotyping of the black community is as insidious now as ever. Len Woodley should count himself lucky. Bruce Wright, a black judge in New York, took ill with heart pains while on the Bench and was rushed to the local hospital. He was placed in a cubicle next door to an elderly, white vagrant who was obviously drunk and had been picked up off the streets. Through the spasms of pain, Judge Wright was conscious of his cubicle curtains being opened by a young doctor, who took a look and quickly closed them, and then the curtains next door being opened and a voice saying to the old drunk, 'Well, Judge, tell me the problem.'

Most black men, however, have no establishment links or celebrity status and their harassment often turns very sour indeed. As I mentioned in Chapter 3, Delroy Lindo – a civil rights activist and the friend of Winston Silcott who was cleared of killing a policeman, Keith Blakelock – took legal action against the police after being stopped and searched more than 37 times in eight years. An internal report by the Metropolitan Police upheld his complaints. Leroy McDowell and Wayne Taylor successfully sued the police for assault and false imprisonment when their car was stopped in east London and searched because they were in a 'drugs-related area'. Nothing was found but because of their protestations they were arrested and charged with public order offences, which were later rejected by a court. It is a classic tactic that when police are worried about their own behaviour and fear they have overstepped the mark, they fabricate charges against their victims. The two men suffer from a very painful disorder, sickle cell anaemia, and had asked whilst in custody for medical attention but their requests were refused. In the end they were awarded £38,000 damages.

Similarly, Carl Josephs, a Birmingham caterer, was stopped 34 times in two years despite having a clean driving licence and no criminal record. He became so fed up he decided to lodge his documents with the West Midlands Police permanently. He sued the force but the Birmingham County Court refused to accept that there was any racial harassment, although they awarded him £1,000 nonetheless. He is taking the case to the European Court of Human Rights.

One of the children who went through school with my oldest son recently called our home from a police station in great distress. My husband and I went to the station, as his own mother could not be contacted. The boy, who has never been in trouble in his life, had come out of the tube station where he was set upon by another youth, who felt he had been 'dissed' or not offered due respect by our young friend. The police had arrived at the scene and, seeing two young black men in a scuffle, yanked both out of the station, put them in handcuffs and threw them into the back of a police van. When we saw our friend he had no skin down the centre of his face.

With his hands locked behind his back he had been unable to protect himself as he had skidded along the floor of the vehicle. His wrists were cut and bleeding where the handcuffs had been applied too tightly. He was in a state of shock at what had happened to him and the police were shamefaced that they had not sought to find out what was going on before treating him like a thug. I have no doubt that despite their profuse apologies, his view of the police will never recover. I also have no doubt that our arrival made a difference. That small instance is but one in a sea of experience which is usually uncharted by the white professional classes.

The recitation of such cases could continue and it makes shocking reading because as well as making individual lives a misery it feeds deep resentment and distrust amongst a whole section of society.

Politicians forget that their rhetoric – developed to appease the law and order lobby or to assuage the tabloid press on the subject of asylum seekers – inflames public fever. It also feeds into the way policing is undertaken and the way courts go about their business. They talk endlessly about 'joined-up' government but fail to join up their concerns about racism with their initiatives on immigration, asylum, anti-terrorism and general crime. The new Anti-Social Behaviour legislation passed in 2003 and proposed amendments to the Police and Criminal Evidence Act will increase police powers to stop and search to cover items that they think might be used in criminal damage. This means that stop and search will now be permitted for objects that are not of themselves criminal, such as paint. As a consequence a far greater use of the power will be permitted and it will inevitably have a stronger impact on ethnic minorities.

When challenged by Doreen Lawrence, Stephen Lawrence's mother, that government was losing interest in beating racism, the

Home Office minister, at that time Lord Falconer, insisted that 'the government's commitment to race equality is as strong as ever and increasing confidence in the criminal justice system is central to that agenda'. He acknowledged that with tensions running high because of the Gulf war, the police and the courts needed to be seen to treat all communities fairly.

When you unpack the stop and search figures, they suggest a greatly increased interest in young Asian men (which would include men from the Middle East) in the aftermath of 11 September. Americans would call this racial profiling. The Asian communities are feeling very beleaguered, sensing a growing hostility and Islamophobia not just from the authorities but also from their neighbours. Statistics for 2001–2002 show that race hate crimes doubled in Lincolnshire, Staffordshire, West Midlands and North Wales. Nearly 9,000 people were cautioned or prosecuted for racially aggravated offences in the same period nationally, double the amount the year before. Most of the victims are Asian but many are Middle Eastern and include asylum seekers. So the communities feel they are getting a rough deal from all sides. According to a report called *Policing for London* (2003), by HM Inspectorate of Constabulary, relations between the police and the Pakistani and Bangladeshi communities are deteriorating so rapidly that the tensions are as bad as those existing between the police and young blacks. If handled insensitively the 'war on terrorism' could greatly exacerbate race relations, particularly in northern cities and towns with large Islamic communities.

Today black people are eight times more likely to be stopped than whites, compared with only six times more likely when the Macpherson Report was published in 1999. While it is true that the number of stops on black suspects fell slightly after the inquiry, senior police at the time said this was as a result of switching to a more targeted approach to searching. This appears to be borne out by the fact that stops on whites and Asians also fell. But during the past two years – at a time when police have continued to complain about lack of manpower, crippling amounts of bureaucracy and low morale – officers have stepped up their stops of blacks and Asians at a serious pace. Stopping and searching on reasonable grounds is an acceptable policing power but when the ground is merely being young and black or DWB – driving while black – that is not reasonable. It involves the stereotyping that rightly enrages law-abiding people from ethnic minorities; it is lazy, unjudged policing with poor results and dire consequences for community relations.

When these figures were published, Paul Cavadino of Nacro, the charity organisation for the care and rehabilitation of offenders, said, 'Despite all the excuses and rationalisations, these figures are indefensible. No one can seriously claim that black people commit eight times more crime than white people.' However, ministers do not want to see this as evidence of racism.

Ian Burrell, the Home Affairs correspondent of the *Independent* who follows crime initiatives closely, sees as the link the pressure placed on police to ride specific Downing Street and Home Office hobby-horses. For more than a year Home Office officials have been chasing the chief constables of the largest urban forces, urging them to do more to tackle street crime. The policy generators have decided that it is street crime that drives public fear and exposes the government to accusations that they are soft on law and order. Tony Blair went before the House of Commons to promise that street crime would be under control within a year. However, success in reducing street crime is being purchased at a very high price, with forces swamping crime 'hot spots' in inner city neighbourhoods with large Afro-Caribbean communities. It is the sort of crude policing which has in the past led to riots. Ian Blair, the Met's Deputy Commissioner insists that it is impossible to deny the fact that in some areas of London 63% of mugging is carried out by young blacks. What, he asks, are the police to do? Ignore that fact? His comments show how the police have shifted the agenda back to black criminality and while he is right that in some poor areas highly populated by black people the black crime rate will be proportionately higher, he is allowing for careless policing. The police never seem to be taught to ask themselves, 'Why am I making this stop? Is it only because this person is black?' In a speech in the House of Lords on 16 June 2003, Baroness Ros Howells, a leading member of the black community, gave us a flavour of these simmering attitudes when she recounted a recent statement made by the Home Secretary that 'black boys are all muggers'. She was devastated, and before walking out of the meeting was quietly insistent that her 'sons are not muggers'. In fact, she has no sons of her own but is the symbolic mother of many.

The post-Lawrence focus on fairness, equality and respect is already being overridden by a panic about black crime, which is in turn used as a justification for discriminatory powers. The police say this is because of pressure from government, which is oblivious to the consequences of its demands.

Patricia Lamour is Assistant Director of the anti-racist charity, the 1990 Trust. She compares the latest Operation Safer Streets in London with previous crackdowns: Operation Swamp at the start of the 1980s and Operation Eagle Eye in the 1990s. She points out that despite the police's equal opportunities rhetoric, officers are encouraged by such operations to see young black men as 'the enemy'. 'The impression is always given of a thin blue line, holding back a tide of crime that's implicitly and explicitly described as black.'

Another problem is that ethnic minorities feel under-protected as victims as well as over-policed as suspects. Stephen Lawrence was not an isolated case. For example, West Mercia Police completely mishandled the investigation into the deaths of two black men from the same family who were found hanged within weeks of each other: one of them, Errol McGowan, had repeatedly asked the police for protection from a racist gang and was ignored.

With regard to police attitudes, a study by Her Majesty's Inspectorate of Constabulary, called *Diversity Matters*, published in March 2003, explains a lot. According to the report, some chief police officers are undermining attempts to improve race and diversity awareness within their forces by behaving disruptively during training sessions, using sexist and other inappropriate language at internal and public meetings and generally dismissing the issues as without importance. The HMI identified 'a lack of genuine commitment from some police managers and leaders' to learning about minorities. The Macpherson Report highlighted the problem of institutional racism but many people in the Home Office and the police have been rowing back from the concept. What the Macpherson panel was describing was the practice and culture within organisations which sustains racism or allows it to go unchallenged.

The HMI study found examples of borough commanders, with no recognised experience or expertise in diversity training, unilaterally undermining anti-discrimination measures. They encouraged staff to believe that race and diversity training was an unnecessary and low-priority distraction. At constable level, too many police officers 'believe race and diversity issues to be on the periphery of their working practices'.

It seems unbelievable that a report published within only a few years of the Stephen Lawrence inquiry should make such sorry reading. It woefully adds: 'The absence of an overarching long-term strategy and the failure fully to implement previous vision and guidance means that, in the eyes of the communities, the service has not set out what it wants to achieve or how to get there. Worryingly, it appears that most of the efforts expended so far have had little real impact.'

Although most objective observers would say that the Metropolitan Police record on dealing with racist crime and black-on-black gun crime has greatly improved, the force itself has repeatedly been convulsed by arguments about race, and in September 2003 faced serious criticism over the abandoned prosecution of a black police superintendent, Dr Ali Dizaei, for fraud. He has maintained that the case was racially motivated and has the support of the Association of Black Police Officers, which then urged potential recruits from racial minorities to boycott the Met.

On 21 October 2003, the BBC broadcast a documentary about an undercover journalist who became a probationer at Bruche police training college covering Greater Manchester, Cheshire and North Wales and secretly filmed his fellow rookies. The programme exposed police recruits praising Hitler and dressing up as the Ku-Klux-Klan; racist views were expressed about Stephen Lawrence and his parents as well as 'Pakis', and the willingness to pick racial minorities out for special police attention was shocking. Trevor Phillips, chairman of the Commission for Racial Equality, expressed concern that there seemed to be 'official condemnation of racism but unofficial condoning' and a clear divergence between policy and practice. When the existence of the film came to the attention of the Home Office, its first response was to complain about the journalist's undercover behaviour, despite the fact that the material was clearly in the public interest. The Home Secretary referred to the investigative work as 'a stunt' and berated the BBC; he later had to apologise when he realised that shooting the messenger was not the correct response to such vicious racism in the police, for which he is ultimately responsible.

An inquiry into attitudes in the Crown Prosecution Service

published in October 2003 cleared the CPS of any direct racism; but, nonetheless, found black defendants more likely to be prosecuted than white and on weaker evidence. The failure to tackle racism is felt most in the delivery of policing services to the community. Black and Asian people are stopped and searched more often than white people because a minority of racist police target them. Similarly, there are more deaths of black and Asian people in police custody. There are recruits who cannot wait to get on the streets to put their prejudices into action.

There are hopeful signs for which New Labour should be given recognition. The Race Relations (Amendment Act) 2002 is the biggest change in race relations law in 25 years. It places a duty on public bodies to promote equality and requires them not to act in a discriminatory way. The police have been put on notice by the Commission for Racial Equality that it will take action within a year if the stop and search scandal continues. The government has also promised to create a new framework for delivering race training to high standards across the police service. It is also talking of putting its own spies into police training programmes to blow the whistle on colleagues.The maddening fact is that the need for race awareness has been discussed now for over 20 years, ever since the 1982 Scarman inquiry into the Brixton riots of the previous year.

The reason why people like myself concentrate so hard on the use of stop and search is because this is where the distrust is sown in innocent black citizens and it is also where disaffection begins amongst the young. It is a barometer. If you are assumed to be a criminal and treated like one, then why bother to resist the pull of friends involved in anti-social behaviour? If magistrates are more inclined to believe the police, is it any wonder that black people are more likely to choose trial by jury?

Research shows that police are more likely to overcharge black arrestees. This means charging them with the more serious offence of robbery where theft would be more appropriate, or charging them with assault occasioning grievous bodily harm rather than actual bodily harm. As a result, pleas of guilty are not entered at the outset in many cases. When black people get angry and object to how they are being treated they end up with additional charges of threatening behaviour, assaulting police or disturbing the peace. They then arrive at court angry. They have bail refused more often and their resentment is read by the court as insubordination and aggression.

In March 2003, Silbert Farquharson, a middle-aged black man with no criminal record who was violently assaulted by the police, subjected to racist abuse and prosecuted on trumped-up charges won nearly a quarter of a million pounds in damages from the Metropolitan Police, one of the biggest awards for misconduct.

The events described are familiar to many of us at the criminal Bar. The difference might have been that the black man happened to have previous convictions. There might have been no independent witnesses. There might have been no one to overhear the racist abuse or see the violence used which was consistent with the injuries. The people who saw these things might not have been respectable members of the community, white and black, who themselves had no convictions. The outcome then might have been very different.

As it was, Mr Farquharson's case screamed injustice even to the sceptical who always insist that people bring these things on their own head.

A delivery van driver, he arrived in a road in south London just after his cousin, Stephen Smith, had been arrested for protesting to police about the handcuffing of a black café owner who was being searched on suspicion of involvement in dealing cannabis. The café proprietor, Clinton Washington, who was in his fifties, had no criminal record. But police said they had seen him wave to a black man in a BMW and thought he might be involved in drugs. Black men in BMWs are immediately suspect in the eyes of the police – ask the comedian Lenny Henry!

Stephen Smith told police that the handcuffs on Mr Washington, who offered no resistance, were too tight. Officers then arrested him for obstruction.

When Mr Farquharson arrived on the scene, he saw his cousin and went to find out what was happening, only to be assaulted by three police officers and thrown face down in the gutter in the presence of appalled members of the public. He was restrained with two sets of handcuffs. They were supposed to be double locked so as not to ratchet up and cut into his wrists but the police neglected to do this. He suffered permanent damage to his wrists and has been left with chronic pain syndrome.

A police officer knelt on his back and called him a fucking black bastard. At Brixton police station he was subjected to further abuse with his shoe tied to a belt loop: 'He's a fucking coon. Let's give him a fucking tail.'

Mr Farquharson and Mr Smith were prosecuted on false charges based on a completely invented account of events to justify the police actions, but the charges were thrown out of court because public-minded witnesses came forward. The judge awarded the high level of compensation because he was satisfied that the physical and psychological injuries meant Silbert Farquharson would never work again. No drugs were ever found. The whole yarn was a concoction.

The judge, Michael Dean, good man that he is, said, 'There is a clear public interest in condemning racist behaviour on the part of persons in authority in order to assure the diverse elements of our community that the police have no warrant to treat our citizens with contempt and oppression.'

Contempt and oppression are sadly on display more often than is realised and lead to serious scepticism amongst black people about the speed of change. Because of the nature of migrant communities even professional black people are likely to have family or friends who have been in trouble, so this knowledge of how the system works permeates the black experience of life in Britain.

A significant part of the work in human rights chambers is about abuse of power by the police, prison officers or immigration authorities or failure to provide the protection minorities need from racism. The Prison Service is still under scrutiny for an incident in 2000 when a vulnerable Asian teenager, Zahid Mubarek, was put in a cell with a known racist who had openly displayed his hatred of minorities and written letters, fantasising about committing a racist murder. Zahid ended up dead.

The Asian communities have always been at the receiving end of more race hate crimes than any other minority. Over the last 20 years there have been a number of major trials where members of Asian communities were prosecuted for riot or affray when they took action against white racist groups which, in the spirit of George Bush in Iraq, they argued was pre-emptive self-defence. These cases – the Bradford Twelve trial in 1981 and the Newham Eight in 1983 and others – all arose from a belief that the police could not be relied upon to protect their communities.

Continued disaffection was shown in 2001 when Asian communities in three northern towns were involved in riots, challenging the assumption that race relations and policing had improved. The sentences on those who were arrested in the riots were in many cases too high and had to be reduced by the Court of Appeal but not before a great deal of anger had been felt at the perceived injustice. The judges in the northern courts had dealt with everyone alike, black and white, taking no account of the background of racism and racial harassment which had preceded the events.

At one of the appeals relating to rioting in Burnley, Lord Justice Clarke accepted that the community had been in fear of a white mob and that the men who were appealing were lawfully on the streets to defend their homes. Their offences were not racially motivated, unlike those committed by the whites, and to sentence them as if their behaviour was equally reprehensible was wrong. Yet according to press reports, David Blunkett's response to complaints about excessive sentencing by the northern courts had been to tell the Asian families to stop 'whingeing'.

Judges who are being urged to avoid discrimination sometimes think that equality before the law means treating everyone the same; they fail to look at the reality of human existence beyond the doors of the court. I was once told by a crown court judge after a debate on justice for women that if I wanted equality for women, he would start sending them to jail with the same alacrity that he imprisoned men. I suggested that failing to take account of whether women had children for whom they were the primary carer would be very unjust but the discussion descended into goose and gander notions of equality. Treating people as equal who are not equal only creates further injustice.

One of the great judges of our times is the recently retired Justice Claire L'Heureux-Dubé of the Canadian Supreme Court. She has been among the most influential judges on women's issues and human rights and her judgments have had an impact on the development of fair laws in many jurisdictions. I have been lucky to count her as a friend and mentor. She always emphasises the importance of 'context' if we are to do justice. Failing to acknowledge the reasons for defensive behaviour and the history of racism in Blackburn, Burnley and Oldham only aggravates resentment in the communities affected.

Suresh Grover of the Monitoring Group, which helps victims of racial harassment, documented 5,000 emergency calls to its helpline in 2003, a 100% increase since 2002. Examples of repeated outrages included the dead body of a Muslim woman being desecrated as she lay in the mortuary of a north London hospital, with slices of bacon placed on her skin under her shroud. Suresh sees a massive increase in racism and religious-based attacks since the Macpherson Report, largely he feels as a result of the war on terrorism and the vehement and hostile political debate about asylum seekers.

Makbool Javaid of the Muslim Lawyers Committee says that there needs to be an equivalent of the Macpherson Report to tackle the problems being faced by the 1.6 million Islamic people in Britain. It is not only West Indians who are in the eye of the storm any more; brown-skinned people are now being stopped, searched and subjected to police harassment. 'Muslims are seen as fifth columnists. The terrorism and immigration legislation has created a lot of anxiety.'

The fears are not exaggerated. The war on terrorism has upped the tempo and there is public talk about a clash of civilisations. Muslim community leaders recall the history of Northern Ireland and the ways in which suspicion fell widely on innocent Irish Catholics, and how corrupted intelligence and unacceptable methods of intelligence-gathering led to the finger of blame falling on the wrong people. A hostile environment means that people withdraw into their own enclosed ghettos, angry that they are distrusted and fearful that they will be made scapegoats. Older Islamic immigrants want invisibility for the time being but the younger members of the community resent being treated with suspicion and are taking assertive stances, with more girls wearing the hijab and young men vocally critical of the United States, displaying their Muslim allegiance with pride.

Concern is repeatedly expressed that British mosques are incubators for the politics of fundamentalist Islam among young Muslims. Young British Muslim men were certainly amongst the ranks of the Taliban and two were involved in 2003 in a suicide bombing in Tel Aviv. More and more will be lured into the politics of violence by smart and insidious mentors if we allow feelings of unfairness and injustice to foment. Rage can feed immovable conviction.

The rise in racism is closely linked to the handling of the asylum issue. Two sets of instincts are battling it out on the subject of refugees. On the one hand there is the fear of people who are different, which gives rise to vindictiveness towards them, which is distorted and exaggerated by the lens of the right-wing press; on the other hand there are values which are equally a part of the British tradition: tolerance, fair play and justice. People in this country are not uniformly hostile to refugees fleeing persecution or to hardworking immigrants who want to make a contribution to British society.

However, the flames of public fear are fanned by government rhetoric and behaviour. It is not enough to make intermittent statements about the positive contribution of established immigrant communities. Berating the judiciary for finding that there is unfairness in aspects of asylum policy creates the impression that asylum seekers are being allowed to get away with something. David Blunkett's display of political authoritarianism towards the judges which I described in an earlier chapter arose from the government's Nationality Immigration and Asylum Act 2002, which allows the Home Secretary to refuse support for an asylum seeker 'if he is not satisfied that the claim to asylum was made as soon as reasonably practicable' after the claimant's arrival in the UK. The decision to withdraw support is taken by officials relying on answers on a form. The officials do not see the applicant and there is no appeal from their decision. Mr Justice Collins, applying the common law principle of justice and fairness, decided that the individual's reasons for not claiming at the port of entry had to be considered. It was not enough simply to argue, as the government's lawyer had, that failure to claim was reason enough for refusal (the Kafkaesque law of the bureaucrat). Sometimes an applicant has been unable to present a claim because of his or her mental state after persecution and torture. Sometimes he or she is still under the control of the agent to whom they have given their every penny: traffickers enter with their prey, and to protect their own backs insist that no claim is made until they are clear of the authorities. Sometimes the reasons are so compelling and genuine that exception should be made if justice is to be served. That was all that the judge was saying. He was pointing out that it would be inhumane if genuine refugees were forced into destitution with a serious risk to their health. He was not saying that the doors of Britain should be thrown open to every asylum applicant or that every applicant should be given state benefits. He was saying that processes had to be fair, that law had to be just.

Detaining and essentially imprisoning people who have committed no offence and many of whom are fleeing persecution is wrong. The fact that our Prime Minister and Home Secretary have both indicated that they may have to consider a derogation from

Article 51 of the Convention on the Rights of Refugees and a derogation from the European Convention on Human Rights to handle the problem is scandalous. It plays into the hands of those who maintain that most asylum seekers are bogus, criminals or even terrorists. Instead of reminding us all that these conventions were designed to protect the vulnerable in precisely such an atmosphere of public anxiety as we now have, the government has capitulated to an agenda set by the right. Never knowingly overestimating the British voter, ministers defend New Labour's hold on the centre ground by consistently matching the Conservatives' illiberalism. David Blunkett has even talked about asylum seekers' children 'swamping' local schools.

Watching the rise of the far right in Europe Tony Blair settled on a Third Way to combat the British National Party (BNP): this meant neither confronting racism nor championing anti-racism too actively. The Prime Minister spoke of 'neutralising' the far right by 'addressing the electorate's anxieties about crime and immigration'. He failed to learn from the French experience that appeasing the far right over asylum only helps them in the long term. So, in May 2002 three British National Party candidates won local election seats in Burnley. Since then they have won a seat in Blackburn and another in Burnley. The issue of asylum seekers was used to clothe naked racism. Yet nobody stood up firmly to the BNP because both major political parties are conceding to their sentiments. As the journalist Johann Hari put it succinctly, 'asylum seekers are the new blacks and Irish: everyone feels free to spit in their direction'.

All states have an absolute duty to give refuge to those fleeing from persecution, under the UN Refugee Convention 1951, from the threat of torture, false imprisonment, rape or death. The duty of accepting genuine refugees requires impartial examination of their claims. The problems facing the government have their roots in the failure to create proper systems to deal with asylum applications humanely, a failure that predates this government, as ranting Conservatives should be reminded. It was they who commissioned the disastrous computer system that was meant to track asylum claims quickly but created chaos. Jack Straw had four years to deal with it, failed comprehensively and allowed himself and ministerial colleagues to use terms like 'bogus asylum seeker', creating a culture of disbelief about those who applied.

This atmosphere of suspicion now permeates the whole system, from the Home Office through to the courts and into public debate.

The mess and hyperbole has meant that many people now believe that Britain is the asylum capital of the world and imagine that we are being disproportionately flooded with applicants. In 2002 a Mori poll found that the public thought Britain hosted about 23% of the world's refugees, although the real figure is 1.98%. The entire European Union accepts 3% with Britain coming eighth in this league in terms of refugees per head of population. They are told by the tabloid press that there are three million illegal immigrants in Britain – a completely 'bogus' figure. They are told that asylum seekers are on 'wall to wall' benefit, when they get £37 per week and are put into flats on estates that no one else wants to live in. The public thought they received three times this amount of benefit. The press claim that the UK is the 'soft touch' of Europe, when many other countries are much more generous in their welfare provision. Nor do people realise that asylum seekers are barred from working for one year. But the lies are rarely rebutted. Most of the asylum seekers who come make no active choice but pay simply to get out of their own country. If they choose Britain it is because they speak at least some English – our great export – or because they know someone here. They want to go somewhere to work and live, not scrounge.

In such a hostile environment, many people who are fearful that their claim might not succeed, or are aware that they do not fulfil the criteria to the letter, have certainly 'disappeared' from the state's view into the nether world of the black economy. They are paid a fraction of the minimum wage, exploited and treated as inhuman. The economy of London would probably collapse without the large number of cleaners, minicab drivers, kitchen staff, hotel workers, sweatshop machinists and building site workers who are illegals.

The hysteria engendered by the media should be toned down by the government but instead, by mollifying the tabloids, they reinforce the belief that most asylum seekers are terrorists or criminals from Albania. The panic has driven the government down the route of detention camps, the course taken by Australia to deal with Afghani families fleeing the Taliban.

A report in 2003 by the Chief Inspector of Prisons, Ann Owers, exposed the routine mistreatment of asylum seekers in removal centres. It included routine strip-searches, poor welfare help or assistance with mental health problems, and lack of legal advice. Only 10% felt safe. At Campsfield House, a privately run centre, 12% of detainees claimed they had been sexually harassed. My concern is that we are likely to see this mistreatment replicated when we detain applicants on a large scale.

As legislation was going through the House of Lords in 2002 I pointed out that, since 82% of asylum applicants are male, the placing of women and children in detention camps dominated by the presence of men was a recipe for insecurity on the part of the women and children. Separate accommodation will soon be available for families and single women, but just living in such an unrepresentative environment can be very hard for women and children and carries inherent risks. My proposal was that at least families and lone women be taken out of the detention plans, since their numbers are small. But the suggestion was dismissed. Many expressed concern about the separate schooling of asylum children and the negative effects on their well-being, but government was unmovable. It is astonishing to sit in the Lords and watch Conservative peers make the arguments for compassion to a Labour government.

Church leaders and politicians in Scotland are now campaigning against the detention of asylum seekers' children. They are particularly concerned about the use of a former jail for detentions. Bishop Mone, President of the Roman Catholic Church's Justice and Peace Commission, said, 'It is a disgrace that children from perhaps the age of five to 14 are held in a prison environment and deprived of many of the rights enshrined in the declaration of human rights.'

One of the reasons for intransigence on young children is that when they go to local schools they are the best ambassadors: they make friends and their parents become part of the school community. A human face is put on the whole issue. The most poignant removals are those which tear children out of a school where they have created attachments and that is what the government PR machine wants to avoid. The unsightly photographs of weeping children. That is the cold calculation in keeping families in the detention centres.

Instead of pouring money into such centres the government should be engaging many more asylum application assessors and streamlining the claim procedure. They should be reappraising the thoughtless dispersals which drive people underground, because they would rather be where their own communities have clustered. We should allow asylum seekers to work while awaiting a decision. We should be devising sensible immigration policies which let people come to Britain to make a life, but this should not mean sucking the talent out of developing countries for whom skilled workers are a precious resource.

The government should be countering the distortions and untruths in the media, ensuring that the facts around the whole question of immigration and asylum are widely known and understood. You only have to spend an afternoon at Medical Aid for the Victims of Torture or the Refugee Council or the offices of a law firm working with asylum seekers to feel the raw pain and anguish of those who have fled their homes through persecution and fear. If ministers need a restorative to renew old passions or stories to stir the public conscience, it is to be recommended. Decent ministers have swallowed the line that left-of-centre governments in other parts of Europe have fallen over this issue and for this reason they have to grasp the populist nettle, out-toughing the other guy. 'We have to swallow stones,' they say, 'in order to get some good measures through, like the amnesty for the 15,000 asylum seekers who have been waiting years for a decision.' They seem to be unaware that the way the issue is discussed by politicians strengthens support for right-wing extremists whose racist hunger can never be satisfied. The political space in which sensible discussion can take place becomes arid and unfertile because if you have to adopt your opponents' policies to win, you have not won. No one points out that total government spending on asylum is 0.425% of total government spending and 200,000 immigrants can never 'swamp' a population of 60 million.

The threat to take the children of asylum seekers into care if their parents refuse to accept a ticket back to where they came from was shameful and gave rise to the extraordinary scene of Michael Howard, the Conservative Party leader denouncing the inhumanity of Labour policy. The explanation that the government would have to do this to square its desire to remove benefits from asylum seekers with its duty to care for the welfare of children was risible. Whatever David Blunkett said about his not being the 'King Herod of the Labour Party', his joke wore very thin when it was pointed out that the care system is supposed to be used for children in extremis not where relationships and bonds are strong and supportive and to use it for other purposes would be unlawful. In most circumstances it would contravene several articles in the UN convention on the rights of the child, particularly Article 9, which states that every child has a right to live with his or her parents unless this is deemed incompatible with the child's best interests. But the British government entered a reservation to the Convention on the Rights of the Child to exclude refugee children from benefiting from the full rights. However, a social worker faced with a destitute parent would have a duty under the Children Act 1989 and the Human Rights Act 1998 to ensure that the children remained with their parents and to that end would be expected to access monies that are specifically set aside for that purpose. We should not be shocked because the use of the welfare system for coercive purposes has become a theme within government as I shall explain in Chapter 11, on punishing the poor.

David Blunkett has said publicly that he hasn't a clue how many illegals there are. The life of illegals is thoroughly wretched: waiting constantly for the knock at the door, unable to seek police help if they are victims of crime (which many are), unable to obtain proper medical help through the NHS because they have no health number, desperate about becoming pregnant because they will be unable to receive the support needed at the birth.

In the last few years I have represented several prostitutes who have been caught up in the trafficking of sex workers. They inhabit a world which is now expanding daily to include women and girls who have fled persecution, violence and rape, but who are utterly controlled by men who have bought them. They feel incapable of stepping out of the shadows because they are caught between the slavery of prostitution and the fear of being deported. Ill health and fear of pregnancy stalk them and they are forced to have illegal abortions because they are too frightened to go near doctors. This is the sort of inhumanity we collude in when we take away legitimate routes and means of support.

And we should insist that although a handful of asylum seekers may be suspected of links with terrorism, our drawbridge must not be raised on their account. It is chilling that there are malign people who abuse the system but the real scandal is the way we treat those with legitimate claims.

We are not in fact bound by treaty to admit genuine refugees if we can find them somewhere else to go, a country other than the one from which they have fled, and one where they will be treated humanely and sympathetically. The receiving country must to be willing to accept. This caveat is pushing David Blunkett towards the idea of creating huge detention centres in places like the Ukraine, where people would be sorted and sifted by some form of officialdom and if they pass muster as legitimate asylum seekers they will be divvied out amongst willing nations on a pro-rata basis. As the black trade unionist, Bill Morris, has forcefully pointed out, this subcontracting of the issue, rendering it invisible to British voters, is a way of avoiding our responsibilities. So far the European Union is resisting this policy. But not to be left out, the Conservatives are now putting together a manifesto which will pledge that asylum seekers will be put on a remote unidentified island for processing.

Labour used to know where it stood. It was against reducing asylum seekers' rights of appeal or introducing a 'white list' of countries from which it would be assumed that all applications for asylum were unfounded. It condemned the Conservatives and Michael Howard when Home Secretary for playing the race card and pursuing such policies. These are now the very policies which David Blunkett has introduced, denying asylum applicants their due process of law. Applicants who are refused asylum are now deported and expected to appeal from abroad. It is difficult enough to appeal from within the UK, when immigration advisers are often miles away from the dispersal centres – from overseas it is virtually impossible. And ministers know that third countries will not accept our rejections. New legislation going through parliament will squeeze asylum seekers even harder, with plans for no more than one appeal step and the creation of an 'ouster clause'. This means there will be no judicial review, and is probably the most egregious part of the Bill. It means there will be no control over any illegality by government. If judicial review is taken away, many cases which have been wrongly decided by officials and adjudicators will not be picked up and genuine asylum seekers will be expelled to a very uncertain future. Those who arrive without travel documents and identity papers will be prosecuted and jailed. Jan Shaw of Amnesty International believes that the new obstacles that Britain is introducing will make it almost legally impossible for asylum seekers to enter the country. Punishment for destroying papers when there is good reason for doing so may breach international law. Torture victims are extremely unlikely to have the usual travel documents.

The reason why there are so many appeals is that many honest asylum claimants are refused first time round because there is a culture of disbelief in the Home Office. The starting assumption is that the person before you is a lying hound. There are, of course, marginal cases and claims which are dishonest but the new measure will hit authentic asylum seekers as well as economic migrants. The government's policies invariably penalise the victims rather than the people traffickers and do little to tackle the real problem in the British asylum system – the poor quality of decision making.

The government wants the world to know that Britain is no soft touch. Maurice Saatchi, the Conservative public relations guru who is now the party Chairman, used to say the difference between the main parties was that the Conservatives were 'cruel and efficient' while Labour was 'caring and incompetent'. The description clearly stung, and swift corrective action is being taken. What any of us could have explained is that competence is the real challenge; cruelty comes easy.

The 'white list' system is notoriously inaccurate in its definition of safe countries, but 17 new countries are about to be added. Even last year the Home Office was returning applicants from Zimbabwe and Iraq. The law is the only protection these vulnerable people have but even that route is now being removed.

When Suresh Grover and other leaders in the minority communities speak of the links between the treatment of asylum seekers and racism in society at large, they are describing the fostering of a climate of intolerance, which cancels out many of the gains made over the last two decades in creating a diverse, multicultural society. By allowing the atmosphere to change, we create the space in which racist political parties like the British National Party can grow. We give them a vocabulary and a *raison d'être.*

Most waves of immigration have come as a result of wars or social unrest overseas or in response to our own economic needs. We are a nation of immigrants. Most of our forebears came either as refugees or as economic migrants often from parts of the former British Empire. New groups are now joining us and our behaviour towards them will affect our future. A Britain that grows in xenophobia will become increasingly unattractive and will not be the place of choice for the brightest and the best. It will also become a place which is less safe or conducive to live in for the rest of us.

As Islamic fundamentalism grows around the world it could be easy for us to be drawn into a new Cold War by those who theorise about 'clashes of civilisation'. It is a trajectory with frightening consequences not just internationally but right on our own doorstep. It is crucial that our own Muslim communities feel that they belong and that they are not discriminated against, ignored or demonised. They should be embraced not as Muslims living in Britain but as British Muslims. The experience of the Afro-Caribbean community should be a warning to us of how a criminal justice system which is perceived to discriminate is the surest way of embedding deep and powerful grievances.

10

WE ARE ALL VICTIMS NOW

THE IDEA OF the 'victim' is a complicated and touchy subject, as we can see if we look at the history of how the victim has taken centre stage in government rhetoric, and at the special needs of women and children as witnesses. The way the state has co-opted the cause of the victim to make significant and dangerous changes in the criminal justice system causes me some baleful musing about the law of unintended consequences.

It may come as a surprise to the *Daily Mail*, but the victims' movement was the direct consequence of the women's movement in the early 1970s, when feminist lawyers, like myself, whether in the United States, Canada, Australia or here, turned the spotlight on the way in which the law failed women and particularly examined their experiences in rape trials and criminal cases involving domestic violence. From that, we expanded the critique to other victims of crime, especially children. It then became clear that if campaigners linked their drive to the cause of human rights there was a much better chance of bringing these issues into the mainstream: the women's movement campaigned vigorously for a bill of rights and the incorporation of international conventions into English law. Victims' Support and a variety of other support agencies, which were developing at the same time, drew on the women's movement's analysis of why law failed women, widening the focus to the systemic failures affecting all witnesses going through the courts, whatever the nature of the offence. The issues, therefore, moved on to the wider agenda, which has been a welcome breakthrough.

Unfortunately, the law and order lobby quickly saw the victim movement's potential as a Trojan horse which would allow them to attack the rights of defendants. The temptation for any of us who are anxious to get a fairer deal in the courts for women and children is to accept as bedfellows people who adopt our arguments about the law's failure, but who refuse to accept the gendered nature of law and the patriarchal power relations at its heart. They simply want the law's rules to be bent in favour of easier convictions.

Successful political campaigns often involve strange alliances and they certainly bring progress, but they can also bring regression if there is no vigilance and clarity about the diverse interests which are being served. Campaigners must be alert to the trap that they can fall into – the danger of sacrificing central safeguards in our system of law because we want to effect change for those for whom we have special concern.

The introduction of human rights law has presented a powerful tool and a language to remind the state that it has a duty to look after the interests of victims. Ostensibly, the government has always been on the side of the victim – it takes on his or her case and seeks to punish the perpetrator – but it has not always done so with enough rigour or sufficient sensitivity to their needs. In seeking to protect victims it must be committed – but it also has to be alert to its other duty, to those who come before courts accused of crime. This has drawn it into the delusion that its role is to act as an umpire between the two groups, victims and offenders, forgetting that its duties to each are different. The reason its duty to the accused is different is because the state has the power to punish. That is the element in the process which is sometimes forgotten amidst the clamour about law and order.

Governments of every stripe see votes in crime and in women – though not when women are committing the crime. It has now become fashionable for politicians to talk about the treatment of women in the criminal justice system but only if they are victims, and if they fit into a very stereotyped view of victims at that. The number of women in prison has tripled in the last ten years and most of them have been victims too.

The present government wants to improve the position of women in the system, particularly the victims of rape and domestic violence. They know that these are issues which all women, whatever their background or class, take very seriously and women have been a large part of New Labour's constituency. Those of us who have fought on justice issues, including many women MPs and peers, have seen a number of gains made, which have increased women's confidence. Having Harriet Harman in the role of Solicitor-General has meant that a surge of energy has gone into the subject of domestic violence, to great effect. There is real recognition that this is an area of offending that has for too long been relegated to the 'soft crime' zone and one that spawns many other social problems, of huge cost to the individuals and to society.

Since I wrote on women and the justice system 12 years ago the culture has begun to shift both in the courts and amongst the general public. Awareness of child sexual abuse, particularly as a result of the pioneering work of people like Esther Rantzen and Valerie Howarth, has brought a level of sensitivity that did not exist in legal circles even a decade ago. There is now an appreciation that policing and crime investigation need to engage and support victims. Trial processes are being improved. But there is still a long way to go. The victims of crime and those who support them have many legitimate grievances about the 'revictimisation' which takes place in courtrooms, grievances to be addressed to the state and which the state should meet and grievances which also need to be met more successfully by the legal profession. However, egged on by the right-wing press, government's chief response is to mount assaults upon the balances between the state and the accused in the criminal trial.

The all-embracing notion of 'victim' sometimes stops people disentangling the different factors at work in different areas of crime. What I consider 'abuse of intimacy crimes', such as child abuse, sexual violation and domestic violence, fit very uncomfortably into the criminal justice system as it has been constructed, because of the nature of the allegations and the relationships which are usually involved. Stranger rape provides less of a challenge precisely because there is no prior connection. The solution to these problems is only going to be found if there is sensible debate.

There is often fraught discussion between those who support civil liberties and those who are concerned with child protection, polarising the two when there should be greater collaboration. As I said in Chapter 8 on sex and violence, I feel very strongly that the abuse of intimacy does require special procedures because sexual violation of adults and sexual abuse of children reach into such deep parts of the human self. This can be done without transgressing the fundamental principles of fairness. The Bar should also be looking at ways in which advocacy should accommodate children. Too often they are still questioned as if they were adults. The cross-examination of children should be conducted in ways which recognise their needs and ensure their well-being: perhaps special training is needed for those who wish to be on a specialist panel of advocates for child abuse trials so that children are protected from aggressive, unacceptable questioning. Margaret Kennedy, the campaigner for the rights of children, especially those who are disabled, tells a shocking story of an incontinent child who was abused by a carer. The boy was cross-examined at length about his condition and the suggestion made that no one would go near such a smelly, functionally uncontrolled child.

No criminal trial ever compensates people for what has happened, but a just conviction does go a long way to satisfying deep feelings of anger. However, there will be occasions when the victim or their family is disappointed because a prosecution fails. Not surprisingly the focus of their anger is the accused, when often the real problem is the absence of strong enough evidence, faults in the investigation or a wholly inadequate prosecution. But since the intermediaries for the victims are policemen and prosecutors, it is hardly likely they will outline their own shortcomings to the victim or explain the ways in which prosecution testimony failed to satisfy the standards of proof. The state's failure is, therefore, often seen as the fault of the accused.

Let me immediately make it clear that witnesses have many reasons to be scandalised at their treatment by the state, never mind their treatment at the hands of criminals– they are often left in the dark about the process, marginalised and sometimes exposed to inappropriate cross-examination. In October 2003 government ministers suggested that witnesses should be imprisoned for three months if they failed to go to court to give evidence. The proposal is aimed at cutting the number of prosecutions that collapse every year because of missing witnesses. The effect would be to scare the scared.

For too long those who had been deeply and personally affected by crime were treated in the same way as the witness who was producing the till roll or the witness who saw a blue Ford Mondeo outside an address. Too readily they were cross-examined by unskilled lawyers as if they were bent policemen, practised in the art of lying to courts. No one acknowledged the emotional impact of their experience. Their special and very personal link to the proceedings was not understood. Modern developments in our knowledge of trauma have opened the courts to a greater recognition of victims' needs, an acceptance that they find the business of coming to court seriously disturbing. As a result the legal profession has had to look at some of its own rules.

Whatever the impression gleaned from Hollywood movies about the coaching of witnesses, barristers cannot rehearse a witness's evidence; it is not allowed in Britain. Solicitors, or police officers in the case of the prosecution, take statements from witnesses. It is against the code of professional conduct for barristers to discuss the content of a witness's evidence with him or her, in order to avoid allegations of securing changes to better the case. The exception is that a defence counsel is allowed to take her client through their testimony and explain where their account will be tested in court. Counsel are also allowed to speak to experts so that we can better understand their assessment of an issue. As a result of the rules against coaching, prosecuting counsel used to avoid even saying hello to Crown witnesses for fear of having her probity questioned. Happily that starchiness has now been abandoned but the principle remains that while those who are going to testify can refresh their memory from their statement before coming into court, rehearsing by lawyers is out.

The Crown Prosecution Service has recently announced a new initiative to bring vulnerable prosecution witnesses to a pre-trial meeting to go through their testimony. The purpose is to see whether they will be able to withstand cross-examination rather than have cases collapse because they fail to come up to proof. They also want to assess whether they have particular areas of susceptibility. A pre-trial meeting would also enable the Crown to assess whether special aids are needed, such as screens for especially fearful witnesses, to make them confident enough to give evidence. There is no reason why any of this should break the rule that there must be no coaching or tailoring of the witness's account. However, Lee Moore, President of the Association of Child Abuse Lawyers wants to take it further and provide personal witness training for victims of rape and abuse so that they can deal better with the courtroom experience. She is clear that there should be no rehearsing of evidence and there would be total openness. No one should be expected to walk into a courtroom totally unprepared for what is going to happen but any such preparation would have to be handled with great care so that the evidence of the witness could not be impugned.

All these incremental changes go a long way to improve the experience of witnesses, and increase the chance that they will be able to give their evidence in the best way possible. Victims now receive much more help, and the CPS often warns them about the sort of cross-examination to expect and areas where their testimony may be vulnerable. The creation of specialist teams within the Prosecution Service, for rape or child abuse or domestic violence, for example, will greatly improve the experience of those who have been violated and have to testify. We have already introduced victim impact statements to set out the longer-term consequences of the crime on the lives of the people affected and this goes before the judge for sentencing purposes.

It used to be the rule that those who alleged they had experienced crime should testify live in court, unless their evidence was agreed by both sides. An accused was entitled to be faced by his accuser; the idea being that a false allegation would be harder to make in the presence of the person being lied about. Sensible discussion on this topic is sometimes hindered because parts of the civil liberties lobby and the legal profession are unwilling to make any concessions at all to the imaginative ways that new technology can be harnessed to lessen terror for children and other vulnerable witnesses. However, huge inroads into the right to face your accuser have now been made. Initially the changes were made in respect of children. At first, screens were introduced so that the child could not see the alleged abuser when it became clear that powerful psychological ties could be created between abuser and abused and that these could be re-created in the courtroom if the child saw the alleged abuser. The child could then be too afraid or conflicted to testify. Eventually even the screens failed to meet the problem. I acted in a case where the leading member of a paedophile ring addressed the judge from the dock, asking if he could have a brief adjournment to use the lavatory in the cells. Normally this is done by passing a note to counsel, but when he spoke aloud the child behind the screens heard his voice and became too distressed to continue giving evidence.

Now, new technology enables children to give evidence from a room beyond the court. A video link makes it possible for the evidence to be received without the child being overawed by the numbers of people in the courtroom and the intimidating ambience. The only person visible on the child's screen is the barrister or judge who is asking the questions. Wigs are removed and the process works reasonably well. To make the proceedings shorter and less arduous, the video of the child's disclosure to specially trained police officers or social workers is accepted instead of the child having to give evidence in chief – their testimony setting out the history of events for the court – before being cross-examined by the defence.

We have also learned that the younger the child, the sooner a case should be brought to court because the ability to retain a clear recollection of events is harder. Speed in bringing cases to trial also enables children to have psychological help sooner. There is a serious problem about the issue of psychological help for the victims of crime. If a child, or indeed an adult, has therapy before the case comes on, it raises questions for lawyers as to whether there is the risk that repetition and discussions in therapy about what has taken place will affect the purity of the account: the child's testimony can be challenged on the basis that it may have been distorted by the therapist's intervention. A way round this could be to have a video recording made of therapeutic sessions. However, the more the material that exists, the more there are opportunities for challenge on inconsistencies. Children do not always give a narrative sequentially or include everything first time around. They also forget and they do sometimes add on details which are products of the imagination. Good prosecutors can help a jury to evaluate whether inconsistencies are of any real significance. But equally, good defenders can point up what is reliable and what is unreliable in the evidence of the vulnerable and the young.

Children's cases are now being fast-tracked but the problem with speed is that defendants can rightly claim that it puts them under pressure to go to trial before they are ready. In this regard, the needs of the child are understandably being put before the rights of the accused and that is how it should be.

There are also new plans to avoid a child coming to court at all by having the child questioned much less formally by counsel at a place comfortable to them and filming the process. But the problems around this proposal still need to be ironed out, because an accused who is not present may feel cut out of a procedure which has enormous consequences for her.

*

Cases involving sexual abuse of children are the biggest test to the system. Considerable inroads have been made into the liberties of those accused but they never seem to be enough. One of the gravest problems is that despite all these changes many cases of child sexual abuse cannot make it to the courts because of the way in which the child first disclosed the sexual interference. It is very common that something alerts an adult to the possibility that sexual abuse has taken place and they ask the child leading questions. 'Susie, the park-keeper has been putting his hands inside Sally's knickers, has he done that to you?' The child may agree but police know that a court will be left wondering if she has adopted propositions put to her when the events did not in fact take place. Or did she hear people talk about the behaviour of the park-keeper before she was questioned? Allegations by defence lawyers that an account has been contaminated because of inept questioning are legitimate and can mean a whole prosecution is put in doubt. The defence now have specialist psychologists, who analyse disclosure interviews to see whether a child or vulnerable adult accuser may have elaborated on or adopted information or formulations put to them by their questioners. Those concerned with the welfare of children see prosecutions failing for what seem legalistic niceties when they feel confident in their hearts that the core of the child's account is true. An adult abuser may well avoid conviction but if the standard of proof is lowered there will be wrongful convictions. For some who see children's pain at close quarters, that price is worth paying.

In cases of abuse of intimacy the preferred truth that a person on trial is innocent until proved guilty presents a tough emotional pill for a complainant to swallow. Let us imagine a woman has been forced to the floor in her own home and penetrated orally and then anally by someone she trusted. It is hard for her to accept that he should be the one to be believed from the outset; that his denial should in the first instance be believed over her accusation. Similarly social workers working with children find it hard to accept that a person they profoundly believe has been abusing children should be given the benefit of any doubt.

We can improve all the extraneous factors – the quality of the investigation, the behaviour of the police and medical examiners, the 'customer care' of the complainant in the run-up to the trial. Separate waiting areas can be provided, as can support staff, specialist teams of Crown prosecutors and barristers, video links or screens. But we are still left with the fact that the witness's account must be tested. We still must presume innocence. Why? Because not all allegations are true.

The huge frustrations about the working of the system in the area of sexual offences have sent us in search of reforms. The screens and video links introduced initially for children can now be used in other appropriate cases where the witness is a vulnerable adult, and in sex cases an accused can no longer cross-examine in person. This was another contentious inroad because it took away a defendant's right but it was introduced in the interests of victims. So, some changes have already been introduced and no doubt more will continue to be devised. But there comes a point where a line has to be drawn defining how much encroachment on the rights of an accused can be countenanced. Deciding where that line must be takes me back to the issue of core principles. Some reforms cut too deeply into defendants' rights. We have to attach high standards of proof to any situation which entitles the state to punish. Changing the ground rules so that there is virtually an assumption of guilt in order to get convictions is a recipe for injustice. The Criminal Cases Review Commission is currently reinvestigating a significant number of cases which relate to child sexual abuse allegations.

It is often suggested that a move to the inquisitorial process – the civil system of Europe – would be the answer in sex abuse cases. Yet the recent trials of paedophiles in Belgium have not suggested it is much of an improvement from the point of view of either the child or the accused.

If society were to decide that, in the interests of victims, establishing responsibility for sexual abuse and rape was to be followed not by the punishment of imprisonment but by a diagnostic and therapeutic response for the abuser, then we could contemplate a different process. But, since most people would never accept such a radical reform, we should continue to struggle for more cautious improvements.

It is easy to pour vitriol on lawyers who defend in child abuse or rape cases and there are those who make themselves scarce, particularly when a child abuse brief is offered. Yet, if criminal lawyers start picking and choosing those for whom they will act, defendants may go unrepresented by the best lawyers. There will always be someone who will take a brief but if the most able lawyers sift their cases and unload those that are harrowing or likely to bring opprobrium, people accused of sexual offences will be even more at risk of wrongful conviction.

I hate doing sex cases. I get depressed and miserable and if it is really grotesque I go off sex completely during the trial but I believe in the 'cab rank rule' which says briefs should not be turned down because of the nature of the offence or the client and I think everyone should take their turn on the front line. It also means that I am exposed from time to time to the raw experience of what happens in these cases and can explore ways of improving the process.

I also believe that lawyers have an ethical responsibility in how they conduct cases. I fight cases hard but I struggle with the limits of what is acceptable. I was briefed once to represent a male physiotherapist who was accused of fondling a woman vaginally while she was receiving treatment. Included in the papers was a statement taken by the solicitor from a witness, who described seeing the woman at a drunken party in a pub, where she had got on the table and removed her top, revealing her breasts to the assembled throng. I asked why the statement was there and the solicitor said that he and the client wanted the witness called to show what a tart the woman was. I said it was not relevant to the issue of whether the assault took place and I thought the accused would be acquitted without it. It was clear to me that its purpose was to prejudice the jury against the woman on extraneous material and I suggested that the judge might also take that view.

The case was removed from me to a more amenable counsel and the new barrister used the evidence at trial, the judge did not stop it being called and the man was acquitted. Colleagues at the Bar vary in their responses to my course of conduct. Many are very disapproving and say that a counsel's duty is to fight a case using everything at his or her disposal and it is for judges to show the red flag. On that basis, they would try to get the evidence before the court, and some judges would allow it because they are impervious to the fact that this kind of evidence fosters the stereotype of the loose woman who not only leads men on but is generally unreliable on sexual matters.

There is insufficient discussion amongst lawyers and judges about what practitioners think is ethically acceptable, and where the lines should be drawn in cross-examination. There has been uproar about new rape legislation listing when a man should not be able to invoke consent – when a woman is mentally impaired but the man is not, where a woman is asleep, where a woman has been drugged or rendered senseless through drink, and so on. While I agree as a practitioner that real life cases may run a coach and horses through such efforts to spell out what is unacceptable, the reason why women have pressed government to resort to legislation is because judges have been so slow to challenge their own deep-seated attitudes to sexuality.

My criticism of government in this area is that they have been happy to roll all victims up together, when they should be brave enough to say that cases involving abuse of intimacy and the historic discrimination against women deserve special treatment. However, ministers live in fear of being ridiculed as being in the thrall of 'feminists'; they recoil from the reality that the most ill-treated victims within our system are women and children, and that this is still a reflection of some very disconcerting facts about male violence. What is the gender of most children killed by parents or relations? Jasmine Beckford, Heidi Koseda, Kimberley Carlisle, Victoria Climbié. Go through the files of the NSPCC and you will find that they are almost invariably girls. What is the gender of the partner most often beaten in a relationship? What is the gender of those most often sexually violated? When we hear a body has been found, someone killed in a park by a stranger, what sex is the victim? The gendered nature of certain crimes and their victims and the gendered nature of law, because it is largely created and administered by men, are still insufficiently recognised or discussed.

Redressing the profound historic failures in relation to women means having to take special steps and the government should say so clearly.

Until women and children get justice in the system certain special processes are justified, including anonymity for complainants in sexual offence cases and anonymity for children at all times. However, at regular intervals we have to rehearse the arguments about why accused men should not be given the cover of anonymity in some spurious call for equality. Open justice means anonymity should be used sparingly. The coverage of a rape case at times leads to the discovery that the male accused is a multiple offender, because other women are given the confidence to come forward.

In response to women's campaigns on domestic violence, a new process was invented to provide quicker, more effective justice for battered women. The magistrates' court on receiving evidence of violence, which need not be from the woman herself, can make an order against an abusive man to stop him molesting his partner. Although the procedure is civil – and so has less strict rules of evidence – if there is evidence of breach, it is a criminal offence punishable with up to five years' imprisonment. This procedure, which involves treating a criminal matter as civil, can be criticised because it avoids the safeguards that apply to criminal proceedings both in terms of evidence and the procedural guarantees that normally apply. However, in my view, until society confronts male abuse effectively this departure from the norm is justified. What is not justified is for government to say we have got away with it here, let's apply this idea in other areas. Yet this is precisely what has happened.

The most notable example concerns the anti-social behaviour orders called ASBOs. The police or local authority may obtain an ASBO on the basis of second-hand evidence that a person has caused or is likely to cause harassment, alarm or distress. If satisfied on the balance of probabilities of the need for an order, a magistrates' court can impose any prohibition necessary, such as detention, for the purpose of protecting people from further anti-social acts. ASBOs can be obtained in respect of children as young as ten, and since the matter is civil they will be dealt with in the magistrates' court rather than a youth court. Again, breach of the civil order is a criminal offence punishable with up to five years' imprisonment. Thus considerable restraints can be placed upon the liberty of a person, including lengthy terms of imprisonment, on the basis of evidence that would never be admitted in a criminal trial. If anti-social behaviour is sufficient to constitute crime it should be dealt with as such and proper criminal standards should apply. The pressing justification which exists with domestic violence does not apply.

In all our contemporary discussions about crime we talk about victims and perpetrators as if they belong to different species. Yet, particularly in the area of child abuse, the abuser is often someone who has himself been subjected to serious abuse in childhood. Amongst women offenders generally, it is the exception if a woman does not have a history of family violence or abuse. Girls who are abused within the family often leave home early, disrupt any chance of education or training, are full of self-loathing and feelings of worthlessness and can easily end up in trouble. In fact, most of my clients would fall into the category of victimised rather than victimiser.

One of the depressing developments is that having campaigned to have child prostitutes recognised as victims of abuse rather than as offenders, children's organisations now see girls of 16 and 17 being assessed as to whether they are victims of abuse or whether they are freely choosing prostitution. If the former, they will be kept away from the courts but if the latter, they will be criminalised. The police find this business of working out which is which hard, and no wonder.

It has long been seen that the nature of the victim sharply affects the approach of the media and the court and can even affect the severity of punishment. The increasing visibility of the victim could have a disproportionate effect on outcomes in the courts. The more pristine the victim, the greater the empathy with them and the more rage against the offender. When the victim is someone with whom the public, the jury and the court can identify, they are apt to see the crime as more serious and deserving of harsher punishment than if the victim is homeless, unemployed or a member of an unpopular group. When prostitutes are the victims of crime they rarely invoke the sympathy afforded to others, yet they are probably subjected to more violence and indignity than any other group, from pimps, drug dealers, motley exploiters and thieves as well as clients.

The press constantly feed into this black and white separation of the victim and victimiser. They know that if a person is not a victim pure and simple they will forfeit public sympathy. Dream families are created. Idyllic relationships, doting parents, bereft wives, the heartbroken fiancé. The courts are still alive with unrealistic stereotypes. If a battered woman is not a quiet mouse, work has to be done to counter the assumption that only passive women stay in abusive relationships. Black men have to overcome the belief that they are bound to be criminals or sexual predators. And apparently, some tabloids only like their victims to be white.

Mary Ann Seighart, the *Times* journalist, tells the story of how a friend who was working for the *Daily Mail* had been asked to find and interview a woman who had been raped and was prepared to relinquish her anonymity. The friend eventually discovered the perfect candidate: an intelligent, articulate 38-year-old who had taken a shortcut home and been raped by a stranger. The journalist interviewed the woman, told her boss every detail of the victim's story, which had been backed up by the police, and he was thrilled. Then the journalist let slip that the rape victim was black and his reply was unprintable. He even suggested she must have made it up and the story never ran.

If the case is one that the tabloids are pushing, a conspiracy of silence operates whereby facts that are known to the detriment of victims are buried, while there is no such impunity for the alleged victimisers. There are rarely any good reasons why the personal lives of victims should be raked over, but if a parent has seriously neglected a child who is then killed by someone else their feelings of personal failure to protect their child may exacerbate their grief, and partly explain their rage to punish endlessly.

For this reason decisions about the final release of prisoners on parole have to be in the hands of an independent body or the judiciary and not the Home Secretary or politicians or victims' organisations, who may be more susceptible to manipulation by the public or the press.

Already, Home Office ministers are toying with extending the witness impact statement so that victims might have a say in parole. Lord Falconer suggested as much in his Parole Board annual lecture on 8 April 2003. This will invite inevitable biases. The police and press can play an important role in keeping vengeful feelings alive. In a case which went to the Supreme Court in the United States, Justice Lewis Powell pointed out that 'the degree of suffering experienced by the victims and survivors may be wholly unrelated to the blameworthiness of a particular defendant'. Judges, and an independent body like the Parole Board, are the best people to evaluate on society's behalf what the degree of blameworthiness is. There is also talk of opening parole hearings up to the public, a move that the chairman of the Parole Board, David Hatch has opposed after seeing how they do it in the United States. Open parole hearings have been a travesty there because of the chilling effect they have upon the members of the Board.

One of the concerns in the United States is that victims' rights movements have become so strong that they are virtual proprietors of the criminal justice system, insisting on the maintenance of the death sentence, resisting reforms on sentencing, demanding a say in the trial and sentencing process, and holding out against deserving releases on parole. The police often lobby against parole and stimulate the families of victims to object, so that no account is taken of the rehabilitative process which may have taken place in prison. The parole process is used as a way to 're-sentence' offenders. We saw this powerfully in the opposition to the release of the boys who killed Jamie Bulger, although the psychiatrists and educators who had worked with them felt that to move them at 18 into adult prisons carried the risk of undoing much of the good restorative work that had taken place.

We should not be tempted to take the American route, but the Prime Minister has already started. There should never be a direct role for victims in punishment. If victims are to have a direct say in sentencing decisions, how is consistency to be achieved between the victim bent on vengeance and the person willing to forgive? Should victims have a say in bail decisions, when a person's guilt has not yet been established?

In 2003 the case of Tony Martin, who shot and killed a young burglar, put the parole system in the dock. He was convicted of murder, later reduced to manslaughter on the grounds of diminished responsibility. He elicited great sympathy from the right-wing press, who argued that a home-owner is entitled to adopt a shoot-to-kill policy against housebreakers. The law has always allowed for self-defence against intruders. If a person hears a burglar in his home and thinks he may be seriously harmed, he can do what is reasonable in the circumstances to defend himself. If in his fear he shoots an intruder dead, a jury will invariably feel sympathetic. What is often left out of the Tony Martin story, as recounted by the press, is that he lay in wait for the boys. He lay in his bed fully dressed in combat gear with his boots on and his gun cocked ready for battle. He had become a vigilante. A crazed vigilante, which is why his conviction was reduced to manslaughter on the evidence of psychiatrists. And it was clear that he intended to kill and he did so by shooting his victim in the back. He was going to exact capital punishment for burglars. Little is said about under-policing in rural areas, or about the failure of the local constabulary who should have responded actively to Martin's calls. Little is said about the steps he could have taken to protect his property, like the installation of metal grilles, which would have cost him less than the price of his illegal pump action firearm. We heard even less about the implications for society if this became a common practice. Yet there is an outcry about gun crime. Tony Martin was posed as a lonely hero against the tide of rising crime. (As we saw in Chapter 9, Asians in the north of England also took the law into their own hands when the police failed to respond to their concerns about Fascist attacks but since they were not white-skinned country dwellers they got a very different press.) When Martin expressed no remorse whatsoever, he was denied parole because he was deemed to be a risk. The press went wild at the injustice of it. They made the crude comparison with the early release after a drugs conviction of one of the men who had burgled him and after tabloid complaints the Home Secretary instigated an investigation. The government is even revisiting the law on self defence, which is perfectly clear, as a result of popular campaigns.

The Manichaean divide between good and bad, victim and accused, is one of the features of Blairism that transcends domestic and international politics. In Tony Blair's thinking the divide between good and bad is always hard and fast and in his pilgrim's progress the Prime Minister is very attracted to simple polarities. Those with long experience in criminal law know that the intricacy of the weave of human life is one of the constant challenges to those trying to deliver justice. Victims are rarely passive victims pure and simple, and victimisers are often worth some compassion if we are ever going to end the cycles of abuse. If human dignity means anything then we have to recognise the humanity of those who offend.

We have seen considerable change in the last decade. I have seen at first hand, for example, how people who have suffered personal loss need a public process to help them come to terms with their bereavement. In the 1980s I chaired a community inquiry in Northern Ireland into deaths as a result of the use of plastic bullets. Above all, what the families of those who were killed wanted was some recognition of their pain and anger at pointless loss of life. That experience, and a close following of Truth and Reconciliation hearings in South Africa, have convinced me that we need better ways of marking the human suffering of those who experience crime without tying all hope of assuagement into the criminal trial. I have often thought that judges in murder trials should bring the family of the person killed into the courtroom at a preliminary hearing before there is any trial, to say publicly, 'Whatever happens in this case, whatever the outcome in relation to the accused, we want to acknowledge that you have experienced a terrible wrong and we, the community, share your sense of horror and outrage.'

In New Zealand ten years ago I saw for myself programmes of restorative justice which drew upon Maori customary law and practice for the resolution of conflicts or wrongdoing in their communities. In crime, the idea is that a person who offends must meet with his victim and be confronted with his wrongdoing and its effect. Restitution should be made and ways found to end the offending behaviour. The community and wider families are drawn into the process so that solutions are found collectively. In New Zealand the process called Family Group Conferencing is used for youth offending and I saw a young boy who had broken into a house meeting with the householders whose belongings he had taken and sold. The couple talked about how a silver dish had been a wedding present from a grandmother who was now dead. It could never be replaced as it was a family treasure. They described to him how upset they were that he had trampled through all the seedlings their children had been growing and how frightened their daughter had become about sleeping in the dark. The boy was thoroughly ashamed. He offered to work in their garden digging over the destroyed flowerbeds and agreed to pay back something towards their loss. A family friend who was there offered him Saturday work to earn some money to make amends. His mother talked about how she felt he was angry about her having met a new man and that he was still confused about his father leaving. He agreed that he was, and said he wanted to stay for a while with his older sister who was now married, until he felt better about his mother's relationship. A plan was developed to help the boy get his life sorted, with offers of assistance which might otherwise not have been forthcoming. The meeting was very successfully chaired by a skilled mediator and everyone left with greater insight, feeling the better for the process.

Such a practice could not work with very serious crime, where the full force of the state is employed and society demands that punishment follow an offence; even when used with lesser offences, success is probably highly dependent on the quality of the mediation team, not only at the hearing but in preparing the victim and the offender for the process. However, in Australia and New Zealand this engagement with another justice model has certainly led to some very imaginative and effective interventions, which means victims can feel more central to the proceedings and more instrumental in the outcomes. It also means young people can be diverted from the criminal justice system in appropriate cases. I came back enthused by the possibilities. These and similar ideas have fired many interesting initiatives around the world. As I have said elsewhere in this book, it is not possible to graft ideas from other systems on to our own without great care, respect for our own legal values and sensitive piloting. The starting point is to draw the essence out of the ideas and see whether there is anything to learn. Restorative justice is not new in any culture. It has ancient roots. What it reminds us is that most trial processes – whether civil or common law based – leave victims feeling cheated and too many offenders fail to take responsibility for their actions.

The philosophy of restorative justice is that it should work with people in their communities in the aftermath of crime. It recognises that crime can have profound effects on individuals, on their families and communities, on the offenders themselves and on their families. Restorative justice tries to redress the harm done to each of these parties and to empower each of them directly to make decisions about reparation and future behaviour, rather than having such decisions imposed by courts or professionals. Informal resolution may look like an easy option but for offenders the formality of court proceedings allows them to avoid the real impact of what they have done. For victims there is no sense of why this wrong was inflicted on them. Even after sentencing there is little sense of closure, opportunity for forgiveness or chance to put the whole experience behind them because they feel so marginalised. Research shows that, more than anything, victims want reassurance that the same harm will not be inflicted again on someone else. The principles of restorative justice are based on the offender taking responsibility for her actions and the finding of ways to put right what she has done. Conventional justice often ignores the harm not just to the victim but to the wider circle of family, friends and employees when crime takes place.

However, mediation can never be a substitute for the court process for those who say they are innocent. It is only possible where an offender accepts her guilt. It also has to be completely voluntary. It has to be planned and conducted by well-trained and skilled professionals because abusive offenders can re-victimise the victims. The mediation must work in a neutral way, balancing concern for the victim with concern for the offender.

Direct communication between an offender and a victim can be very powerful in letting an offender see the effects of her behaviour and, if her own victim is unwilling to take part, victims of similar crimes whose offenders have not been caught can take part instead.

How could such ideas be integrated into our system here in Britain? Already, the UN Convention on the Rights of the Child encourages diversion of young people from courts wherever possible. Child development theory and experience show that in dealing with young people, flexibility and non-stigmatisation are as important as due process. A conviction or finding of guilt is a step of huge importance in a child's sense of his or her 'redeemability' and restorative justice provides a whole new approach in the handling of youth offending.

The good thing is that the government has wanted to explore restorative justice approaches and, in the Youth Justice and Criminal Evidence Act 1999, it brought the idea into the system by making it another possible option available to youth offender panels. The new Intensive Supervision and Surveillance Programmes for juveniles, which combine tagging with a full programme of work, training and reparation for victims, have been very successful but despite the best efforts of the Youth Justice Board, the Home Secretary continues to lack the courage to make the principles behind the programme mainstream, applying them to adults too.

As Kate Akester, author of 'Restorative Justice, Victims' Rights and the Future' (2000) has pointed out, there is widespread uncertainty in government circles about what restorative justice means, both in theory and practice. Human rights standards require due process, with legal representation, while the restorative justice method sensibly tries to avoid lawyers, keeping the proceedings informal. The government scheme currently requires a plea of guilty in the Youth Court, which is unfortunate as one of the gains acknowledged in other jurisdictions and elsewhere is the avoidance of the court process altogether. In New Zealand 80% of less serious cases are diverted from court to informal measures, usually of a restorative nature. Of the remaining 20%, family group conferences are used instead of court or in more serious cases to develop the recommendations to be made to the court in the pre-sentence report. If the judge accepts the plan it will normally form the basis for a three-month court order. If all the conditions of the plan are fulfilled, the case is discharged. Justice is deemed to be done.

Mediation can also be used in many other ways. Roger Graef, in his handbook *Why Restorative Justice? Repairing the Harm Caused by Crime* (2001), tells the story of Claire, a single mother with an eight-year-old son, Max. They experienced an aggravated burglary where their house was broken into at night by a burglar named Sean and they were terrorised. Sean was caught and sent to jail for three years. But Max's nightmares persisted. As the time approached for Sean's release, Claire grew anxious. She approached the local Citizens' Advice Bureau, which referred her to the local Mediation and Reparation Service. The mediators visited Sean, who had just been released. He was shocked and upset to hear that Claire and Max remained in fear and agreed to a meeting at a local community centre. Sean apologised in full and reassured Claire that he had no intention of burgling her again or causing any harm. Claire accepted the apology and reassurance and found the meeting helpful. Max's nightmares stopped soon after.

John Major, whilst Prime Minister, suggested that as a society we needed to 'condemn more and understand less' but in my frequent encounters with the victims of crime, their desire is often to understand why the criminal acted as they did. Jo Berry, the daughter of Sir Anthony Berry, a Conservative Member of Parliament who was killed in the Brighton bombing in 1984, a case in which I acted, described very poignantly her anguish over the death of her father, in a documentary film for the BBC called *Facing the Enemy*, (broadcast in December 2001). She had tried to get on with her life but her mind was very much on the conflict in Ireland and the man who had planted the bomb which had taken her father from her. In 1999 she had joined a victim support programme in the Republic of Ireland. Many of the participants had experienced trauma as a result of acts of terrorism. Through a reconciliation group she met some ex-IRA prisoners, which initially created conflicting emotions, including anxiety that she was betraying her family by even talking with those they would consider their enemies. Eventually she met Patrick Magee, who had been convicted of the bombing.

In a piece in *Good Housekeeping* in October 2003, she describes the impact:

> Over the past two-and-a-half years of getting to know Patrick, I feel I have recovered some of the humanity I lost when the bomb went off. I don't feel so hurt any more and I can see behind Patrick's

> motives. I also know that Patrick sometimes finds it very hard to live with the knowledge that he cares for the daughter of one of the people he killed. He says that while he regrets killing my father, he still stands by his actions. In part it is comforting, but it is still something I wrestle with.

Jo Berry has now become involved in setting up Causeway, an organisation committed to facilitating meetings between people who have been caught up in the Northern Ireland conflict; she is also training to be a trauma counsellor. She says she is learning to accept the parts of her that wish to blame and judge.

There will always be victims even in lesser crimes who want no part of such a process, but research on victims shows that of those taking part in mediation 73% wanted an apology, 80% said they wanted answers, and 90% wanted to tell the offender the impact of their crime. Most want to prevent recurrence and 65% wanted restitution.

The impact of crimes on vulnerable victims can be enormous. Their security is shattered and they often blame themselves for what happened, going over and over events and wondering whether if they had done something different the outcome could have been changed. With some kinds of crime they suffer stigma. The growth of Victim Support, which has large numbers of volunteers, has been of considerable help to many who suffer crime, offering friendship and counsel. For many victims punishment is not their goal, safety is.

Roger Graef suggested that restorative justice might be successful where there are blurred distinctions between offenders and victims, for example warring neighbours or young men in a fight. In many circumstances a criminal prosecution is not the best way to resolve the conflict and because there is an unwillingness to invoke criminal processes the enmities remain alive. 'We can all be human and inhuman, violent and yet vulnerable and remorseful. We may at one moment be callous and insensitive but then become aware of and regret the damage we have caused. Mediation can address these ambiguities.'

While the government has trumpeted the use of anti-social behaviour orders as the method for dealing with 'neighbours from hell', the most effective way of resolving conflict over children or issues about noise is through mediation, with the parties coming around a table with respected community members to sort out differences and to find a way of living together in mutual respect. The presence of people whose views matter – another neighbour, a community worker, a local doctor or priest – can lower the temperature and firm the resolve. In the summer of 2003, children who were raising hell on scooters in a north London estate were brought together with residents. As a result a piece of waste land was found for them to play on.

Gerard Lemos, a partner at social researchers Lemos&Crane, also thinks that there are better ways of dealing with racists than just locking them up. RaceActionNet is a network produced and managed by Lemos&Crane. Lemos points out that racists are not all skinheads and thugs wielding knives and that racial harassment is not the same as racist crime. Racial harassment by neighbours often involves women over 50. Mediation, sometimes followed up with acceptable behaviour contracts, has most effect. Young people hanging around and racially abusing people can also be diverted by good negotiation. Youth workers who are any good know how to distract and deter them. The problem is the absence of sufficient youth workers.

In the early 1990s I was asked by a well-known media organisation to conduct a hearing and mediate where there had been an allegation of sexual harassment. The young woman had been subjected to continuous unwelcome attention by an older man, who had a position of influence in the organisation. She wanted to stay with the publication but wanted the harassment to stop and she did not want her complaint to affect her prospects. The mediation hearing led to a sensible *rapprochement*, some insight for the man in question and an opportunity for everyone to move on.

Another area where restorative justice may be helpful is in the complex situations around violence in the home, such as domestic violence and child abuse. Again, the victims may have ambiguous feelings about their abuser. In addition, the collective shame and destruction of wider relationships involved in bringing a case to court means they suffer in silence. There is huge guilt on the shoulders of victims if they feel they have caused the break-up of the family or the imprisonment of a partner. It may even be that in some rape cases, the woman wants acknowledgement that she was forced to do something against her will, but not a full-blown court case. Until now my view has been that the criminal trial processes must always be used in such cases so that the seriousness of domestic and sexual violence is accepted within society. However, I agree that there could be cases where alternative routes to justice should be considered. All these processes of course need co-operation from both sides and considerable skill on the part of those professionally involved. They would only be possible if the accused accepted guilt and if the victim's involvement is completely voluntary. My fear is that the process could be manipulated by the abuser. During the meetings, control has to rest with those affected, but often they find that surrounded by family and friends they feel safe enough to air their pain in a way that is impossible in court.

Linda Mills, a professor of law at New York University has shocked feminists by suggesting that restorative justice can sometimes work effectively in domestic violence, because women disclose their abuse at an earlier stage and often men do want help with their violent behaviour. She shows that middle-class couples often take this route privately, with family therapy and psychiatric intervention, while working-class men face the courts.

As the world is changing, within society, business and private relationships, we are looking for new methods of conflict resolution and, where it is appropriate, we should be doing the same within the justice system. If such alternatives were given more government encouragement and support, many more offenders would plead guilty, take responsibility for what they have done and help their victims recover. We would all reap the benefits.

11

CRIMINALISING THE POOR

WHEN NEW LABOUR introduced the Human Rights Act in 1998 they made a point of explaining that rights also entailed duties. They had caught the drift of the American communitarian critique that obsessive 'rights talk', with a concentration on the individual, could be detrimental to the concept of 'community'. But this adoption of American thinking ignores the fact that the European human rights model to which we signed up is very different from that of the United States, where certain rights are immutable and their impact on the well-being of the community as a whole is detrimental. The right to bear arms is an example where the cost to American society has been considerable. The right to free speech means that the Ku-Klux-Klan can spew forth racist slurs with impunity and be protected by rights organisations. Religious fundamentalists' attempts to prevent abortions were thwarted only by the primacy of an individual woman's right to privacy, rather than by concern for women's reproductive freedom.

The human rights philosophy which developed in Europe since the Second World War is quite different. It accepts that rights conflict with each other and that a careful balancing is necessary in pursuit of justice. The interests of the community are part of the balancing act.

The communitarian movement in the United States was developed to counter the specific experience of an American rights culture, which took no cognisance of the greater needs of society. However, to a party like Labour, seeking to make some peace with its collectivist past, communitarianism provided some positive ideas.

The emphasis David Blunkett places on civic responsibility and duty to the community in which we live is to be welcomed after the onslaught on such values during the long years of Thatcherism, when consumerism and individualism were lauded. We do need to reclaim the concept of 'the common good'. However, all the declaiming about civic responsibility seems to be directed at the poor. There is rarely a word said about the ways in which others should be playing their part: stepping forward as witnesses, sitting as jurors, offering to be magistrates, helping to run community rehabilitation projects, volunteering at local schools and youth clubs. And what about the super-rich, including party benefactors, paying their taxes?

Bob Holman works and lives in Easterhouse, Glasgow, developing community projects and changing lives in the most inspirational way. He is tired of the refrain of politicians and commentators that 'respect, order and self-discipline' are no longer extolled as virtues amongst the working class. He sees these characteristics in thousands of low-income people who run community projects in deprived areas. He sees that when young people are allowed to work as helpers and treated with respect, loutish behaviour declines. Unfortunately, the money given for such projects by central government is minimal.

When I first went into the House of Lords I had the hugely pleasurable experience of supporting the passage of the Human Rights Act, devolution and the other early constitutional reforms. It was like being in clover, having campaigned on the issues for so long. But then my long dark nights started with the cuts to the child benefit of lone mothers. I made speeches about how much harder and more costly it was when you were left on your own with a baby and could not do a big supermarket shop but were reliant on the corner store. Then came vouchers for asylum seekers so that they were further stigmatised. Then the removals of legal aid and the rolling out of the Public Defender Service which would always mean an inferior system for the poor. I seemed to be in constant battle with the ministers for social security and criminal justice.

The reform of the welfare state had been flagged up but nowhere did any manifesto indicate that the benefit system would be used as a source of punishment. The mistake we were making was in turning our welfare system into the American equivalent, a meagre safety net. The risk in going down that road is that the majority have no vested interest in protecting it; they are no longer stakeholders. The approach started with the New Right in America in the 1970s, led by the economist Milton Friedman, making it clear that welfare should be no more than 'a floor' in a free market system. A theory about the 'underclass' was promulgated by another right-wing American, Charles Murray, in his book *The Bell Curve*, demarcating a social category of people with attitudes and behaviour quite distinct from the rest of the population. The membership of this class was described as coming from two sources, from young, healthy low-income males who are idle and from single mothers who choose to have children outside stable relationships. Murray stated that he wanted 'to reintroduce a notion of blame'. This thinking seeped into the political soil.

The government is right to be concerned about people who are abusing benefit, working while receiving allowances, claiming incapacity allowance fraudulently, becoming dependent on benefits while they could be working, but the way to deal with such abuse is to ensure that the terms are drawn up as specifically and as tightly as possible, and that the medical profession and others are brought on side in protecting benefit and prosecuting real abuse. As successful Treasury-driven initiatives have shown, the road back into employment is facilitated by good training and skills development, as well as job counselling.

Wrestling with the problems of welfare reform is hard. I believe in welfare reform but I also believe in welfare. Again and again government ministers have devised plans to remove housing benefits or child benefit or other state benefits as a stick with which to beat the poor into submission. Far from promoting a 'responsibilities agenda', the proposals invariably undermine the capacity of the most hard-pressed in our society to function at all.

The desire to care for the poor, the vulnerable, the old, and those with disabilities, relies upon the finest of our human impulses. It relies upon all that reservoir of good stuff – ideas about the brotherhood of man, that we are all 'Jock Thompson's bairns' as we say in Scotland. It is a basic principle of morality and is at the heart of 'society', that concept so readily dismissed by Mrs Thatcher.

The need to care for the disadvantaged is a precept shared by every creed and extolled as a central principle of humanity. Social security is our collective way of giving it force by creating a set of rights and entitlements. But concepts of right and entitlement can be meaningless if there is no means or power to make them effective, and cannot be seen in isolation from the economic system in which they operate.

I happen to believe in universal benefits because they are less likely to be eroded and there is no stigma attached to their receipt. However, a low tax society is prepared to sacrifice universal benefits because real communitarianism is deemed too costly. Mutuality of obligation is secondary to self-interest even under a Labour government, and strong public services are secondary to tax cuts.

There is a tendency to see social security simply as wholesale charity, when in fact a nation alert to its self-interest recognises its other purposes. No economic system has ever kept people permanently in employment. Since human capital is the raw material of any economic system, an enlightened government ensures that the pool of unemployed labour is kept fit and fed and ready for re-employment. In a new world of employment where the flexible labour market is god, people will go in and out of work, dependent upon the needs of the employer. Large companies are encouraged to downsize and to employ their remaining workforce on short contracts or a part-time basis. The jobs may disappear but people who are made redundant do not. Unlike other raw material, employers expect the state to look after the potential labour force: they do not expect the government to store and care for their equipment or plant but they do expect the state to take responsibility for the needs of those who are laid off. It is therefore important to the economy and to employers that people do not 'deteriorate' when they are not employed. They need enough money to keep themselves clothed and fed. The sums are not large.

The state has also been challenged by the new flexible work arrangements into finding ways of providing supplementary benefit for those on low incomes. Because many people are only able to work part-time or on short contracts for pitiful wages, the government has invented family tax credits, which are intended to keep people in the work environment but help them survive on pitiful wages. In many ways this lets employers off the hook for paying people badly and the rest of us off the hook for not paying enough for services and products. Another problem is that the scheme is so complex that so far there has been poor uptake. However, what seems clear is that we can expect a future in which far more people than ever before will have bouts of unemployment and experience being hard-up.

I have argued for a new ethical contract between employers and employees where, if security of tenure is to be removed, employers should be required to provide retraining and educational opportunities for staff at workplace learning centres or supported local colleges. This would seem to me to be a useful role for the trade unions which are too often stuck in old ways of negotiating.

However, if we are to devise new economic models which involve a different kind of relationship between employer and employed we must recognise the impact on social security. It is also vital that we are alert to the new ways in which welfare benefits are increasingly being used as a form of social control.

I am as keen as anyone to revitalise moral responsibility in society but a social security system must not have a moral agenda. Already New Labour's social welfare policies are reverting to nineteenth-century Victorian notions of who is worthy of help and who is not. We should ask ourselves whether we think the state should have the power to use the withdrawal of welfare benefits to enforce a moral agenda. We doubtless all offend someone else's moral principles in the way that we conduct our lives. We live with those differences because there would be no peace for any of us if we did not. People with an unusual lifestyle have the same right to live as the rest of us and if their conduct moves into criminal behaviour then they should be punished using the criminal courts and criminal sanctions, not withdrawal of their welfare benefits.

We expect the National Health Service to be morally neutral in its treatment of patients. We would be on very dangerous terrain indeed if we decided that those who used drugs be moved down the waiting lists or those who had committed crimes deserved less urgent care. However, even this principle is being challenged with the rehearsal of ideas about making medical charges for people who smoke or who are obese. The duty of the NHS is to preserve life, not make moral judgements on how life is used. This is just as true of social security.

Conrad Russell, the Liberal peer who has been a constant and determined advocate on behalf of the disadvantaged, has led the way in opposing financial sanctions on the poor. He asks what the response would be if cabinet ministers were required to give up drinking alcohol as a condition of receiving a salary from public funds. The replies are probably unprintable.

The original author of the shift in thinking about welfare is Frank Field, who argues that there is an implied social contract between the state and the unemployed in which the state is bound to support people while they are out of work and they in return are obliged to do everything they can to find employment. This is a sentiment with which we would all agree but it is the follow-through that creates the dilemma. If the answer to lack of rigour in finding work is the removal of benefits, other social problems ensue – debt, prostitution, homelessness and crime.

The impetus to use benefit withdrawal as a stick started with single mothers. Under the Conservatives, the myth was generated that girls got pregnant deliberately and lived off benefits without menfolk, the state having become some kind of sugar daddy, which because of its generosity had emasculated men by removing their proper fathering role. At the Conservative conference in 1992, the Social Security Minister, Peter Lilley, mocked lone mothers by singing of them as 'young ladies who get pregnant just to jump the housing list'. The many diverse social factors which have led to the growth in single parenthood are complex. It's true that women's employment is an important antidote to child poverty and this was recognised by Labour in government. However, the government creates a false dichotomy between employment and benefits. Evidence suggests that women's employment, especially in the case of lone mothers, is only a counter to child poverty when supported by decent benefits and services. Low-paid women's work is not, on its own, a sure route out of poverty. Nor are all women in a position to take up paid employment. Sometimes when a woman has just extricated herself from a violent relationship what she and her children need is recovery time. Similarly, when a father has walked out on his family having met someone else it is not just the mother of his children who feels abandoned: a woman may feel her children need her full time until they have adjusted to their new circumstances. Benefits continue to be crucial to the well-being of the woman and her family. But in addition, it should be acknowledged that benefits make a vital contribution to the security of everyone in a more complex society.

Many who have the good fortune to be in regular well-paid employment have no idea of the hardship involved in living on state benefits. One of the cruellest cuts by the Conservatives in 1986 was the abolition of entitlements to pay for essential domestic items like a cooker or a bed. Since then people have had to take a loan from the Social Fund to pay for these necessities and repayment is deducted weekly from their benefits, leaving them often with the most meagre level of subsistence. That debt can often tip the poor into complete poverty and a spiral of further borrowing from loan sharks. Labour in opposition had promised to abolish the Social Fund but changed its mind in government.

Unfortunately, Frank Field's 'social contract' thinking has taken hold and is now being expanded to imply a contract whereby benefits depend on good behaviour. Recipients must send their children to school daily and on time until the age of 16; they must stop their children being public nuisances, gathering on street corners; they must keep their housing in good order, contain the noise that they make and be respectful of the needs of the rest of the community. All of us would agree that people should conduct themselves in ways that are sensitive of others and should help their children develop social responsibility. However, the key question is how this is to be done. If the answer is the removal of benefits what are the consequences; where does such interference and social engineering end? The American neo-conservatives have proposed that one condition of benefit might be that certain single parents give up their child for adoption. They have also suggested that families with more than five children should receive no additional welfare. Can we foresee a world where people who refuse certain prenatal genetic tests forfeit disability benefit for a child? The shrinking state can very easily become the invasive, thoroughly controlling state.

We should think hard about how far we are willing to see the state interfere in the way we raise our children, otherwise we may find that it starts to meddle where it should not. Most people want to live decent lives. They want to have children who do not get into trouble, who are upright citizens and who will have jobs when they leave education. The state's task is to help people do what they want to do, not mould people into a particular pattern. Forcing mothers by court order to attend residential weekend courses on parenting when their children are misbehaving, but when they themselves have committed no crime, is an interference with liberty which many middle-class parents would balk at. In a letter to the Deputy Prime Minister and others, which was leaked to the press in May 2003, Lord Irvine, then Lord Chancellor, suggested that some might find compulsory attendance over a weekend 'draconian and an extreme example of the nanny state'. He sensibly asked who was going to look after the children who remained at home while a parent is undergoing compulsory training for several days. It would be far more effective to persuade the mother that she could discover ways of tackling some of the hard challenges of adolescence and have a good time if she went to a course on a voluntary basis at her convenience. But this is part of Tony Blair's 'something for something' society. No free handouts.

While we may endlessly debate the morality of removing benefits from poor people, the main argument against the use of welfare withdrawal to punish is that *it doesn't work*. It does not make people behave better if you make them poorer. If people are left with barely enough money to scrape an existence, they are driven further into hopelessness and the kind of wretchedness that fosters crime and depressive illness, alcoholism and drug abuse and all the ensuing anti-social behaviour that so exercises people. Top-down legislative mechanisms of social control and coercion will not solve the problems of anti-social behaviour which emanate from people who are deprived in so many ways.

The other facet of using the removal of benefits as a rod is that only the judiciary should punish. At first the government dabbled with the idea that the Department of Social Security and Pensions should threaten the benefit reduction to coerce recipients into better behaviour and automatically remove money if there was any default. However, now the powers are to be vested in the courts through Anti-Social Behaviour and other legislation, despite the expressions of concern by many organisations, including the Citizens' Advice Bureau, about the use of the benefits system for imposing penalties for criminal offences.

Anti-social behaviour has become the newest subject of ministerial fervour and is a now a proxy for talking about class, a taboo subject. Although crime is going down, few people believe the good crime figures. They still fear out-of-control people roaming the streets with graffiti and vandalism as constant reminders of social disorder. Residents on run-down housing estates recount the misery of living next to terrible neighbours or the destruction caused by delinquent kids. Police action is necessary – but most of the legislation is already in place. It just needs to be enforced appropriately. Instead of spending huge sums of money on new orders, which will ultimately lead to an increase in the imprisonment of young people, the emphasis should be on finding ways of addressing the discontent and nihilism of people who have largely been neglected.

Bob Holman says that through his work in Easterhouse he is confident that communities just need to be engaged in the solution of these problems. When people are treated in a positive way they respond. 'Let kids design adventure playgrounds and then let them build them.' Half the problems with young people relate to the inadequacy of meeting places or youth clubs. But as he points out: 'Our communities need to be resourced'.

The Citizens' Advice Bureau points out that the purpose of housing benefit is to enable tenants on low incomes to meet their responsibilities to pay their rent. Withdrawal of housing benefit by the courts would make this virtually impossible. They point out that victims of anti-social behaviour want fast and effective remedies: but withholding benefits provides neither. Once housing benefit is withdrawn arrears would have to build up before there was an eviction. This would probably be six months down the road. So it certainly will not meet the needs of complaining neighbours.

The penalty also bears little relation to many of the known causes of anti-social behaviour. If these have to do with parents being unable to control their children or with the unmet needs of people with mental health problems or drugs or alcohol problems, docking benefits will hardly have a deterrent effect.

Alistair Jackson, Policy Director of Shelter, pointed out the punitive authoritarianism in plans to remove housing benefit from families found guilty of anti-social behaviour. 'Taking away housing benefit will make families homeless because they will not be able to pay the rent. This will not address the causes of their anti-social behaviour but merely move the problem on.' Landlords will lose rent, which will make them even more reluctant to have tenants on housing benefit. There will be additional pressure on the courts, an increase in local authorities' homelessness problems and social services will have the burden of dealing with evicted families. Local authority housing officers want to build orderly communities and, while they see ASBOs as useful as a last resort, what they say is needed is intervention right at the start, when families first cause trouble. They need good social workers to come quick and often, professional mediators, youth workers and places for young people to go. However, services are so overstretched and money so scarce that early prevention is not taking place. Youth services have been starved of funds. Yet, Alan Milburn in a 'think-piece' for the *Independent* in October 2003 suggested that zero tolerance policies had not gone far enough. He suggested that local councils should be rewarded for every bad neighbour that is evicted. Pause for a moment and consider the potential abuse of such a policy and the madness of putting money into such a punitive course rather than funding preventive measures.

The riposte of the Home Secretary to anyone who raises concern is that those who have no experience of anti-social behaviour and the misery it brings should not get in the way of those who are trying to do something about it. This rebuke allows the middle classes to feel comfortable about the use of sticks against the poor when the problems are all about poverty and the growing divisions in our society which need much more than punishment. The fact that the measures may be unworkable in law is something David Blunkett does not want to hear.

Clearly, one of the frustrations for the courts is what to do when it comes to finding punishments for the poor who commit crime. With heavy hearts many judges and magistrates find themselves handing out fines, but exacting only a pound or two on a weekly basis, which of course only adds to the round of debts. Judges and magistrates know, as they send people off with what seems like a small financial penalty, that they are adding to their burdens and the same people are likely to be back before the courts in short order for yet more thefts and burglaries. By cutting down funds we are driving people below the survival line and creating social outlaws. As Conrad Russell has powerfully argued: 'If we talk about welfare and liberty, the case against disentitlement to benefit is perhaps as strong in terms of freedom from fear of the rich as in terms of freedom from want of the poor.'

Anti-social behaviour does generate high emotions because communities can be wrecked by the wild actions of a few. But policy must be based on evidence of what will work and it must be fair and reasonable. The use of ASBOs is useless if the people causing the trouble have serious problems that require massive intervention which is not forthcoming. Whenever a case of anti-social behaviour comes to court, a story of chaos and impoverishment invariably emerges. If the government took a close look it would see that quick fixes will not work and real solutions will involve supporting communities more effectively with family centres and club houses, sports pitches and gyms. One of the great mistakes in the 1980s was reducing school sports and selling off sports fields, which withdrew one of the crucial outlets for the energies of testosterone-fuelled boys.

In South Africa I witnessed a programme supported by the British Council which took young people from townships, many of whom were heading towards crime, and gave them a training as sports coaches for younger kids in poor areas. It turned their lives around and while we are busy exporting these ideas we are failing to see how effective they could be at home. The New Deal has drawn many young people into work but not enough of the jobs contain any opportunity for progression. The jobs which used to be available to young working-class men in docks and shipyards no longer exist. The rites of passage into adult malehood – of apprenticeships and joining the union – have gone. Doing rotten jobs for which the minimum wage is often flouted and which go nowhere does nothing for a young person's self-esteem.

In all the debate about anti-social behaviour, class is what underlies the issues. A revolution has taken place in the world of work and we have seen the death of heavy industry which employed working-class men. Many of their sons and grandsons are now reaping the effects of that change and we as a society are blaming the young men who would otherwise have gone into those jobs for not being fully occupied or completely happy. We blame them for their hopeless lives instead of taking a share in the responsibility for the turn their lives have taken. When the industrial revolution took place in the early nineteenth century, it created significant numbers of dispossessed people. All the same problems were pushed into the faces of the luckier ones – petty crime, drunkenness and begging – and a clamp-down in the form of vagrancy legislation sought to do precisely what all our current anti-social behaviour laws are supposed to achieve. It did not work then either. While governments have focused on the benefits of the technological revolution to certain sections of society, there has been insufficient focus on the downside. When New Labour came into government it was seen as a new, refreshing, modernising force, oriented to change; but as its social and criminal justice policy emerged, it has increasingly become a continuation of the preceding 18 Conservative years. One of the founding purposes of the Labour Party was to concern itself with the conditions of the poor. A potential radical and democratic agenda of really ameliorating the negative effects of the market and expanding its benefits to everyone remains unused.

None of the vitriol poured on the poor is directed at the fecklessness of the rich. No mention is made of the yahoo yobbery in West End wine bars, no reference to the loud and invasive drunkenness of City bankers. A BBC programme entitled *The Third Degree: The City Exposed*, which was aired on 23 October 2003, described the bullying, aggressive culture of the City of London. A leading City employment lawyer was quoted in the *Financial Times* on the same day saying: 'You only have to go out on a Friday night at 6 p.m. and see all the boys, and sometimes girls too, behaving like louts to know it's true.' Apparently this has led to the late night northbound train out of Liverpool Street Station being dubbed the Vomit Comet. Horseplay is an endemic part of the culture that exists in the highly charged environment of the dealing room. Not only are such anti-social boors immune from criticism, but so are their friends who pollute the air with their highly charged cars, double park, shout into mobile phones, allow their dogs to shit on pavements, award themselves offensive pay rises and evade their taxes. Many anti-social acts by the middle classes go unremarked.

In July 2002 the government had to back off proposals to cut child benefit payments to the parents of persistent young offenders and the parents of truants. These would have been particularly tough on lone mothers who are urged by government to find work, which often makes it even harder for them to police their children's behaviour. Experienced social policy makers like Ruth Lister, a professor at Loughborough University, had to point out to ministers that the many objectives of child benefit did not include the inculcation of good behaviour. Moreover, when child benefit replaced tax allowances, it was widely acknowledged that it represents a form of tax relief for all families with children. Alistair Jackson of Shelter also pointed out that taking housing benefit away from families is a punishment that will not deliver the solutions that tenants and communities need; instead he proposed the use of existing court sanctions along with advice and support, as well as confronting perpetrators with the effect of their behaviour on themselves and others.

I had my own battles with government in 2000 over the removal of benefits from people who broke the conditions of a community service order. The idea was that if someone failed to attend their community service or was late twice, the benefit office would be informed and the civil servant there would dock the person's benefits.

When a court makes a community service order it is explained that breach of the order through non-attendance will mean a return to court and the imposition of imprisonment. The courts should have the role of punishing, not the clerk at the benefits office. The whole point of the return to court is that the judge or magistrate can measure whether the failure to attend is wilful or whether there is an acceptable reason.

People who are placed on community service often have multiple social problems and the idea of the punishment in the community is to bring together retribution and rehabilitation – to help them reconstruct their lives, creating some order out of chaos. That process is not easy for people who have drink problems or who have been abused or battered and are suffering from depression. Getting up in the morning and getting to the project on time can be hard when you have had no such rituals and rhythms in your life for years, or if you have been up all night with a sick child, or your teenage son did not come home and got himself arrested. Ask the middle-class parents of a child with drug problems whether there are ever relapses and how long it takes to establish self-discipline or order. Sometimes the steps back to a decent life are faltering, and indeed removing benefit is the most effective way of driving people back into crime. And the impact on the children of families where funds are reduced can be very damaging.

We are seeing the creation of double punishments for the poor, for there is no equivalent sanction for those who are not dependent on benefits. The government tried to maintain that no court finding of breach would be necessary before removal of the benefit as this would be an 'administrative' procedure. The probation officer would simply be required to inform the local benefit office. An alliance of peers in the House of Lords led a revolt, recognising that we were seeing a breach of the due process provisions in the Human Rights Act, and the government came to accept that the offender would have to be brought back to court for breach of community service. However, if a person has no good excuse and is wilfully failing to comply with their community order they are usually sent to prison anyway, so removing their benefit becomes irrelevant. A pilot scheme was started in October 2001. By January 2003 550 people had had their benefit withdrawn. The cost of processing each case, as reported in the *National Association of Probation Officers News*, 2003, was £730 but the amount of benefit saved in each case was £132.

Another example of unworkable policy is the creation of curfew orders, which were to be used against kids on estates. The reason they have not been used is because police and social services in most areas have recognised that they would be a barrier to effective policing rather than a help, while social workers were concerned that on occasions forcing young people indoors was returning them to home situations which were abusive. It was more productive to disperse the groups, make arrests for real criminal behaviour or to engage social services with the problems many of the youngsters face. The huge cost in parliamentary time and money creating all this legislation would be more effectively used in the recruitment of more social and youth workers, as well as probation officers.

One criminal case has gone all the way to the House of Lords on the strict liability offence which imposes fines on parents of adolescents who truant. The people affected are mainly single mothers whose teenage sons just refuse to get out of bed. What is not needed is a financial penalty. Again this policy impacts on poor people disproportionately, but because it entails strict liability it means that there is no defence. Some of these women are actually being intimidated by their sons and what the family needs is intervention and support. One mother who was sent to prison in 2002 for not sending her daughter to school expressed gratitude for her incarceration because it was in Holloway that she was diagnosed as suffering depression and delayed grief over her mother's death. It is a sad comment on our system that she had to be jailed before any attempt was made to discover why she was failing to get her child to school.

Large numbers of people have now been deprived of their benefits as a result of benefit sanctions. Despite persistent questioning, the government has no idea how these people are getting by. Crime and begging are the most likely answer. The majority of people living on the streets are young – between the ages of 15 and 24. Many have been in the care system. Recent research shows that over 70% have mental health problems. Many have been physically or sexually abused. Most have drink or drug problems. What are we doing in simply punishing them? Most of those on the streets are so demoralised that they have come to believe punishment is no more than they deserve. Ladling a conviction on top of their wretchedness is not going to have any effect.

Harry Fletcher of the National Association of Probation Officers sees a growing trend in government to criminalise non-conformist behaviour, no matter how low key. He says: 'This intolerance will further exclude disadvantaged young people from mainstream society.' There is certainly a marked expansion in the definition of anti-social behaviour. Youngsters congregating in groups might be undesirable but it is difficult to see this as criminal. Anti-social behaviour should be tackled but not by making criminals out of litter louts or people who ride bikes on the pavement, which is what the Anti-Social Behaviour Act will do. It will be possible now to imprison for up to three months groups of two or more youths who do not disperse from street corners. There are few men from a working-class background who have not idled away adolescent hours in this way; they should be counting themselves lucky that their youth predated Mr Blunkett's ingenuity. There will also be power to remove children under 16 from the streets if a member of the public believes the young people might intimidate or harass them even if nothing has as yet happened.

The law has never been used successfully to solve social problems like destitution, disaffection or social exclusion – all it does is move the misery out of sight. As the Professor of Law, Gary Slapper, has pointed out, 'when a community kicks problems like this out of its back door, they are prone after a delay to come charging back in through the front door . . .' It is already a crime under the 1824 Vagrancy Act for a person to place himself in a public place, street or highway 'to beg or gather alms'. Aggravating the status of the offence or the current punishment, which is restricted to a fine, is bound to create an even larger and more deeply stigmatised number of outcast people. A criminal record will be yet another barrier to rehabilitation and will mean more work for the criminal justice system.

For most anti-social crime the new concept of restorative justice discussed in the previous chapter will be the way forward. In New Zealand and Australia, it came out of the Aboriginal justice systems which saw the community coming together to solve problems of crime, with the offender being confronted by his victim and ways found to restore not just the damage but also the trust which has been destroyed. Walls are repainted, graffiti is scoured off, parks cleaned up, gardens replanted. Youth clubhouses built. Counselling made available. The problem with really creative responses to crime like these is that the ones which do the business are labour intensive and need wise mediators to make them succeed. Mediation UK reports that its Cardiff scheme has closed for lack of funds, and there is no longer a scheme in Glasgow. Yet early mediation can reconcile young and old neighbours at low cost, avoiding the courts and achieving an 80% satisfaction rate. The investment in serious alternatives to low-level crime, however, would be more effective than all the cockeyed schemes now pouring forth from the Home Office.

If it is not feckless families, it is beggars and vagrants who are in the eye of the storm. New laws to criminalise begging are being introduced, with the government claiming that there is no reason for anyone to beg in this country. The majority of those who beg have serious drugs, drink or mental health problems and what is needed is the creation of multiple units to address their problems intensively. That is where some serious money should be channelled, not into anti-social behaviour orders which cost £5,000 a time. The single big initiative the Home Office should embark upon is addressing drug addiction. Then we would see returns for our money. At the moment there are not even enough schemes for those who want them voluntarily, never mind those directed to them from the courts. An addicted beggar will have to be caught three times before drug treatment is available to him. And then there is deep resentment that someone might jump up the waiting list because they have committed a crime, while a young person who has stepped forward and said 'I need help' will have to wait sometimes for a year. There is evidence of people committing crime just to get help. Drug rehab units should be seen as of the highest priority and multiplied throughout the country and with speed: 200,000 drug treatment places have been promised by 2007 but few of them will be residential, which is what addicts need most.

Inventing new ways to punish the poor is a disgraceful activity for a Labour government. A Green Paper to look at the fundamental causes of crime has been scotched by the Treasury; perhaps they feel they already know why there is crime and that the largest part of it derives from hopelessness, thwarted opportunities and unemployment. The Chancellor, Gordon Brown has been by far the most effective Home Secretary in the last 20 years because of his employment initiatives. He has also been a driving force on child poverty. Perhaps he could cast his net a little wider and see what is happening to the rest of the poor in our midst.

12

WITCH-HUNTS AND THE PRESS

ON 11 MARCH 2003 Rebekah Wade, the editor of the *Sun*, giving evidence before a select committee of the House of Commons, admitted paying police officers for information. The only surprise to anyone practising in the field of criminal law was that she made the admission publicly. For years the relationship between the media and the police has been a source of controversy, but leakage from police inquiries is now endemic: a Metropolitan Police anti-corruption investigation in 1999 revealed that a detective agency run by former officers was acting as an intermediary between the police and the tabloids.

It has long been understood that there is at the very least 'a drink in it' if a police officer passes on information, but at a more sophisticated level most crime correspondents have contacts who give them regular tip-offs and solid police intelligence on suspects. They keep the reporter up to date on developments and provide the colour about crime scenes that sell newspapers. And just as the press use the police, the police use the press, leaking information about operations when it might be in their interest. Like 'unnamed sources' in Downing Street, unnamed police sources provide a slant on investigations in order to stimulate response and sometimes fly a kite to see where it leads.

Contempt of court is a strict liability offence. Under the 1981 Contempt of Court Act, a journalist may not write anything that creates substantial risk of serious prejudice once a suspect is arrested or a warrant issued. However, increasingly the press take risks about what they print because the consequences are not sufficiently serious to rein them in. A friend on one tabloid was present when the paper sought legal advice on the consequences of running a story against a celebrity where the supporting evidence was shaky. In the end, they worked out – in a financial evaluation – that any libel damages would be worth the scoop and resultant increase in circulation.

As the media respond to (or even create) the near hysteria generated around paedophilia, they argue righteous concern for the well-being of children: but their righteousness can lead to the destruction of innocent lives and untold impact on the justice system.

Matthew Kelly, a well-known television star, was playing Captain Hook in the pantomime *Peter Pan* in Birmingham when the police turned up in the theatre and arrested him. The manner of the arrest ensured maximum publicity and there is no doubt the press were not there by chance having a staff night out. The details filled the papers for days. Hundreds of articles were written. As part of the inquiry an officer was even flown to Sri Lanka where Kelly has a holiday home. His house was searched, his computer taken and his life dissected. His video collection was investigated and the presence of Disney classics deemed highly suspicious. Kelly spent five weeks with the fear that his career was over because someone made a claim of abuse by him 30 years before. No part of the allegation whatsoever could be substantiated. Nothing incriminating was ever found. But for weeks he lived the nightmare that people might tell more lies about him and that he might end up in prison. All this took place under a glaring spotlight. Finally, he was completely exonerated but the experience will have taken its toll. Whether the police or sections of the press felt the least chastened it is hard to know, but there is no more vulnerable suspect than the person accused of child abuse and it is outrageous that his name ever appeared in print before a decision to charge.

This coalition of the media and police means that certain people are put on trial without the benefit of a judge and jury. It used to be that calls for sacking and ostracism followed conviction but now the press gleefully make such demands after arrest. David Jones, the football manager, was also falsely accused of abusing children. He lost his job and a year of his life before being cleared but his father died prematurely, broken by the pain of the allegations, and his wife and children have suffered greatly from the publicity.

Everyone wants to see child abusers brought to justice but the moral panic generated by sections of the media is making it very easy for individuals to invent stories, particularly about those in the public eye, either for money or because they are envious, malicious or just yearn for attention. Neil Hamilton, the former Member of Parliament, and his wife Christine had this experience over a false rape allegation, when an emotionally troubled woman, Nadine Milroy-Sloan, opportunistically invented her complaint. Simply Red's Mick Hucknall and the Jam's ex-singer Paul Weller faced similar claims and press attacks, with little apology when the allegations were eventually dismissed. Already the Court of Appeal has overturned cases involving accusations of paedophilia because the complainants, now adults, were shown to be motivated by the desire for compensation.

The saturation coverage given to allegations against the famous, or in cases of special notoriety, puts a fair trial at risk. Juries are usually very good at distinguishing media hype from evidence, and judges can alert them to the risks of having their judgement swayed, but there comes a point when coverage is so sensational and so emotionally charged that no amount of jury vigilance can cancel its effect. And jurors can now use the internet very easily at home to remind themselves of what they may have forgotten.

The vilification of Michael Barrymore is a case in point. The inquest into the death of a young man in Michael Barrymore's swimming pool led to a tabloid campaign of attrition which 'convicted' the television presenter of being complicit in his death, when the evidence left many questions unanswered. New evidence has now come to light which casts doubt on the autopsy. Many of the witnesses giving evidence at the inquest had entered into financial agreements with newspapers before testifying – an abuse which has been criticised since the trial of Jeremy Thorpe all those years ago in 1979 and which is only now being outlawed. Had criminal charges been pressed, it is unlikely Barrymore could have had a fair trial. As it is, he more or less stands 'convicted' in the court of public opinion as a result of the press annihilation.

In another instance, the television presenter, John Leslie, was named by newspapers after the celebrity Ulrika Jonsson described in her memoir being raped in a hotel room by an unnamed television colleague. After a police investigation – which it was said included two allegations of sexual assault relating to other women – the Crown Prosecution Service decided there would be no charges. No charges, no trial: but John Leslie has already lost his job and without an acquittal he will go around forever branded with the accusations. He undoubtedly feels that his reputation has been destroyed by the widely reported tittle-tattle. None of this helps the cause of women trying to get justice in the courts, because trial by media leaves us uncertain as to what really happened, with the accusers suspected of invention and the accused left ruined anyway.

We are seeing the replacement of due process in the courts by public shaming as a means of social control of abhorrent behaviour. This is a coarse form of justice, which displays a contempt for legality; do we want to live in a culture where people are destroyed even before any charges are made against them, and where the chance of a fair trial is put in jeopardy?

Naming and shaming reached it worst depths when Rebekah Wade, then editor of the *News of the World*, started a campaign in her newspaper in July 2000 to publish the names, photographs and addresses of known paedophiles. Despite warnings from the police that the move would drive offenders underground and would, therefore, undermine the sex offenders' register which enables the police to monitor convicted paedophiles, the paper went ahead and published. Limiting access to the register is an essential element in child protection because it means real tabs can be kept on offenders. All the evidence suggested that publication of such information, far from working in the interests of child safety, actually put children's lives at risk. The *News of the World* described its front page coverage as a 'crusade' inspired by the abduction and murder of a little girl called Sarah Payne and claimed wide public support on the grounds that police monitoring of paedophiles was ineffective.

As a direct result of the campaign, vigilantes mounted attacks on suspected paedophiles. For six nights in a row they marched through an estate in Portsmouth, forcing four innocent families to flee after being wrongly identified as harbouring sex offenders. Violence also flared in Plymouth and a man was pursued by a mob in Whitley, Berkshire. Two men accused of child sex offences committed suicide. A millionaire businessman arrested on child sex charges was found shot dead at his Kent home. A paediatrician who had nothing to do with paedophilia was hounded because his persecutors could not distinguish between the two words. Police also believed that an arson attack on a flat in Norwich was linked to the 'naming and shaming' campaign: burning paper was pushed through a downstairs window as a father and his three children slept. It turned out that the flat had previously been occupied by a paedophile who was then in prison. The communal hysteria meant that thugs used parents' fears as an excuse for lawlessness and the group dynamic drew ordinary law-abiding people into the violence.

The paper ran the campaign for three weeks until it was forced to back off because of the horrifying effect on the lives of innocent people. It was clear that individual police officers were the source of the information published, although police organisations were as concerned as child protection agencies at the damage being caused. The *News of the World* only agreed to refrain if government took action on sex offenders and insisted that what was needed was a 'Sarah's Law', making public the names and addresses of paedophiles by giving parents direct access to the register. The principle is based on 'Megan's Law', which was introduced in the United States after the murder of a seven-year-old girl, Megan Kanka, by a paedophile in 1994. It makes it mandatory for offenders to be placed on a register to which the community has access. The government did agree to look at tougher police powers in dealing with paedophiles, although the risks of such a law are transparent. The success of the register depends on offenders remaining in contact; but once they fear that they may be victimised they are likely to change their names and go into hiding without alerting police.

After Roy Whiting was convicted of Sarah Payne's killing the paper resumed its 'naming and shaming' campaign. This time it stopped short of listing names and addresses but published pictures of men who had failed to enter new addresses on the sex offenders' register so that the public could help locate them. The trouble was that three of the photographs included had not come from any official police source and one of the men was co-operating with the police and not presenting any problem.

The new campaign was praised by the Home Secretary David Blunkett, although he made clear he would not bow to pressure to introduce a Sarah's Law. However, he indicated he was considering the use of new technology, such as satellite tracking and 'reverse tagging' where an alarm sounds if an offender enters particular buildings or off-limit locations. Tags are already used for those on bail in exceptional cases and the practice has even spread into non-criminal settings – it has been suggested that asylum seekers and elderly patients with Alzheimer's could be tagged to stop them wandering off, and over-anxious parents talk of having their children fitted with a microchip to prevent abduction. Before we know it, a Home Secretary will be promoting the huge benefits of every one of us having a tag or a microchip or a barcode tattooed on our little finger.

The killing of two little girls in Soham in August 2002 roused all the same fears and emotions around the country again. Another furore developed over media coverage, with the press publishing such prejudicial details about the suspects that when they were eventually charged the question was raised as to whether they could receive a fair trial.

In the midst of these frightening cases of child abduction and murder people often forget that the majority of children have most to fear at home. Most sexual abuse is by family members and most children who are killed are killed by relatives. The bogey is not out there but within the fold, and that is much more frightening if we pause to think about it. But perhaps that is the very reason for externalising the threat.

The ongoing Operation Ore – the United Kingdom's largest ever hunt for internet users who download child pornography – has added to the feeding frenzy of the tabloid press on paedophile mania. Credit card details used to access material gave police leads on over 7,000 people. Making it an offence is absolutely right because real children are used and abused in the creation of these images and the damage to their lives is rarely healed. In the United States it was found that one-third of those found in possession of indecent images of children were actively abusing children and it was assumed that all those who viewed such images were potential abusers. However, it is also possible that the viewers include people who only want to see that which is forbidden out of some dark curiosity or for reasons that are complex and connected to their own unresolved feelings about abuse, which they will never act upon.

So far approximately 2,000 have been arrested, 50 of whom are police officers, and the others are being investigated, but needless to say it is mainly the celebrities whose names have been leaked to the press. The rock musician, Pete Townshend, knew his name was circulating amongst journalists and came forward to make a statement that he had downloaded child pornography as research for a book he is writing about his own abuse as a child. He has actively supported campaigns against abuse and there was no evidence against him of paedophilia but he was still cautioned and his name has been placed on the sex offenders' register. He knows he will now forever be branded a paedophile by some people, despite the absence of any conviction or evidence that he has ever laid a finger on a child. This is a man who has also given large sums of money to campaigns for battered women, again because of his childhood experiences.

While Operation Ore has been a crucial tool in identifying child pornography users and potential abusers, the police have complained that because of the numbers involved they have had to take large numbers of police officers off child protection units in order to make arrests. Working out the priorities in this area is difficult but, given limited resources, the chief aim must always be to protect children who are at risk here and now. The police only receive credit card numbers and not actual names, and they have to work through the lists with financial institutions, a time-consuming, resource-intensive activity. The sheer volume is presenting serious problems to the police and it will do the same in turn to the courts and the Probation and Prison Service: we are going to see a large bulge of this group going through the system.

In fact one of the most effective ways of closing down the internet porn industry would be to put the onus on the credit card companies to block their cards' usage for these purposes. If Visa and Mastercard refused to provide credit services for pornography they would lose huge amounts of money but the porn industry would shrink overnight. As with all major crime, many legitimate businesses make huge sums of money off the back of dirty trade yet they are never done for living off immoral earnings and nor are they publicly excoriated.

The naming and shaming bug is not confined to newspapers. Essex Police had plans for a new poster scheme where the faces of repeat offenders would be posted throughout Brentwood. Their first offender to be shamed was a 27-year-old man, whose lawyers immediately obtained an injunction to stop the police from putting up the posters. The judicial review was mounted on the basis that the 'name and shame' poster campaign breached his human rights under Article 8 of the European Convention (the right to family life) because of the effect it would have on the man's wife and children, who have done no wrong. The case was not only of interest to the

Essex police but also to eight other forces waiting to launch similar campaigns. It raised fundamental questions not just about the stigmatisation of those named and shamed, but also about the purpose of the judicial process and the role of community opprobrium in deterring anti-social behaviour. There is no doubt that the intention of the poster campaign is to put criminals off re-offending and to persuade others that the indignation of the community will follow any transgression.

Some people, as I have said, do hold the view that there is insufficient shame around in our modern world and ways should be found to reintroduce social stigma. On this basis the Home Secretary is planning to lift reporting restrictions on juveniles who repeat-offend. Previously their anonymity was protected by the courts but the new idea is to shame them into better behaviour. In my experience there is no shortage of shame amongst those who fall foul of the law but it is understandably in short supply where there is social exclusion. Then, having convictions is just another of the ignominies life presents, reinforcing personal difficulties. For young offenders the shame often drives them towards more offending rather than making them stop.

The Essex police say they carried out a risk assessment on the selected offender to make sure he did not have mental health problems just in case he decided to end it all in the face of such humiliation. They say they also evaluated whether their posters could turn vulnerable relatives into targets. But even the police accept there could be a downside if they are not careful. Organisations involved with offenders pointed out that it is unfair to pick off isolated individuals for this treatment and that it amounts to an additional punishment which is not given to every person with criminal convictions. Finding the balance between the rights of a prisoner and her family and the feelings of a community is tough; the editor of the local paper pointed out that the offender in question had shown little consideration for the human rights of his victims. However, the strongest argument was provided by the *News of the World* experience where naming and shaming led to vigilantism. For this reason the courts held that the campaign in its present form did contravene the right of the offender's family to security.

Justice has to be seen to be effective and since few of us sit in the public galleries of courts, the media fulfil the role of informing the public; according to Bob Satchwell of the Society of Editors, court reporting is an important part of local newspapers' work. But, he adds, the nature of communities has changed because families no longer live in close proximity and people may be convicted in courts a long way from home. 'In the past those who were anti-social and convicted risked the disdain of their uncles, aunts and family, who would have all lived nearby and got to hear about the miscreant. But that has all changed. It is now the local paper's job to keep the community informed.' However, because they lack resources the local paper has difficulties covering every court and new regulations make their task harder.

We should remain reluctant to provide anonymity for the parties to a trial or those who are convicted because the public nature of the process is an essential element. It may prevent people lying and making false allegations; it can bring further crimes to light and it means that a person is convicted of wrongdoing under the public gaze. It is also the reason why the acquitted person should have his or her vindication made public too and without any sense that the acquittal is conditional. While the worst excesses of this exercise in shaming are directed at celebrities, many ordinary people are destroyed in the eyes of their local community in the same way. Any decision to grant anonymity until charges are made would have to be afforded to everyone and that would have implications for our desire to have open justice. If the police can arrest and the press cannot report it, it may mean the members of the public who have information about an offence will not come forward because without a name they will not hear about a particular inquiry. However, the abuse of press freedom has reached such a fever pitch that a restraint should be put on the press until there is a charge, or until an application is made to a judge to publish a name for a special reason in the public interest. In Sweden the news media voluntarily refrain from publishing the names of defendants until they have been convicted.

Because of the serious fear of reprisals by vigilantes the courts have recently taken the exceptional step of granting lifelong anonymity and a publicity ban in relation to Robert Thompson and Jon Venables, the young killers of the toddler, James Bulger, and to Mary Bell who was convicted in 1968 of the manslaughter of two small children when she herself was 11. The orders were granted in both cases because the court was satisfied that there was serious risk that the offenders would be killed if their secret identities were ever revealed.

Bell has had to move with her daughter five times because of a string of reprisals. She was hounded from a village in the North-East of England, attacked in a pub and subjected to such hate that when the book *Cries Unheard* was published in 1998 by Gita Sereny, with her co-operation, the police could no longer guarantee her safety. Her partner had been abused, by a woman who had to be restrained from attacking him with a broken bottle, and her teenage daughter faced torment at school, including a parents' demonstration to bar her from lessons. She has had to change her name three times since her release in 1980. Ms Sereny's book documented the terrible, abusive family life which preceded the killings and the court heard about the fragile mental health of Mary Bell now. There was every risk that if the press hounded her to name and shame her or to reveal her whereabouts, she would take her own life: the court was so convinced that it took the rare step of granting the order banning her exposure. The judgment revealed the ugliest side of press intrusion and the lack of trust there is in the tabloid press maintaining declared ethical standards.

The other witch-hunt which has sold newspapers is the onslaught against asylum seekers. The anti-refugee campaigns have been misinformed by hatred, lies and exaggeration which have played on people's fears and prejudices. In 2003, Rebekah Wade, by now at the *Sun*, launched a petition urging the government to stop bogus asylum seekers 'flooding the country' and secured half a million signatures within a week. Toxic rabble-rousing in the tabloids accused refugees of being responsible for terrorism, welfare scrounging, all manner of crime and the spread of diseases such as tuberculosis, Aids and hepatitis. The appeal to the basest of human instincts resulted in such noxious xenophobia that the government became nervous and – as with the paedophiles – simultaneously denounced the worst excesses and sought to appease the tabloids with reactionary policies. Any asylum seeker or recent immigrant who is charged with crime has to meet a wall of prejudice in the courts as a result.

The horrifying killing of DC Oake in Manchester on 14 January 2003 shocked the public. Stephen Oake was engaged with other officers in an anti-terrorist operation searching for the deadly poison ricin at a flat where three suspects were detained. One of them suddenly broke free and attacked officers with a large knife, injuring several officers and inflicting a fatal wound on Constable Oake. This led to papers running vicious stories about two of the arrested men having been in the country because they had applied for asylum. The conclusion to be reached was that asylum seekers were in fact terrorists. The newspapers contained so much speculation that the Attorney-General Lord Goldsmith had to issue a statement expressing concern about some of the coverage and the assumptions that had been made which could prejudice a fair trial. He threatened action under the Contempt of Court Act. But nothing happened. Similarly when Sajid Badat was arrested in Gloucester at the end of November 2003 the Home Secretary immediately linked him to Al-Qaida and said that he 'posed a very real threat to the life and liberty of our country', echoing the kind of statement President George Bush has made about the guilty nature of detainees in the camps at Guantanamo Bay. It is crucial for a Home Secretary to uphold justice, due process and the rule of law; he more than anyone should understand how a fair trial might be put at risk. The matter was referred to the Attorney-General under the Contempt of Court Act and the Lord Chancellor, Lord Falconer, muttered about it being 'wrong to comment in detail on a case in relation to the particular facts at this particular moment' but the complaint blew away.

None of this is new. In the same week as Mr Blunkett was holding forth on the man arrested and ultimately charged with possessing explosives and conspiring with the convicted 'shoe-bomber', Richard Reid, who was sentenced to life in the USA, the Attorney-General was uttering warnings about the coverage of the Soham murder trial. Here the press was exposing the infidelity of the alleged killer, Ian Huntley, and although it is not an issue central to the case, his lawyers were alarmed about the coverage. Again, the warnings came to nothing.

The power of the tabloid press to influence public opinion is considerable and is often abused. Editors of mass market papers are reluctant to become more accountable and always dismiss any debate as interference in a free press and the creation of state control and censorship. The press understandably wants self-regulation but since 41% of complainants to the Press Complaints Commission are not satisfied with their rulings, it would make sense to have an ombudsman to deal with appeals. It is also clear that current editors should be prevented from sitting on the PCC.

From time to time cases are successfully appealed because press coverage has been so damaging that it may have affected the outcome. In 1992 I acted in the Irish case of McCann and others. The convictions were quashed because at the moment when the jury were about to retire to consider their verdicts there was so much hostile debate in the media about terrorists and how they escaped conviction by using the right to silence. This has included interviews on prime time news with the Cabinet Minister, Tom King, who had been Secretary of State for Northern Ireland and who was supposed to be the assassination target in the McCann case. The court of appeal judges watched the newsreels and had to agree that the saturation coverage called the safety of the convictions into question. In fact, there was not an abundance of evidence.

The justice system needs the media but the media should not sit as judge and jury, or blight fair trials by inflammatory reporting. As a result of press behaviour new types of court order are growing up that restrict the basic rights to report criminal cases. In newsrooms up and down the country there is consternation about the number and breadth of restrictions that make it more and more difficult for journalists to fulfil the important task of reporting criminal courts. Not only are names and addresses of the accused restricted but so are photographs and court sketches. The new Courts Act 2003 introduces powers to make costs orders against third parties in criminal proceedings. This could be used to charge the media for the cost of a retrial if something appears in print which puts a fair trial in jeopardy. The trial of Leeds footballers Lee Bowyer and Jonathan Woodgate for an assault upon a young Asian man had to be halted at the eleventh hour on 8 April 2001 because of an interview with the assault victim's father, which appeared while the jury was deliberating. It accused the men of being racist. The concern is that, faced with such financial risk, local papers particularly could be deterred from covering the courts. It is the national tabloids, which make calculated decisions to run stories because of increased circulation, that are undeterred by financial threats. Imprisoning editors would be the only effective remedy.

Another source of alarm in the courts is the payment of large sums of money to witnesses by the press. A number of recent cases have been tainted because the credibility of witnesses has been called into question by the disclosure that they would personally gain from their testimony. In 2002 during the trial of a teacher, Amy Gehring, who was accused of having sex with under-age boys, three prosecution witnesses were offered thousands of pounds for their stories. She was acquitted amidst recriminations about the paper's conduct. The Victoria Beckham kidnap trial collapsed because the key witness had received £10,000. None of this is new. In 1979, Peter Bessell, who was at the heart of the prosecution of the former Liberal leader, Jeremy Thorpe, was offered £25,000 if the politician was cleared but double that if he was convicted. When cases are blown by the press, there are inevitably calls for payments by journalists to be outlawed but while there are aspects of chequebook journalism which are reprehensible it is also a crucial part of the press's investigative work. To formulate any law would be impossible without a serious infringement on the freedom of the press, and our right to know. The Press Complaints Commission code states that payment before someone becomes a witness is not a breach but payment after an arrest has been made is banned.

The only way to stop creeping restrictions is for the media to regulate themselves more effectively. Otherwise, governments may legislate yet more restrictively to restrain court and crime reporting and the freedom to report cases will go the way of so many of our other fundamental rights.

13

BIG BROTHER

WHILE MODERNITY HAS presented us with many problems in the field of crime, it is also providing society with considerable means to solve them. Investigation is being revolutionised by scientific and technological development. Genetics has given us methods of DNA identification which are now so sophisticated that a unique DNA fingerprint can be obtained from a single nucleated blood cell. An offender is shedding DNA in snowdrifts – as indeed we all are everywhere we go – and detection possibilities are being multiplied hugely as a consequence. Old rape and murder cases are being reopened to see if new technology will provide evidence.

The downloading of text messages from mobile phones and messagers, the accessing of e-mails and the entire contents of the hard drives of computers are radically altering the policing of organised crime from fraud and money laundering to the use of child pornography. Placing people at the scenes of crime through mobile phone call locators is now a routine part of criminal cases. The use of SIM cards taken from mobile phones to establish association, contact and the numbers of co-conspirators, as well as telephone contact at a critical time is part of the daily round in crown courts throughout Britain. When a conspiracy exists to commit crime the pattern of calls made between people at crucial times can be critical. If someone has just made a huge deposit of dirty money into a bank it is hardly likely that the first call she makes as she steps into the street is to have a casual conversation with someone she barely knows. If a man has just planted a bomb he does not immediately phone Ireland to find out what won the last race at the Curragh. He may say that was what he was doing but juries piece the jigsaw of connections together and are more likely to conclude he was reporting back. Satellite photographs, satellite pick-up of international phone calls and the recording and translation of content are blowing holes in the activities of drug importers and terrorists who could not survive without their phone fix.

Police surveillance used to be based on the targeting of specific individuals or groups but, although that continues, we are also seeing the emergence of mass surveillance, with systems in a growing number of fields profiling millions of people at a time. The ever-present eye of closed-circuit TV on every building is now a regular source of evidence in criminal cases and it has huge public support. Britain has more CCTV cameras per head of population than any other country in the world. Images on CCTV from Strand shopping mall in Bootle helped lead police to the boys who killed James Bulger. Without CCTV footage police might not have caught the nail bomber David Copeland who targeted the black and gay communities in April 1999. Pictures from cameras were also central in the Hungerford Bridge drowning in 2000: not only did they locate the murderers but they showed their casual demeanour within minutes of mugging two students and throwing them over the bridge into the River Thames to die. The Real IRA men who left a bomb in a taxi outside the BBC headquarters in 2001 were sighted on video when one returned to collect a forgotten jacket from the vehicle. According to a House of Lords report, when private systems are taken into account, there are more than 1.5 million lenses covering public spaces in the UK. The launch of congestion charging in London, using a scheme which logs car numberplates with cameras, will have added to that number.

For over ten years now attempts have been made to harness technology for facial mapping. The idea is to use facial measurement to compare the photograph of a suspect with photographs taken at the scene of a crime, for example CCTV footage. The length of the brow will be measured usually by counting the pixels or dots which make up the computerised photograph. The length of the nose will be measured in the same way and so on. The FBI is now sponsoring a new facial recognition research project in Britain at the Magna Centre in Rotherham, which is part of Sheffield University. It will involve 3,000 British volunteers. The same research would not get off the ground in the US because the American constitution makes people too mindful of their rights and there would be concern about the use of such research and its implications for civil liberties.

Having been engaged in one of the earliest cases where facial mapping evidence was used, I am highly sceptical about the reliability of such evidence. My client, Michael Groce, was the son of a Cherry Groce, who had been shot accidently by police during a stakeout of her home when her son was being sought for a robbery. The incident led to the Brixton riots in 1981. A few years later the police arrested Michael Groce on another allegation of robbery and the evidence was of CCTV footage which the police had forensically compared to newsreel footage of Michael Groce, visiting his mother in hospital after the shooting. The claim was that these were one and the same man. The face of Michael Groce was blown up to the same size as the man on the CCTV film of the robbery and the length of nose and forehead were measured and claimed to be exactly the same.

Being married to a surgeon who is involved daily in the reconstruction of faces, I showed him the compared photographs which were going to be used to persuade a jury to convict Michael Groce. He explained that the slightest infinitesimal movement of the head can lengthen or shorten the length of the nose in a photograph which is why we all have favourite pictures and ones we hate. The same happens with the length of the forehead or jaw. He put me on to a specialist medical physicist called Alf Linney, who works with surgeons, helping them through the use of measurement to plan facial reconstruction operations. Alf was just as unconvinced about the reliability of the methodology as my husband and set to work to show the fallacy of the comparison. Another scientist, Joseph Schwartz, was able to show that without statistical support the results were meaningless anyway. Each photograph may show a black man with a nose measuring twenty pixels in length but 20% of the population may have noses that length.

By the time Dr Linney gave evidence he was able to produce a photograph of another black man who also resembled the robber and whose facial measurements were exactly the same. It was Steve Biko, the South African freedom fighter who had died many years before after being beaten-up in a South African police station by the police. The jury had seen enough to know that the evidence was thoroughly unreliable and acquitted Michael Groce. In March 2003 the Court of Appeal warned about the risks of miscarriages of justice, saying that there was currently little or no scientific basis for these comparisons, but no doubt efforts will continue to be made to get this evidence before the courts.

There are now machines which can test banknotes for the presence of drugs, and sniffer machines which can sense the presence of explosives. A whole range of technologies formerly only used by the military or intelligence community are now becoming available to police. We have computer identification through facial mapping, iris identification, voice identification from telephones – all of which could take us straight to culprits. We have infrared surveillance so that the presence of persons in buildings or hiding in container lorries is established from outside, and tiny 'up and under' magnetic tracking devices which when popped on to a car disclose its every move.

Convergence is leading to the elimination of technological barriers so that different systems can mutually exchange and process different forms of data. Through data-sharing and data-matching between government databases, through access to our telephone bills, shopping loyalty cards and other accounts, we can all be kept under covert surveillance.

All these techniques can now be used in evidence-collecting for cases that appear in court, but we have to find effective methods for receiving it into evidence that do not mean intelligence agents giving evidence from behind screens like the Wizard of Oz. Already the Director of Public Prosecutions has expressed a willingness to disclose and use evidence in telephone taps in court. Currently, the police claim public interest immunity and do not disclose how they come by certain information or they keep the information from taps purely as intelligence in the background. Disclosure of telephone taps would require a change in the law. If covert evidence-gathering is going to move into the mainstream, police and intelligence services must be willing to have their methods made public and scrutinised. There is always a tension here because criminals try to find ways to subvert and outfox the police once they know more about policing methods. Yet it is amazing just how careless even the most sophisticated criminals are. They need to make phone calls, they need to touch items, they need to travel and take risks. If they were risk averse they would not be offending. In fact, many of them have the characteristics of those who are successful in business. At the moment old-fashioned fingerprinting – discovered in 1900 – is still the most successful method of securing convictions; wearing gloves would sort the problem but it is just so damn difficult to do the fiddly stuff with them on!

Improved investigation will only come about if the police and supporting science and technology officers are trained appropriately. There is currently a serious skills shortage across the board within the police. If police are to be supplied with palm pilot technology (one plan being put forward now) so that they can record every stop and search, with the information instantly feeding back to the station, then officers right down to the lowest level are going to require effective technology training. This is where a real difference could be made in cracking crime.

However, along with excitement about the ways in which technology can be harnessed to tackle crime are the questions about limits. How willing are we to surrender personal privacy to increase our security? The Regulatory Powers Act 2001 and the Electronic Communications Act give extensive powers of interception of e-mails and other telecommunications to government.

After 11 September it became clear that people were prepared to make significant concessions. ICM research for the *Guardian* in September 2002 indicated that 72% of people would sacrifice some privacy to fight terrorism and crime. When people worry about the security of their personal information on the internet and e-mail, their real concern is about the risk of someone using their financial information dishonestly. Their fears are not irrational. Plastic card fraud is booming in Britain – it has grown by 50% in the last two years, to £430 million. As well as scams like copying card details when purchases are made off- or online, stealing cards in the post or registering charges twice for items, the most common fraud involves hacking into the computers of companies which process retailers' payments. In 2003 a hacker recently gained access to the credit card details of eight million Mastercard, Visa and American Express card holders in the United States, sparking fears of fraud on a massive scale.

The problem of insecure systems is not confined to the private sector. Fifty-eight per cent of those polled by ICM did not believe the government could be trusted to keep our personal information secure. This is particularly alarming when according to the civil liberties' organisation, Liberty, 65% of records on the Police National Computer are inaccurate. Liberty has documented cases of people failing security checks because their names and addresses are similar to those of convicted criminals.

A few years ago President Clinton visited Birmingham for a G7 Summit. He took a photo opportunity, drinking some real ale in a local pub. After the President left, one of his security men paid for the beer, adding the price of the glass from which the President had been drinking, and then carefully slid the item into a holdall before his own departure. Ever the criminal lawyer, this snatch of information in a newspaper induced some interesting speculation on my part. The Monica allegations were still raw, and murky accounts of semen stains on a blue dress had surfaced. Perhaps the President's cohort was protecting his interests. DNA on the rim of a glass had figured in one of my own cases. Alternatively, perhaps the security agent's secretion of the glass was for a sinister purpose, unknown to the President – or to protect him against one. Hillary Clinton has always maintained that her husband was the victim of a concerted right-wing attack, with powerful forces at work to ruin him: perhaps this is an indicator of the fear even a President entertains that his DNA in the wrong hands could be used unfairly against him.

Imagine the security agent had not collected the glass but the publican sent the President's saliva off for analysis and sold the genetic information to a tabloid newspaper or to those with access to the famous blue dress. Would the law provide any sanction? The short answer is that nothing currently on the statute book is adequate.

The Human Genetics Commission of the United Kingdom, which I chair, has recommended that the government consider introducing a criminal offence with strong penalties to deter the deceitful and surreptitious collection of genetic information and the use of it without proper consents or legal permission. This would supplement current laws, providing further deterrence and symbolic condemnation of genetic trophy hunting. It would also protect young children better from inappropriate paternity testing, which can occur without adults' consent or court-ordered procedures.

At the moment an estranged husband could have a child tested on an access visit without any consents, or a mother-in-law, who suspects the truth of her grandchild's paternity, could surreptitiously send hair samples for testing. The private testing services which already exist in the UK operate to a code which requires appropriate consents but via the internet it is possible to have such testing done in other parts of the world where no such regulation applies. The proper way for an estranged father to establish paternity is to do so through a solicitor and, if necessary, through a court order. The devastation wreaked on children and other family members by revelations made without proper preparation, support and counselling can be long-lasting. Yet after the Human Genetics Commission announced in the press its recommendation to outlaw surreptitious testing without consents, I received poison pen letters, all from men who think the feminist lobby is depriving them of their rights. In fact the concern of the Commission was with the rights of the child.

It is vital that the wider implications of genetic testing are understood before people consent to a test. Genetic testing can reveal unexpected information and clinicians should recognise that people have an entitlement *not* to know as well as to know. Everyone involved, at all levels, needs to understand the requirements of medical confidentiality, across the entire medical and biomedical research field. Adherence to confidentiality should become an essential part of employment contracts and of membership of relevant professional bodies. This will probably have to be backed by sanctions and possibly by the creation of the broader offence of breach of medical confidence.

It is going to be impossible to create special protocols for the handling of genetic information by medical practitioners because it is part and parcel of the whole patient profile and soon, with the wide use of information storage technologies, test results will be interwoven into the fabric of our medical records in our GP's surgery and at hospitals we attend. The potentially sensitive nature of this information underlines the importance of protecting the confidentiality of patient medical information in general.

A serious concern is that if solid walls do not remain around this medical information people will not have themselves tested through the orthodox channels of GPs and hospitals but will use the internet and over the counter services which they assume will provide anonymity. This will not be in the interest of the overall healthcare of the individual patient.

Advances in genetics raise stark questions about the erosion of public trust when civil liberties are encroached upon, and about the cost of such erosion to society. *Inside Information*, the Human Genetics Commission's report on privacy, sets out a concept of genetic solidarity and altruism. Sharing our genetic information can in some circumstances give opportunities for us to help other people and for other people to help us. It is about reciprocity. We have a common interest in the benefits that medically based genetic research can bring.

Rather like blood donation, the gift has a return benefit. But people want to have confidence that their liberties will be protected if they contribute to the common good and participate in the creation of a medical databank, like the Biobank currently being created by the government in partnership with Wellcome Foundation for epidemiological research on genetics. Society should in turn provide some guarantees. Not only should there be independent supervision of such databanks but it should be illegal to use genetic research databases for any purposes other than medical research. This restriction is important in view of the case law on medical confidentiality. In the case of *W.* v. *Edgell*, the inmate of a secure hospital was applying for release and his solicitors sought a psychiatric report from the good Dr Edgell to support the application. The doctor was so convinced that the applicant was as mad as a hatter and likely to burn down Liverpool if given his liberty, he promptly released his report on W. to the tribunal without the consent of the patient. The High Court decided that the public interest outweighed Mr W.'s privacy. In another case, *Regina* v. *Kelly*, the Scottish High Court held that the Scottish Crown could compel pathologists to testify about an inmate's HIV status, despite the fact that the information was collected for a public health purpose and the inmate was given an assurance of confidentiality. The blood samples taken for HIV testing were reversibly anonymised, which meant that a code number was given to the inmate so that his name was secret and he was not readily identified but the Crown was able to de-encrypt the results. (The Cambridge professor Ross Anderson is very clear that there is no such thing as an unbreachable information security system. Anything can be de-encrypted.)

In the Kelly case, the judge rejected the arguments of unfairness, holding that the 'public interest is quite clear . . . serious crime should be effectively investigated and prosecuted'. Neither case went up to the Court of Appeal so at the moment, medical researchers cannot confidently guarantee that in no circumstances whatsoever would they disclose the identity of Biobank participants; all they can say is that applications for access will be strongly resisted through the courts. Criminal investigation warrants could override them and, given the current trend to privilege 'law and order' issues over civil liberties, it is likely that government would support the right to breach the walls of anonymity. The government White Paper has trailed this possibility.

The government's approach to privacy has been exposed already in the field of genetics by the introduction of new legislation, the Criminal Justice and Police Act 2001, followed by the Criminal Justice Act 2003, without adequate parliamentary discussion or public debate. These Acts allow the authorities to take DNA from everyone who is arrested even if they are not charged. Here in the UK, the policing DNA Database is kept by the Forensic Science Services, under the auspices of the Home Office. DNA collecting is done by simply swabbing the inside of the cheek with a cotton pad.

Advances in genetic science are providing a powerful and effective tool in crime investigation. DNA testing is the most important advance in forensic science in our generation. DNA samples found at the scene of the crime can be highly probative evidence in determining the identity of an offender. The DNA at the scene can take many forms. It may be semen on the clothing of a victim, a speck of blood on a door handle, saliva on a cigarette, a hair follicle, flakes of dry skin or skin cells from a fingerprint. A bar code is created from this DNA sample, which can be compared with the bar code created from the DNA sample of a suspect, or a trawl of the database can take place and comparisons may throw up a match. The bar code is made from what are called non-coding sequences, which means they give no information about the health, propensities or appearance of the individual. Sometimes it is referred to as 'junk DNA'.

Occasionally the methodology used for comparison is questionable or the technician making the comparison can be mistaken, but in most cases a positive comparison is fairly conclusive evidence. Nevertheless, it should be recognised that the presence of some DNA at a scene may not prove an accused guilty. For example, in most rape cases accused men do not deny their presence or the fact of intercourse so DNA is rarely controversial in such cases because the issue is almost invariably one of consent. A person's DNA may be present at a scene but it is not possible to say when it was deposited, and if a suspect has been there on any occasion other than at the time of the offence the mere presence of DNA will not be conclusive proof.

The DNA bar codes from suspects' samples are kept on a computer and the samples from which they are culled are kept in a databank. Obviously the samples from scenes of crimes should be kept for ever but there is no good reason why suspects' samples are kept. The Home Office claims that the retained samples allow the authorities to conduct further tests should the computer fail or if the bar code is faulty but that could also be done by having back-up or by just going to the suspect for another sample. The real concern is that the sample could be subject to further tests for research or other more controversial purposes.

The DNA will remain in the database for ever, even if the person is acquitted of any crime. If your brother is on the database, in many respects you too are on the database as you probably share a huge percentage of his DNA. Anyone who volunteers a sample in an intelligence trawl for the purposes of elimination – for example everyone in a block of flats – will be asked to sign a consent form and their DNA will also remain in the possession of the state. This includes the husband of a rape victim, who gives his sample to assist in isolating the attacker's DNA. A person who is arrested on a malicious allegation which is subsequently dropped because it is shown to be false will remain on the database. The Attorney-General agreed that even a victim's DNA would remain there if they consented at the time of the investigation. Not surprisingly there are serious concerns as to whether any such agreement given in the heat of an investigation could constitute informed consent. Members of the public know that to refuse to consent to a voluntary sample awakens suspicions of involvement. Yet no mechanism exists to apply for removal of your sample after a period of time.

The question which immediately follows is: Why not? to which the answer is 'After proper debate and safeguards, maybe yes.' Perhaps we should consider a national DNA database, which is what the police want. But only if the public consent. If people give consent for one purpose, their consent should not be abused. Professor Peter Taylor Gooby of Kent University (Social Policy) at Canterbury and many other analysts point out, though, that DNA matching is probabilistic rather than positive. The larger the numbers on a database the greater the risk of a misleading match.

*

So questions are increasingly arising. Can we trust the security of databanks and databases in our high-tech world? Who can access our genetic information and who are the gatekeepers? Already it is being suggested that there are genes for different types of aberrant behaviour, such as aggression. There can be little doubt that investigators of crime would see the potential of a national databank. If a DNA sample at the scene of a crime shows the offender carries the gene for a rare disease could there be a trawl of the medical records or the Biobank or the Forensic Science Services DNA samples bank for those with genetic diseases? Recent health legislation allows the Secretary of State to give permission for accessing medical records if it is in the public interest as he sees it (section 60 Health and Social Care Act 2001). This means that the procedures are already in place to allow police investigating crime to apply to a politician so that computerised medical records can be trawled. Given the courts' precedents that the investigation of crime trumps privacy it looks as though use of medical and research databanks may not be off limits, unless the government recognises the impact of such incursions on the public trust.

Of course, ministers dismiss any Big Brother ambitions. They also insist, like Police Chief Scarpia in the opera *Tosca*, that the innocent have nothing to fear. Why should we be alarmed that police or other investigators might have sight of our private records if we are decent law-abiding folk?

Of course one of the fears is that once there is access, even for authorised police purposes, there is the risk of the leaching of information to other interested parties for uses that we ourselves do not as yet understand. If the police sell information to tabloid newspapers (as we know they do), they will be just as likely to do so to insurance companies and employers.

As the welfare state is being dismantled most of us will be required to make greater provision for ourselves in old age through insurance. Our genetic code is a powerful predictor of our future health. For this reason the insurance industry is very keen to know whether we are at risk of living long but very dependent lives. The interest is less in when we might die than in whether we might live to our dotage in need of expensive support and care. Insurers hope that as genetic science advances they will be able to make use of the information in assessing premiums. So people should be aware of potential uses of DNA not yet publicly discussed and the likely interest of commercial enterprises in our history and our future. We should also be conscious of the implications for those who will not be accepted for affordable insurance.

Another recognised fear is related to wrongful convictions – of which we have our own all too recent experiences. People are frightened of being wrongly convicted as a result of cross-contamination or even an error in the testing process, and they are petrified of being set up for a crime they did not commit. Unfortunately as this science becomes demystified and police come to understand how readily they can obtain DNA it is likely that this will provide an opportunity for corrupt practice. The possibilities of planting evidence and other abuses will be all too apparent to rogue police and other agents of the state.

Underlying our new hoarding of DNA seems to be the cynical belief that those who are suspected of a crime are probably guilty, even if acquitted, and likely to be involved in further offending. In addition, the new provisions increase the police bank considerably. The Home Office aim is to hold the profile of nearly one in every 15 people in Britain. Already lawyers involved with the black community fear that ethnic minorities will be disproportionately affected by this method of enlarging the DNA database. Huge numbers of people picked up by the police in their youth but acquitted of any crime will remain on the database for life. Even children are being swabbed.

This takes Britain to the top of the illiberal league table: nowhere else in the free world is this happening. Canada and France have already legislated to prevent the retention of samples from persons acquitted of crime and in both jurisdictions samples of juvenile offenders will be destroyed once young people reach adulthood if they remain crime-free for a set period of time. The FBI in the United States has expressed jealous amazement that this legislation is in force in Britain, sure that the American public would find such inroads into civil liberties wholly unacceptable despite the heat of their feelings about crime control.

Sir Alec Jeffreys, the British professor who invented DNA fingerprinting in 1985, was forthright in his criticism of the changes in a recent article in *New Scientist* magazine. In his view it is illiberal and unjust to create a bank by stealth: it would be fairer to take the DNA profiles of every Briton rather than mingle the fingerprints of the guilty with those of the innocent.

Other geneticists are also aghast, amazed that the public has seemed to be so supine in the face of such invasion of privacy. Professor Robert Williamson and his colleague Rony Duncan, geneticists at the Murdoch Children's Research Institute in Melbourne, Australia, also advocate either retaining tests of 'only the convicted or everyone' in the interests of fairness. They argue this on the basis that at least the convicted have done something wrong; if the innocent are to be included, no distinctions should be made and we should all be involved. In reality the public have had little opportunity to absorb the implications of this policy change, as there has been hardly a murmur of public debate. The impoverishment of public discourse, the political spin, the media's time imperatives mean the implications of these developments go almost unnoticed. A mere illusion of open democracy is created. Barely any discussion took place about DNA retention in the Commons and despite our best efforts in the Lords, the clauses rattled through.

In a recent case, the Court of Appeal had to balance individual privacy and the benefits of retaining unconvicted persons' DNA samples in the fight against crime. According to the Lord Chief Justice, Lord Woolf, in a Royal Academy lecture, particular attention was paid to the evidence on behalf of the police, because the court felt the police were in a better position than it to assess the scale of the contribution which the samples could make to the prevention of crime.

As the science develops, the police are bound to want to test samples at the scene to produce a profile of the suspect —a tall, red-haired male, carrier of Tay-Sachs disease, therefore probably Jewish (Tay-Sachs is a comparatively rare disease most prevalent amongst Ashkenazi Jews) who may have a history of mental illness because he is a carrier of a behavioural gene for schizophrenia. The implications for the sense of insecurity among citizens and the potential for authoritarian, invasive conduct by arms of the state is enormous.

Already in New Zealand in a murder investigation, the courts have allowed police access to all the hospital-stored Guthrie tests, which are tiny blood pricks taken from the heel of newborn babies for medical reasons. The access enabled the identification of the killer and it showed how a national database could work. Successfully. I suspect it has not yet been done here only because the police have not thought of it.

It is not surprising that eminent geneticists like Jeffreys and

Williamson express concern about the potential abuses of a forensic databank full of our samples. They know that genetic tests have become extremely sensitive in the last ten years. Gene amplification techniques now allow a unique DNA fingerprint from just a single nucleated blood cell. While they argue that in the interests of equity a bar code of all citizens should be made at birth, they also insist upon very real safeguards. The key safeguard is that once the bar code is made from non-coding sequences, the sample is immediately destroyed. So, there should be no databank of samples taken from potential suspects. The only samples which should be kept are those from the scene of the crime which should be retained for ever in case of miscarriages of justice. Secondly, the database of DNA data must be held independently of police.

The government expresses complete confidence in the Forensic Science Services, as do I. They do their best to act to the highest standards. However, no one knows what the future holds. Already there are plans to privatise the Forensic Science Services and the staff are concerned that their high quality service, which is respected throughout the world, is about to be wrecked. As Nick Cohen, who is a relentless campaigning journalist on civil liberties, pointed out in the *Observer* on 30 November 2003 there are worries that, in the interest of profit, scientists will be expected to cut their investigative cloth very differently and public interest may move down the priority ladder. Investment companies and other potential owners might 'milk their new asset dry'. Cohen added: 'On the big murders – the Sohams of the future – no expense will be spared. But on the ordinary run of rapes, assaults, woundings and burglaries no one I spoke to believed that the same care will be taken in the cost-conscious future.' The Human Genetics Commission has recommended that in order to increase and maintain public confidence there should be an independent body, which would include lay members, to oversee the way the National DNA Database works.

It is crucial that a climate of suspicion does not develop which creates reservations amongst citizens about voluntarily submitting to DNA intelligence screens when a serious crime has taken place. If fears are not allayed, the public is also less likely to participate in important medical research projects like Biobank.

Interestingly, in debate the former Attorney-General the late Lord (Gareth) Williams asserted that he would willingly give a sample to assist the police if a child in his village was the victim of a crime – as would most decent citizens if they were sure that there was no cost to their doing so. However, the Attorney resisted my inquiry as to whether all cabinet ministers would start the ball rolling by putting their DNA on the database. It is worth noting that the police themselves have shown marked reluctance to be included for elimination purposes in case the information might be used in paternity suits, or by the Child Support Agency or in disciplinary proceedings.

The Home Office has agreed to review the processes for the holding and storage of genetic material for criminal investigations but we have as yet to see how effective this will be.

Currently only 1.5% of crime is being detected by DNA. This is because the police do not have the resources at the moment to search every crime scene for DNA. They have to make careful judgements to justify the outlay. Every criminal justice sample costs £40. Looking for DNA would be inappropriate in a whole range of crime but police say they could immediately get the use of DNA up to 5% if they were given the money and staffing, and that percentage would increase steadily once the technology is developed more. It could soon be possible to bring a mini-lab and computer to the scene of a crime so that a bar code is created immediately from swabs and identification of a suspect can be even swifter. Given the powerful evidential value of DNA even an increase of 5% in crime clear-up would be highly significant, but currently the funding is being poured into policy initiatives which will have higher profile and more visible results, like the clearing up of old cases where the files were almost closed.

The Metropolitan Police is currently conducting a 'cold cases' review of 1,500 unsolved stranger rape cases dating back to 1987 where DNA samples can now be retrieved from clothes and other crime scene material. Already Scotland Yard has recovered profiles in eight out of ten unsolved cases so it looks as though the potential for clearing up cases is huge, especially important when the conviction rate in rape has fallen to a record low of 5.8%. Particularly reassuring is the police belief that it will help them track down a number of serial rapists. They now believe they have a lead on a set of between four and nine linked rapes in north Tyneside dating back to the mid-1980s. A man who raped a French au pair in church grounds in 1989 was also jailed for eight years in August 2003 as a result of the trawl.

The paradox is that while individuals want the police to have the power to deal with crime, they – rightly – fear encroachment not just by central government but by other wielders of power. As the state seeks to shrink, power slides into invisible spaces. It is not only government and representatives of the state who might make use of our genetic information. A sample of dental floss stolen for paternity testing by Kirk Kerkorian, the legendary corporate raider, from the rubbish bin of Steve Bing, the Hollywood producer, became the subject of a civil lawsuit for DNA theft. The practice of taking samples for genetic testing without consent is growing. In that case the thief was a private detective and many might feel the ends justified the means, but they rarely do. In another US case, Burlington North and Santa Fe railway company agreed to pay compensation to 36 employees over tests done without their permission to see whether they were genetically disposed to carpal tunnel syndrome, which produces repetitive strain injuries. A recent British case exposed how an insurance company had unlawfully entered a woman's home and secreted a camera to secure evidence showing that she was exaggerating her disability. While the judge criticised the behaviour, the evidence was admitted. If insurance companies are prepared to burgle and employers are prepared to obtain by deception, we may be right to worry about the security of our DNA.

This is why legislation to outlaw the theft and use of DNA without proper consents is so vital. The government has experienced a backlash against genetically modified foods and this has sensitised it to the need to meet public concerns in the field of science. The cynical might say that there is also concern not to undermine research in a field where Britain is at the cutting edge and significant financial interests are at stake. Whatever the thinking, legislation of the kind the Human Genetics Commission has recommended is now being promised.

The government's sensitivity to other areas of public alarm is less acute. Statutory powers to snoop on telephone and e-mail records are to be handed to more than 500 organisations. Local councils, the Royal Mail and a raft of government departments will be able to demand access to sensitive information. Pressure on the Home Secretary (including, we are told, from his son) made him revise the plans as originally drafted but despite the introduction of safeguards the powers mean a huge invasion of privacy. Electronic security experts say that the potential for abuse is considerable, and that criminals will be able to avoid detection by simply scrambling or encoding messages while ordinary citizens will be the ones to suffer.

The more extensively officialdom has access to what is ours, the more likely it is that commercial and other interests will also become beneficiaries. A company called Experian is the biggest credit-checking organisation in the world. It is paid by 300 corporate clients as well as the police, government departments and agencies to dig out information on all of us. According to Katherine Viner (the *Guardian*, 13 August 2003), 40 million people in Britain are on file. That is almost everyone over 18. Online shopping, loyalty card applications, store cards, standing order forms and virtually every financial transaction is recorded somewhere and traceable by Experian.

The keeping of information on citizens may be invidious but even more outrageous is that the information is often wrong; yet no avenues exist to correct it. In addition, the information kept on police files is often of suspect value. It is rare that one can gain some insight into police practice but in 1979 I was one of the counsel in the so-called 'Persons Unknown' Anarchist trial at the Old Bailey. It became known that the prosecution had vetted the jury and the defence demanded access to the material on the 93 potential jurors on the basis that there might be reasons why the defence too might object to a juror. (This was in the days when each defendant could object to a number of jurors; a right which has been removed.) The 'intelligence' on file was extraordinary. One person had an address 'believed to be a squat'. Another had once made a complaint against the police, which had later been withdrawn. One potential juror was listed as associating with a 'criminal': judging by other entries, this did not mean someone with an actual criminal record. Another had a son who once spent six months in a detention centre. The rumour, innuendo and malign inferences from material relating to persons other than the individual in question raised serious concern about the quality of the records. Yet in the Soham case, the accused, Ian Huntley, had been through a police vetting procedure for his job as a school caretaker which failed to disclose that he had nine allegations against him of rape, indecency and sex with under-age girls in less than four years. This was because Humberside police had failed to record them on the central police computer (an indication of police attitudes to sexual allegations).

Information-gathering is not confined to one's country of origin. European airlines flying to America have been compelled to give the US government free access to all the details they hold on every one of their passengers. Not only does that include names, addresses, nationality, passport numbers, credit card details and addresses while in America but other information included on airline databases, such as medical information, disabilities, special meals ordered, price paid, onward flights, past itineraries, banking details, names of persons to be contacted in emergencies. All will be held on file and consolidated with information from other sources.

To top everything the Home Secretary and the Prime Minister in the face of opposition from other Cabinet Ministers including Gordon Brown and Patricia Hewitt have persisted in their scheme to introduce identity cards. Jack Straw, who had his own scheme for identity cards when Home Secretary had 'detoxed' after leaving the Home Office (there is definitely some contaminant in the drinking water there) and rediscovered his libertarian instincts. He too was against the cards and expressed concerns about a public backlash if a flawed scheme went ahead. But going ahead it is.

The Home Office has embarked on a six month trial of new high-tech passports to 'lay the foundations for a compulsory identity card scheme' (*Guardian*, 3 December 2003). The pilot scheme will involve 10,000 volunteers receiving personalised smartcards containing biometric information – initially a digital image of their faces based on a passport photograph. The trial will be run by Mori, the pollsters, and the Passport Office. The Government has now admitted that this is a preparation for a compulsory national identity card scheme after lots of initial bluster about voluntariness.

People are confused about what ID cards are to be used for. As with the reasons given for military intervention in the run-up to the Iraq war, government presents a different rationale every time it is questioned. We only need to ask our European neighbours, whose lives would stop without them. In an article in the *Independent* in February 2003 the television producer, Nicholas Jones, who now lives in Spain described how the card there is issued at age 14. It carries personal details and an encrypted fingerprint but its key feature is its unique number, which it shares with the holder's passport, driving licence and tax files. It is clearly this element of such a card that excites Whitehall. Initially the Spanish card's purpose was to simplify dealings with the state or the state's dealings with you. Wherever there was some interaction with the government or the police, the card had to be shown. Now there is 'function creep' and it is business that has increased the importance of the identity card. Spaniards need them to open bank accounts: they are essential for any credit card purchase. It is impossible to buy a mobile phone without one or to check into a hotel. The hotel passes its number straight to the police.

According to Nicholas Jones, employers love identity cards. The number is on your payslip for tax purposes. This links to bank records. Even the most harmless of activities requires the number, like entering your child for a nursery or renting a flat. Tracking your every move is as easy as pie.

The Home Secretary believes identity cards will cut welfare and NHS abuse, crime, illegal working and immigration. In Spain they laugh at the idea that a card stops crime because they know that there is a huge black market in false identity cards. As Shami Chakrabarti, the director of Liberty has pointed out, 'To obtain a biometric identity card one must first prove identity using existing documentation, like birth certificates, which can be stolen. Criminals will obtain a passport with a false name but a genuine iris scan. Rather than tackle identity fraud this scheme will help to legitimise it.'

Gulling the public into believing that ID cards prevent benefit fraud is disingenuous since most benefit frauds are not about identity but claiming for more than the entitlement or being dishonest about circumstances. The question of illegal immigration is even more complex because of the variety of different immigration statuses held by non-nationals, from asylum-seekers, visitors, work permit holders, etc. For the scheme to work it would involve holding the often-changing immigration status of every person in the UK on a register and assiduously updating it.

And then of course there is the additional complex question of who is entitled to what benefits depending on their immigration status: as with benefit frauds the process of checking eligibility for a service is probably even more complex than establishing identity in many cases. The other point of whether a scheme will achieve its purpose is the issue of compulsion. As a means of detecting crime or illegal immigration, the level of checking would necessarily be in direct proportion to its effectiveness. As well as being compulsory in terms of participation there would be an obligation to produce. This is my objection. I would be prepared to have additional biometric information included in my passport in order to police our borders more effectively but I do not want there to be an internal passport, a licence to live.

However, the government argument is that the new biometric technology will make forgery very difficult. A tiny microchip containing highly personalised information would make a card unique to its owner and undoubtedly it would be harder to forge but organised criminals can always rise to the challenge.

The identity card is the ultimate bureaucratic tool that creates a highly monitored society. As Nicholas Jones points out, 'continental experience shows that identity cards would dramatically change life in Britain. It also reveals why Whitehall really wants them. The daily logging of their unique card numbers will create audit trails that lead to the Blairite dream of joined-up government!'

The government wins support for the entitlement card on the back of asylum scares, maintaining that it stops illegal working, but there is already a legal requirement on employers, introduced by Michael Howard, the previous Conservative Home Secretary, to ensure that people have an insurance number. Employers who want to pay below the minimum wage will be just as uninterested in identity cards.

It is anticipated that a card would record name, address, date of birth, employment, sex, photo, numbers for national insurance, driving licence and passport. It would also carry an iris scan or electronic fingerprint. And there is conjecture that in the fullness of time our genetic profile could also be included.

Lots of people feel ID cards would make life *so* much simpler, since we already have to show lots of documents for financial dealings, and since our lives can probably be pieced together already from all our electronic dealings. However, an identity card would be the ultimate tracking device. (The Chinese are just introducing a new hi-tech card, which is causing alarm to human rights groups because of the impact on dissidents.) The daily logging could lead to the Orwellian nightmare of losing your right to live a life free of intrusion. The Home Office is also the ministry which has had the most comprehensive fiascos in its attempts to introduce new technology into its operations. One of the reasons immigration ran out of control was because of the disastrous mess with its computer system. The attempts to vet schoolteachers for paedophile offences was so slow, it looked as though the school term would not start in September 2002. The prospect of losing your all-purpose card or being barred from public services or healthcare because of high 'false reject' rates when the card is checked against the central computer raises alarm, as does the idea of getting a replacement from the Home Office by return of post.

A report on Britain's proposals for ID cards was compiled by a committee of the Canadian parliament in October 2003 and it said: 'The British entitlement card would not be meant to address security issues such as terrorism, and those who briefed the committee [Entitlement Card Unit representatives from the Home Office] made it quite clear it would not be useful in this regard.' The unit also expressed concerns about the security and integrity of the card because the 'foundation documents' needed to apply for the card such as birth certificates are easy to reproduce. It was also pointed out that a scheme would cost well in excess of the original estimate of £3.1 billion. Money which many of us feel would be better spent elsewhere in the prevention of crime.

A major concern for me is that the card could have alarming consequences for the black and other minority communities who are already subjected to more frequent police intervention than any other citizens. Lawyers in France are clear that 'les marginaux' are harassed to produce the card and it affects the culture of policing negatively. There are likely to be huge problems in ID databases over accuracy, data sharing, statutory overrides of data-protection principles and lack of audit trails.

Many changes to the law take place without the proper scrutiny of parliament because of the rushed way that huge, complex bills are propelled through the House; the public could be forgiven for thinking that these methods are adopted to avoid real public debate. The recent Criminal Justice Bill saw extraordinary numbers of highly significant government amendments being introduced in the Commons at the last minute. Even staff at the Criminal Records Bureau became alarmed that a Home Office amendment tabled within days of Commons votes amended primary legislation to allow, for the first time, the private sector to access criminal information held on the police national computer. Not only will this amendment pave the way for the wholesale privatisation of the Bureau's work but it also raises several data protection and national security issues. It is the stealth used in introducing such changes that makes people understandably distrustful.

The computer chip and other technological advances are

radically reshaping our lives. One way of restricting the state's ability to pry is to create an independent body to oversee developments; too high a level of intrusion is not justified in the name of better governance.

14

THE GREAT PRISON SCANDAL

ON A SPECIAL *Newsnight* programme in February 2003, the Prime Minister was challenged by an invited audience about crime. He earnestly explained that his government had overseen more people being sent to jail than ever before, as though it was something in which we should take pride.

Britain is now the prison capital of Western Europe, with an average incarceration rate of 139 for every 100,000 of population in England and Wales and 127 in Scotland. We even outstrip the jailing rate of Colonel Gaddafi. Our courts are far more punitive than those in Canada or Australia and beat those of all our closest neighbours, including courts in France (which jails 93 for every 100,000), Germany (98) and Spain (133). Portugal used to take the prize but Britain is now in the lead. Of course, Russia, China and the United States knock us into a cocked hat but that should give us no comfort. The rapid growth in Britain's prison population – from 42,000 in 1991 to 74,023 in October 2003 – is due to the increasing use of custody by the courts. The reason for the explosion in the jail population is that judges and magistrates are sending more people to prison and sending them for longer. Yet this is happening while, apart from robbery and the recent surge in gun offences, crime is going down.

As Paul Cavadino, Director of Nacro, the offender rehabilitation organisation, points out: 'If ministers want to cut inmate numbers they need to mount a sustained campaign to persuade sentencers to do just that. Roy Jenkins and Willie Whitelaw did it and it worked.' However, a serious commitment is necessary for such a campaign and at the moment the government is too worried about how it will play in Bognor.

When the Lord Chief Justice's sentencing guidelines on burglary were misrepresented in the media as going soft on burglars, rather than as an effort to distinguish between different kinds of burglary and different kinds of burglar, Downing Street and the Home Secretary immediately distanced themselves rather than seeking to support our leading judge in his efforts to pull back the rush to imprison. All of us who have experienced burglary know how violating the experience is, but a break-in to your home while you are sleeping is very different from the burglary of an office. Making careful distinctions, carefully calibrating appropriate sentences, is at the heart of good judgments. A burglary by a boy with a drug problem who has no previous convictions will always be better dealt with by a community programme and restorative justice initiatives. At the same time a burglary by a practised thief should draw down prison. That was all that Lord Woolf was emphasising to magistrates and judges. Once someone has a prison record their employability is deeply affected. But the auction between the main political parties on who will be tougher on crime means that politicians run a mile from candid debate.

The upturn in imprisonment can be directly traced back to the period when Michael Howard, the leader of the Conservative party, was Home Secretary, with his insistence in 1992 that 'prison works'. His bellicose, tub-thumping demand that offenders be jailed by the courts certainly worked. Despite the evidence that reconviction rates are little different amongst those who are imprisoned than those who receive community sentences, an incredible shift took place in the minds of sentencers. In 1992, 45% of all adults convicted in the crown courts went to prison. By 2001, 64% were being jailed. Home Office figures show that 56% of those imprisoned re-offend within two years as against 44% who are given community penalties. Between 1981 and 1996 there was never more than 3% difference in the reconviction rates of those who went in or stayed out. This change has taken place since Labour came to office. Alternatives to prison are more effective and more humane and allow offenders to give something back. Yet the courts continue to appease what is assumed to be the public expectation and the numbers continue to escalate. According to Paul Cavadino, 'Whether they are taking their lead from the media, politicians or conversations in the local pub, sentencers clearly believe they're supposed to pass heavier terms.'

The talking up of punishment is designed to satisfy a public which seems to be punishment hungry. In our modern world we experience heightened anxiety generally and greater awareness of the risks we all face in our daily lives. The refrain that something must be done about crime is equalled by uncertainty that whatever is done is either politically warranted or socially effective. When there is time for reflection many people agree that jail should be kept for serious offenders and that imprisoning less serious offenders only exacerbates most of their problems. The challenge for government is to lead positively in that debate. However, when Jack Straw became Home Secretary he challenged Michael Howard's 'Prison works', only to say 'Prison doesn't work but we'll make it work'. That Labour took the decision to continue Michael Howard's incarceration binge is one of the blackest marks against the government's record on social justice.

The Blair government has presided over the steepest increase in the prison population in over a century: prison overcrowding is now at crisis levels. The Prison Service is unable to meet its 'performance indicators', which means it has not managed to reduce the level of assaults nor has it increased purposeful activity such as jobs, training and education. The service is close to breaking point and money is now being spent on crisis management. Cells are overcrowded; prisoners are angry about being moved to prisons hundreds of miles away from their families. The risk of suicide and riot increases when such tensions are unleashed. The suicide rate in female prisons reached record levels in 2003, with 14 deaths. Prisoners in some places are locked up for most of the day with no exercise or association because of pressure on staff. The Treasury has had to give in to Home Office demands and a further £200 million is to be spent building two more private prisons and extra wings and houseblocks in existing jails. We have already had 19 new prisons in the last ten years – 16 of which are now overcrowded. Each place in prison costs £75,000 to build and £37,000 a year to run – twice the cost of Eton. The new money alone could buy effective drug treatment, adequate mental healthcare and robust community sentences for thousands of offenders.

It became clear in the run-up to the last election that, whichever of the two main parties won, the UK was lurching into yet another massive prison building programme. The Conservatives can never be outdone in any trading war on the subject of law and order but my heart sank at Labour's announcement to reform the sentencing of criminals 'to provide tougher punishment'. Prison is the right place for people who use violence and pose a real threat to our communities but not for many of the people currently being incarcerated. The building programme will mean 9,500 extra prison places for adults. The implementation of the Criminal Justice and Police Act 1999 requires over 4,000 new places for young offenders aged between 12 and 16.

For most people, prison is the end of a road paved with deprivation, disadvantage, abuse, discrimination and multiple social problems. Empty lives produce crime. For those of us who have no experience of prison it is hard to imagine what it means to lose your liberty, to surrender to a regime where the rules are not your rules, where your autonomy dissolves, where your battered self-worth spirals into further decline. Small matters taken for granted in the outside world become complicated and strangely insurmountable because of the requirements of the authorities. Your timetable is directed by others, privacy disappears, petty resentments build into serious conflict and indignities are part of the daily round. It is my idea of hell.

In 30 years of practice at the Criminal Bar I have spent rather a lot of time in prisons. In the early 1990s I was a particularly regular visitor to Holloway Prison. Since that time I have served on the Health Advisory Board there and I am now involved with the Birth Partners Scheme to help prisoners through their pregnancy and the birth of their babies. The same issues arise repeatedly: appalling family circumstances, histories of neglect, abuse and sexual exploitation, poor health, mental disorders, lack of support, inadequate housing or homelessness, poverty and debt, and little expectation of change. Many women in prison have themselves been the victims of crime, usually violence within the home or sexual violation when they were children. Poor, battered and abused, they find themselves continually punished.

In the face of all this they often show remarkable resilience and courage and frequently do not fulfil the stereotype of victims, which can be why they end up in prison because they are seen as 'bolshie' and in need of discipline. Of course there are some women who have had reasonably privileged lives who end up in jail but they are few. However, virtually all women who go to prison come out damaged by the experience. Offending and imprisonment for women means more than failing to meet the standards of law; it also means failing to be a 'proper woman'. The damage inflicted as a consequence of removal from their children, their families and their communities is immeasurable. They are overwhelmed with feelings of guilt.

Between 1993 and 2001 the female prison population for England and Wales increased by over 145%. As many as two-thirds of women in prison are now suffering from a mental disorder, with record numbers, as I said, being driven to suicide because of a lack of adequate care. The majority of these women need psychiatric support and drug treatment in the community. They do not need to be locked up for hours on end in overcrowded prisons where self-harming, tearing into their own flesh with hairclips and bottle tops, is endemic. They do not need their medication to be pushed through the metal flap in the door as though they are lepers. Between 1990 and 1995 seven women took their lives in prison. In the first three months of 2003 the exact same number committed suicide. Women make up only 6% of the prison population but account for 11% of the self-inflicted deaths. Half of all women in prison are on prescribed medication such as antidepressants or anti-psychotics. Most of the women who kill themselves take overdoses or hang themselves, but one woman recently choked herself by swallowing toilet paper.

The Prison Service is under-staffed and under-trained. Officers have less opportunity to get to know prisoners individually and thus to spot the danger signs that a woman might take her life.

Most of the women enter prison vulnerable to breakdown because of their personal histories, but not all. The *Independent*'s campaign during 2002–2003 on mental health documented the experience of Wendy Kramer, who was imprisoned for two and a half years for conspiring to supply drugs. She left prison with severe mental health problems despite having no previous history of mental illness. She was never diagnosed or given therapy while inside but another inmate helped her find a counsellor.

'In prison I felt anxiety, panic, self-harm, suicide, depression – the unbelievable hurt inside your stomach which is what makes you bang your head against the wall. The main thing that gets to me is that there are a lot of women in there that shouldn't be. They aren't criminals; they are mentally ill.'

Two-thirds of women who are imprisoned have children under the age of 16, estimated at 24,000 children. Whereas many men serve their sentences knowing their partners are taking care of their children, according to the Prison Inspectorate only 25% of women stated that the father of their children was looking after them while the women were inside. I have for a long time campaigned that the criminal courts should be required to obtain reports on the impact on children of imprisoning a primary carer, whether a mother or a father. These children have done nothing wrong but are also punished and the long-term effect is hard to estimate but is not hard to imagine. They suffer all kinds of emotional and psychological damage as a result of their mother's imprisonment.

The reason why it is worth looking so closely at the experience of women is that so few of them commit violent or serious crime. Women in prison are more likely to be suffering from multiple problems of material deprivation than male prisoners, less likely to be career criminals or dangerous yet they are at the receiving end of a growing punitiveness. This has partly reflected the increased hostility to single mothers generally and the judicial inability to understand that equality does not mean sameness and that they do not have to punish a woman exactly as they would a man if, for example, she has responsibility for dependent children.

Pat Carlen, visiting Professor in Criminology at Keele University and one of the most powerful and informed voices on women's imprisonment, has examined what she brilliantly and sardonically describes as the 'carceral clawback': the way in which the arguments for reducing the imprisonment of women have been subverted and used as a rationale for locking women up. She sees the Straw boast of 'making prison work' as the problem. The 'repairing gel', as she describes it, was to be the creation of programmes inside prisons to address the background problems of the women and indeed the men too. This has given sentencers a sense of justification and freedom to lock up women rather than find a community alternative: they persuade themselves that women will be helped inside. In truth, provision is very patchy because of overcrowding and such programmes can never be much use if the sentence is short.

All the arguments women criminologists and lawyers made to persuade the courts and policy makers that the background of most women and their place in society explained their offending are now used, not to avoid prison, but to justify imprisonment. The very language we used in developing a feminist critique of offending has been appropriated and is used to legitimise the use of prison. There is talk of 'empowering' women prisoners and raising self-esteem. Yet as soon as a woman is assertive she is very quickly reminded she is a prisoner and that unquestioning compliance with the rules is the expectation.

One issue that affects both men and women prisoners is the extent of drug abuse, which swamps any benefit from job opportunities and skills development. In a recent special investigation, David Rose, an *Observer* journalist and author of *In the Name of the Law*, was able to show that the increase in class A drug use had played its part in the increase in the use of imprisonment by the courts. In 2002, 79.8% of male prisoners entering Pentonville Prison reception had taken cocaine or heroin in the previous 48 hours. The figures are also high for women. Nationally, the figure for new prisoners requiring immediate detox has risen steadily, from 16,000 in 1996 to 47,000 in 2002. We can safely deduce that many of the crimes committed by these offenders were committed because of drug abuse. However, places in community rehab are so sparse that the courts feel compelled to use prison for detoxification.

The government introduced an option called drug treatment and testing orders so that there could be treatment in the community. The programmes are designed to be intense and well structured to reassure the courts and the public and while they are expensive, at £6,000 per year, they are still much cheaper than prison. Under the scheme, detoxification beds are supposed to be made available within the NHS. Offenders are meant to be tested twice a week for relapses, spend at least 15 hours a week in sessions designed to bring some order into their chaotic lives, and have regular reviews by the courts of their progress. But a recent report by the probation inspectors found the scheme bedevilled by the failure of Whitehall: too many funding streams, too many targets, central micro-management, of which government is so guilty, and constant reporting back. As a result the Probation Service is totally unable to provide for the number of orders that should be made. And so it is that the prisons like Pentonville become the short-term dumping ground for people with drug problems.

In May 2003, the Inspector of Prisons published a critical report of Pentonville, which has to cope with over 40,000 prisoner movements a year: 100 prisoners leave each weekday morning and another 100 come in. As the Inspector pointed out, despite the best efforts of staff, 'it is not acceptable to hold prisoners in conditions which fall so far short of decency and activity'.

We have yet to have an inspector of prisons who has not incurred the wrath of politicians because they have the audacity to speak the truth about what they see. Stephen Tumin and David Ramsbottom had to deal with the brickbats of Michael Howard and Jack Straw respectively. The assumption was that after Sir Stephen, a harder personality was needed and that a military man would be no faint-heart. However, David Ramsbottom was someone with a highly developed sense of fairness, who was unafraid to speak out. The current Inspector, Ann Owers, who was Director of Justice, comes with a full awareness that these are human rights issues on which the government should take action but she too should expect the road to be rocky. Government does not like its shortcomings to be exposed but the Inspectorate is an alarm system so that we know what happens in our name in a hidden corner of the system.

Therefore, it is not surprising that government now intends to draw the teeth of the Prison's Inspectorate by merging it with the Probation Inspectorate and abolishing its specialist role. In January 2004 David Blunkett announced his proposal to create a new National Offenders Management Scheme, uniting the prison and probation services. The problem is that the two services have very different cultures, with probation having its roots in the social services. The blurring of the boundaries of probation with the prison service may undermine the relationships of trust which offenders need to develop with probation officers.

Prison is about punishment. We keep trying to invent the notion of the benign prison because we cannot bear the idea that we are inflicting pain. Prisons are given the veneer of being therapeutic environments, to provide a modern rationale for locking up not just men and women who commit serious crime but men and women who commit minor crimes too. The purpose is not so much to make prisoners feel better as to make us feel better. What has really filled the jails in the last ten years is a profound shift in penal policy, driven by an unwillingness to admit that crime is largely about poverty and deprivation.

The 1991 Criminal Justice Act contained a clear enunciation of sentencing principles. The idea was that offenders should receive their 'just deserts' for the particular crime before the court, with sentencing reflecting the seriousness of the crime. Sometimes this led to rigidity because not enough account was taken of the different circumstances and background of offenders. Doing justice in an unjust society demands the judgement of Solomon and should require the sentencer to strike a balance between the public's right to protection and nature of the offence, the background of the offender, the effect on the victim, the chances of preventing repetition. However, the important principle was established long ago that people should not be punished for what they have not done. This is where there has been an alarming turnaround. As the 1990s proceeded, risk of committing further offences became a more and more dominant theme of law and order politics and has become increasingly influential in penal policy. What people *might* do, if not locked up is to be in the mind of the sentencer. Risk has become the dominant criminal justice motif.

Risk of physical danger, 'dangerousness', was recognised in the 1991 Act and is now central in the evaluation of those who have committed violent offences, but what we have been seeing is a blurring of the differentiation between violent and non-violent offences and a conflation of 'seriousness' and 'persistent'. So a shop-lifter who has a history of stealing and a drug problem to support is seen as being at risk of further offending and is imprisoned. This willingness to lock people up for what they might do and for their nuisance value, rather than for what they have done, is informing other areas of Home Office policy. There is the inclusion of 'grooming' in the Sexual Offences Act to catch paedophiles who are befriending children with the ultimate aim, it is assumed, of having sex. People can already be arrested for conspiring, attempting or inciting another to commit a paedophile offence. The risk of this 'thought crime' charge is that men who show any kindness to a child will be at risk.

There have also been plans to change the Mental Health legislation in ways that have appalled the Royal College of Psychiatrists. Under existing Mental Health law someone can only be detained without committing a crime if they can be 'treated', because there would then be some benefit to be gained from their detention. There is, however, a type of mental disorder which has been described as severe personality disorder. This is not a medical definition as there is no medical consensus on what it is, and some people suffering from severe personality disorder cannot be treated – yet they could be detained if the government has its way. People could lose their liberty not because of anything they have done, and not so they can have medical care, but because of a fear that they just may do something in the future. This is 'pre-crime detention', as in the sci-fi film *Minority Report* (2002). Most of the psychiatric profession want no part of it and see it as an outrageous infringement of human rights. The answer is proper, well-resourced care and monitoring of fragile people in the community, not pre-emptive incarceration. When one in four of us will suffer mental illness in our lifetimes it is worth taking stock before allowing government such power. A draft Bill with these powers has been postponed for a second year because of the criticisms but the government is reluctant to abandon the idea.

At the end of the 1980s there was almost complete consensus that petty persistent offenders should not be imprisoned. The futility of the revolving door syndrome was recognised: giving short jail terms to people who commit crime because of their circumstances outside prison. These sentences provided insufficient time for any serious rehabilitative work and in any case had no impact on the common situations of poverty, homelessness, addictions and abuse, and prison was likely to make re-offending worse rather than better.

The 1991 commitment to avoid prison for less serious offences, even if the offender had a history of offending, did not last very long. Magistrates became frustrated by the lack of scope to deal with offenders they saw as a nuisance. By 1996, because they were told to assess the risk of re-offending, what people might go on to do, they were given the green light to imprison. There were also moral panics inflamed by the press about persistent offenders such as 'rat boy', an adolescent in the North-East who had acquired countless convictions and was seen as completely feral and beyond redemption. Magistrates were fired to solve low-level crime by jailing people.

The Halliday Report on sentencing published in 2002, which recommends ending the use of short jail sentences, shows that between 1989 and 1999 custodial sentences passed by magistrates' courts increased from 18,200 to 53,000. That is a 191% increase. The increase in the imprisonment of women (143%) was over three times greater than the increase for men (40%). These are on the whole property offences. For women it is theft, handling, minor fraud and small-scale drugs offences. As Professor Barbara Hudson has pointed out, 'the revolving door has not just been re-opened it has been given a shove to make it revolve more vigorously'.

Another source of injustice is the remarkable variation in sentencing between different benches in different parts of the country, providing a casino in justice. At the extremes, one magistrates' court was imposing custody in only one out of every 43 cases, while another imposed custody in one in every two. Yet despite evidence that magistrates are imprisoning excessively, the government has now widened their remit by the Criminal Justice Act 2003, giving them greatly increased powers to imprison, which is creating alarm and despondency about the further impact on prison numbers.

The incarceration of women shows so baldly where the system goes wrong but many men in prison are similarly there for less serious offences when they should be receiving support and help in the community. Good community service programmes need not be a soft option.

Under Jack Straw's reign, at great expense and inconvenience the Probation Service was renamed the Probation and Community Punishment Service. Managers were brought in rather than practitioners. All the headed notepaper and office signs had to be changed, reprinted and repainted – a cosmetic endeavour to put the word 'punishment' at the heart of government activity. Probation orders were ostensibly abolished but were really just renamed community punishment orders. It is hard to know who was persuaded by such war-paint but the Probation Service remains the Probation Service to everyone who works in the system. Instead, the money should have been spent on strengthening the numbers of probation officers who are the very people who can oversee good community sentencing, take on the aftercare when people come out of prison and help people gain skills to join the workforce. The Probation Service is now in crisis.

Virtually everyone who has real knowledge of crime is of one view. The priority of the government should not be building prisons but developing intensive, supervised programmes of work and rehabilitation which involve active repayment of offenders' debts to victims and the community. David Blunkett says that is what he wants, but on this subject he does not say loudly and clearly 'Watch my lips. Prison does not work.' His song changes depending on his audience. If he wants to end the scandal, he has to keep telling the courts not to send people to prison, whatever the uproar in the press. Instead, he takes side-swipes at the judges in the belief that mockery will stiffen their sentencing resolve. At a police conference he boasted that he himself had previous convictions for arguing with the judiciary but suggested the Lord Chief Justice, clearly a softie, was unlikely to send him to prison and community service was all he was likely to face.

The new sentencing proposals of 'Custody Plus' and 'Custody Minus', which mean part of a sentence involves prison and part of it is suspended, give fresh sentencing options to the courts which could help ease prison numbers at the lower end but they will only work if there is leadership from the top about avoiding the use of prison altogether. They could easily become a substitute for short sentences. The problem with Custody Plus is that it requires 26 weeks post-release supervision by the Probation Service, when the Probation Service is already overstretched and understaffed. As a result its implementation has been postponed.

In 1995 I chaired an inquiry for the Howard League for Penal Reform into violence in young offenders' institutions and again the overwhelming evidence was that young people who ended up in custody were themselves profoundly deprived and more in need of support and help than punishment. England and Wales lock up more children than any other country in Europe. In April 2003, 3,000 of the most vulnerable, damaged and impoverished 15-,16-, and 17-year-olds in our country were languishing behind bars, despite evidence that offending by children was falling. There has been a ninefold increase in the number of children in prison. Forty per cent of those who end up in prison have been in local authority care. Ninety per cent of young people in prison have mental health or substance abuse problems. Nearly a quarter have literacy and numeracy skills below those of an average seven-year-old and a significant number have suffered physical and sexual abuse. Penal reformers say that the government's obsession with teenagers on street corners has contributed to the sharp rise in the number of young people in prison. This rush to custody is in breach of the UN Convention on the Rights of the Child.

Although 'cutting-up', the turning of anger inwards, is seen as a characteristically female response to stress and self-loathing, it happens increasingly amongst boys in young offenders' institutions but is all too often dismissed as attention-seeking and manipulative behaviour. Locking up children who have complex and multiple needs in worn-down and neglectful institutions is not the answer. In these places children are routinely treated in ways that in any other circumstances would trigger a child protection investigation. Despite the advent of the Youth Justice Board, with its supposed 'child-centred' approach, and warm words from the Prison Service about child protection, the conditions experienced by thousands of children sent to prison each year should shame us all. Recent reports from Ann Owers, the Chief Inspector of Prisons are shocking. Of one institution, Huntercombe, she said: 'It is holding far too many young people in unmanageably large units to be able to provide a safe environment.' Of another called Onley, she said: 'It is a long way from providing a safe environment for all its young people, indeed for some vulnerable children we do not believe it would have met the requirements of the Children Act.' Of girls in Holloway she said: 'No assessments of risk or vulnerability were being carried out, the regime was wholly inadequate, staff lacked essential documentation and no training plan meetings were being held.'

Then there was the scandal of the privately run juvenile jail, Ashfield, near Bristol, which was so repeatedly damned for its failure to meet standards that it ran up fines and penalties of nearly £2 million. Ashfield had such widespread bullying that many children were afraid to come out of their cells. The majority of staff were deemed to lack the experience, confidence or skills to manage a difficult and demanding population. That is what happens when the bottom line is the imperative and money is saved on staffing. Using the private sector to deliver public services can have a significant impact on the very character of an institution. As Professor Colin Crouch of the European University Institute in Florence has pointed out, privatising 'core services' like NHS medical care or the custody of offenders inevitably results in a failure to fulfil the basic purposes of public provision.

In 2002, in a landmark case brought by the Howard League against the Home Secretary, Mr Justice Munby decided that the Children Act 1989 did apply to children in prison, saying that the evidence he had heard about child incarceration 'ought to shock the conscience of every citizen'.

The Children Act places the needs of each individual child as the highest priority. The Prison Service we are told complies with the 'principles' of the Children Act rather as, according to George Bush, Guantanamo Bay complies with the principles of the Geneva Convention. Between April 2000 and January 2002 segregation or solitary confinement was used 4,437 times, with approximately 1,000 young people being locked up alone for more than a week. Control and restraint techniques involving the infliction of pain are frequently used even on girls under 18 by male prison officers. It is difficult to know whether David Blunkett is shocked. In a speech at King's college on 22 October 2003, Anne Owers spoke about children being routinely strip searched on arrival at institutions: 'if a child resists, can you justify him or her being held down by adults, in painful wristlocks, and forcibly undressed.'

It fell to penal reform organisations and children's charities to table amendments to the Criminal Justice Bill to have the principles of child welfare enshrined in the criminal justice system. But still the government resisted the call. The best places for children who need containment are secure units in local authority establishments but places are scarce. In November 2003 the Youth Justice Board decided to cut even more places.

Then there is the shameful issue of racism. Black people are six times more likely to be jailed than whites. They are more likely to receive imprisonment, even though it is their first offence. As I have already pointed out, they are eight times more likely to be stopped and searched and once arrested more likely to be remanded in custody than others charged with criminal offences. As Juliet Lyon, Director of the Prison Reform Trust has said, 'It is impossible to feel confident in a criminal justice system which sanctions the disproportionate imprisonment of black people.'

A quarter of Britain's female prison population and 17% of the male prison population come from an ethnic minority background yet only 5.5% of the population is from an ethnic minority. A study conducted in 2002 by Professor Jeremy Coid of the Royal London School of Medicine examined data on more than 3,000 prisoners and uncovered huge differences in treatment based on ethnicity. Only this year the CPS has admitted to institutional racism and the Commission for Racial Equality is investigating allegations of racism in prisons.

Class and race are the overwhelming indicators for imprisonment but we no longer talk about class in Blair's Britain, or indeed poverty, unless in relation to children or the developing world.

In 1991 Lord Woolf, now our Chief Justice, conducted an inquiry into prisons after riots at Strangeways. His report noted that a substantial number of prisoners leave prison embittered and hostile and 'in a state of mind where they are more likely to re-offend' and with their employment, family and community ties weakened. It was also argued that the 'motivation to change behaviour and often lifestyle, the learning process itself and the positive reinforcement of such choices are all significantly more likely to occur in the community than prisons'.

The current statement of purpose of the Prison Service identifies a rehabilitative objective: 'Our duty is to look after prisoners with humanity and to help them lead law-abiding and useful lives in custody and after release.' The last Director of Prisons, Martin Narey, undoubtedly tried very hard to make that aim a reality. Yet the problem that virtually every prison officer acknowledges is that with overcrowding, limited resources and often poor morale, it is difficult to fulfil that mission with any seriousness. Staff surveys show that only 1% of prison officers believed that prisons were very successful in rehabilitating inmates: 49% believed they were not successful at all.

The redoubtable Jackie Lowthian of Nacro is well placed to provide an overview of prisons, particularly those incarcerating women. She points out that the need to accommodate ever increasing numbers along with budgetary constraints means that there is an overall sense of decline in many prisons. Because of the inexorable demand for places, prisoners are too often given inappropriate allocations in prisons so far away from their family that they receive few visits, or they are placed in prisons where nothing useful is available to them. She documented a deterioration in healthcare and hygiene. Staffing shortages mean that non-mandatory tasks such as help with housing and resettlement support have to be dropped in order to ensure that statutory functions like security and discipline are carried out. In turn, these inadequate standards of care increase the risk of bullying, self-harm and suicide. They also mean there is no cover, so prisoners' education or other activities are curtailed. Home probation officers have so little time or resources to spare that they cannot see women in prison or offer voluntary aftercare. There is no help on offer on a statutory basis for people on short sentences.

One of our responsibilities must be to ensure that while people are in prison, they have opportunities to repair the black holes in their own experience which led to offending: many activities should be taking place in a more developed way. Government is indeed trying to make provision – creating therapeutic programmes addressing violence or past abuse, domestic violence projects for both victim and offender, and therapy addressing childhood trauma, issues of sexuality or substance abuse. However, the schemes require Home Office accreditation and many of the best holistic services and programmes fail to get funding because they fall outside the narrow, prescriptive limitations required for accreditation, which is all about the current obsession with 'cognitive behavioural models'. Cognitive behavioural therapies are all the rage, getting women to have insight into their behaviour, the way their abuse as children leads them into adult relationships with abusive men, the way the violence they have experienced has led to low self-worth and addictions. It is of course right that psychological work with women in prison can be of real help, and may be crucial if they are to develop strategies for survival, but alone it will not address the main problems for women because it excludes the material conditions of their existence – poverty, racism and sexism. If politicians are going to talk about the causes of crime they cannot deny the reality of the women's experience in the communities in which they live. Much more has to be done about housing issues and training for work.

The programmes available are sketchy, totally dependent on who is in charge or the special interests of certain professionals engaged with the prison or based locally. Whether a prisoner can access such a programme is more in the hands of the gods than the result of any real assessment of need. Yet ministers talk about these initiatives as if they were available on tap. In any event, *Home Office Research Findings* 206 show that cognitive behavioural programmes made no difference to reconviction rates.

The provision which makes most difference to people's lives is education. If you can come out of prison with a skill you are more likely to find work and you have more chance of beating your habit, staying clean and resisting crime. The Lattice Foundation at Reading Prison trains young offenders in fork-lift driving, with participants attending day release courses. Seventy per cent have found employment on release and only 6% have been known to re-offend. At Leeds Prison there is a targeted training and education programme which includes testing for dyslexia. It has been found that there is a high level of dyslexia: prisoners have histories of problems at school which led to offending, but their learning difficulties were never acknowledged. Yet the Chief Inspector has described as still lamentable the level of education available to young offenders between the ages of 18 and 21. In her view none of the young offenders' institutions in England and Wales was providing sufficient education and training. Her report on Norwich Prison showed 750 prisoners packed into cells meant for 561. On one wing 200 out of 250 prisoners were involved in no meaningful work or education. Those who did work were making breakfast packs. In the prison's training wing only 8 out of 45 inmates on one landing were in education.

Education and training should be at the very centre of every prison regime, not an add-on. But we are still a long way from providing the kind of educational framework that most of us would consider fundamental.

Most people in prison have had inadequate education and have never had the opportunity to fulfil their potential for a host of reasons. Research by the Prison Reform Trust in 1993 noted that the Home Office had estimated that around half of prisoners have functional difficulty with literacy. The Basic Skills Unit's work in 1994 is perhaps the most informative in terms of setting a figure and putting it in context. Four hundred prisoners received into 16 prisons during a one-week period in that year were surveyed and the findings led to the conclusion that 'more than 1 in 2 of the inmates in this survey had a low level of literacy'. This is in contrast with a figure of one in six for the general adult population. This is not to suggest that poor literacy is the cause of offending. What it does suggest is that improving the literacy of offenders could be a key intervention in enabling them to move away from offending.

North American studies show that adult basic education 'appeared to have the greatest impact on offenders who could initially be defined as at higher risk for reoffending'. A second stage contained reports of follow-up interviews with a large cohort of prisoners who had gone through basic literacy educational programmes. The idea was to explore the impact as the ex-prisoners themselves saw it. Around three-quarters of those interviewed indicated that participation had encouraged them to try other courses, about two-thirds reported greater success in finding jobs after release (with the majority of those in relatively stable employment). A third said that participation had helped improve family relationships and eight out of ten credited the programme with providing them with skills, which enabled them to access activities that had not been open to them previously. Eighty-six per cent now read newspapers and the majority acknowledged the importance of reading for entertainment, for obtaining hobby and job information and for keeping abreast of current events. One in five also rated their learning experience as very important in terms of personal change, affecting their relations with other people more widely.

I have contact with Bedford Hills Prison, a women's correctional facility in upstate New York. All government support for education in the state's prisons has been cut – 'why should prisoners get better education than people on the outside?' was the refrain. Different charities are now being approached to fill the gap because the College Bound programmes have had such far reaching impact. College-educated inmates are much less likely ever to return to prison and therefore saved the taxpayer hundreds of thousands of dollars. Research showed that the college education programme alone reduced the rate of women's return to prison from 33% to 7%. The children of college-educated inmates stayed in school longer and were less likely to end up in prison than the children of inmates without the benefit of the education programme.

The acquisition of education is inextricably linked with the processes of social participation. This is not just a matter of having the skills to understand and reply to job advertisements, questions in driving licence applications, goods purchase agreements, television licence forms, insurance policies, benefits forms and the myriad documents which are part of day to day existence. Literacy is more than a functional skill – it is a force for integration. It is a core element in feelings of inclusion and identity with others and is of underlying importance in encouraging offenders in the direction of resettlement and responsibility. We all benefit.

Whenever I have discussed taking classes with prisoners they always say that the classes made them feel less worthless, and made them recover some self-esteem. Of my many clients those who have enjoyed some educational success in their pre-incarceration lives always feel that learning while in prison will be their means of survival. However, they then write me letters full of their frustration about the absence of appropriate courses and support, the difficulty at times of getting suitable books and materials. In some prisons the library is little more than converted cells with collections of well thumbed paperbacks and out of date reference books. Transfer between prisons takes place without any account being taken of the fact that a prisoner is halfway through a course of study with a particular teacher. The disincentives for learning can be enormous.

Prisoners also often complain that education can be used as a 'privilege' and any misdemeanour can be met with the withdrawal of the lifeline. Cell-sharing with an inmate who does not share your interest can make reading and study impossible if a radio is constantly played full blast.

Just as we have realised that education must be at the heart of any inspired project for regeneration in Britain, so it must also be at the heart of any inspired project of rehabilitation of offenders. But to do that government has to realign its thinking and its spending plans. Fewer people in prison, fewer prisons, and the money spent on alternatives to prison and the creation of a real learning environment inside prison.

A joint plan has been created by the Home Office and the Department for Education and Skills to address the educational needs of prisoners, and the Department for Education and Skills now holds the budget for education and training in prisons. The advantage of this is that it should stop the Home Office raiding the pot for other purposes. But the plans are not radical enough and nor will they work when the numbers involved are so large. Every new inmate should be seen in the first few weeks and given the opportunity of creating his or her own education plan. It should be a mapping system with clear progression routes. The plan should travel with them and there should be a requirement on prisons to meet the inmate's need.

Prisons really are evidence of our failure as a society. David Blunkett expresses concern and a desire to reduce the prison population, but he does not want to put his name to daring alternatives for fear that middle England will see him as a limp-wristed liberal. The decency of middle England is greatly underestimated by this government. Instead, Blunkett talks in punitive language which permeates the courts. His much-publicised intent to keep killers in jail for twice as long or for ever is designed to create a bit of licence to get more low-level offenders out of prison. 'You can't accuse me of being a lily-livered wimp' will be his retort when he is forced to open the prison gates because of crisis after crisis. But his general rhetoric is all about retribution. He should be reminded that for every additional year 5,000 extra lifers spend in prison we could have 5,000 extra teachers. Blunkett's new National Offenders Management Scheme would involve replacing jail sentences by fines for minor offenders. But this is still too little, and too timid.

There are no votes in reducing the prison population unless you really are a bold politician, and boldness is not one of this government's attributes when it comes to Home Office policy. At some stage someone is going to have to be bold or we will end up warehousing huge parts of our population, particularly the poor, within prison walls. Bold would be to make war on the numbers going to prison, bold would be to challenge the idea that prison works. Bold would be to end the imprisonment of children. Bold would be to hold firm on civil liberties even when faced with crises.

15

THE RETREAT FROM HUMAN RIGHTS

'Ah, but a man's reach should exceed his grasp, or what's a heaven for?'
Robert Browning, 'Andrea del Sarto'

ON 2 OCTOBER 2000, with many others I celebrated a truly historic occasion – the coming into effect of the Human Rights Act 1998. I was not celebrating because the Act represented a gravy train for overpaid lawyers, as the tabloids would have you believe, but because it marked a significant milestone on the road towards a popular culture of rights. Harold Wilson came to believe that his greatest achievement as Prime Minister was the Open University and some day Tony Blair will see his triumph as the Human Rights Act. But he does not seem to know it yet.

Before it came into existence the Act's critics were legion and they were not all on the right. Some left-wing groups saw bills of rights as undermining political activism, and as giving too much power to the judges, who were invariably reactionary. The right-wing view was that bills of rights undermined parliamentary sovereignty; they were a left-liberal invention, likely to be used for politically correct purposes, reining in the behaviour of the majority in the name of dissatisfied minorities.

In fact human rights provides us with a new language for discussing our relationships with each other and with the rest of the world. It offers a language that belongs neither to the left nor the right, because it is non-ideological, and can speak to all the peoples of the world irrespective of religious belief or world view because it is avowedly secular. Rights have to be given the force of law for that is how we link our dreams to the acts of daily life. Too often we speak of human rights only in terms of how they are violated and not in terms of how they can affirm and legitimise the aspirations of a society.

For Kofi Annan, the Secretary-General of the United Nations, human rights are 'a yardstick by which we measure human progress'. The language of human rights applies not just to the abuse of others on the grand scale that makes international news headlines, it also relates to the small acts of inhumanity which disfigure our lives even in Western developed societies. The thread that should run through all our human interactions, as colleagues, as parents, as lovers, as spouses, as neighbours or as strangers, should be respect for the essential humanity and moral worth of others. The ideas contained in human rights should penetrate the doors of our homes and inform issues such as domestic violence and child abuse, and enter the workplace so that discrimination and unfair treatment are examined in their context. They should suffuse public services, our schools and our politics. They are like the angelus bell or the song of the muezzin: we should hear the ring of their meaning as we go about our ordinary business, aware that they are a conscience call for all of us.

Of course the legislation only makes legal demands upon the state and public authorities as to their duties and responsibilities in protecting rights, but if ministers spoke passionately about human rights as ethical standards which we should all meet, with government setting the example, there might be a greater enthusiasm. When we talk of legislation complying with human rights standards it should not be a box ticking, minimalist exercise but a challenge to speak to the best in the human spirit. Human rights is a strong and angry commitment to pluralism and tolerance, inextricably linked to democracy and due process. Rights are not expendable entities to be dumped when exigencies require, as has already had been done in Britain in the name of combating terrorism, or as the Prime Minister and his Home Secretary suggested in spring 2003, when the courts repeatedly found against them on the removal of benefit from asylum seekers. Human rights are inseparable from social justice: they do not exist in a value-free zone. The widening gap between the rich and everyone else is also a human rights issue.

Yet, the grandeur of ambition involved in creating a human rights culture has never been seized by the government. Their timidity is again the product of fear and insecurity. Despite having a huge majority, New Labour has repeatedly shown a lack of confidence in delivery of policy, particularly in the area of constitutional change where they have a record of backtracking and dilution, or trading and bungling. The uncertainty started with devolution, where attempts were made to manage the process of leadership selection from the centre, despite the rhetoric that Labour was committed to 'subsidiarity', meaning people making decisions that directly affected them closer to home. These controlling tendencies backfired in Wales with the insertion of the 'on message' Alan Michael as First Minister to keep traditional Labour, Rhodri Morgan, out, a decision reversed by the Welsh electorate at the first opportunity. Similar attempts were made to control selection of the mayoral candidate in London because of antagonism to Ken Livingstone. In the same way, promises of a full-blown Freedom of Information Act were watered down, democratising the House of Lords was abandoned halfway and proportional representation has been dropped like a stone.

The constitutional reform agenda was seized upon by New Labour before the 1997 election because it signalled modernity but sadly they became unnerved by the reach and implications of their own platform. They failed to see how each ingredient links with another; how a modernised, independent judiciary is essential to the protection of human rights, which in turn requires real freedom of information, which links to a parliament that is accountable.

The shame of what has happened in the field of human rights is that instead of using all his skills as a passionate advocate, explaining that human rights was about a new 'way of being' in all relationships, the Prime Minister feared ridicule at the hands of the media. The press speculated that the courts would be flooded with ludicrous cases that would cost billions and that the legislation would undermine the British way of life. Downing Street wanted to place a distance between itself and any unforeseen consequences. It sat on plans for a Human Rights Commission and referred to human rights only in speeches about international affairs.

The feared avalanche of cases never happened. In the first year of the Act (2001) there were only 297 cases and according to statisticians no sign of an increase in litigation against public authorities. The Act has made virtually no difference to the length of cases, according to research from the former Lord Chancellor's Department and the cost has been negligible. While the language of human rights could have lifted the quality of the debate about asylum or the state of our prisons, reminding us of our responsibilities to the stranger at our gate and even to those who have wronged us, instead we have had the protestations of David Blunkett that the Human Rights Act is being used to strike down government policy. In fact, in only seven cases have the courts made declarations that public authorities' decisions were incompatible with the human rights legislation. The judges have actually been very cautious about their interpretation of the Act. They have been unwilling to create a free-standing privacy law out of the Human Rights Act; they refrained from creating a 'right to die' in the sad case of Diane Pretty in 2003, who was desperately ill with motor neurone disease and wanted an assisted death to be made exempt from prosecution, and they maintained the Home Secretary's ban on the entry to the UK of the controversial and inflammatory black militant, Louis Farrakhan, despite his claim that it infringed his freedom of speech.

It is right that politicians should have checks placed on the exercise of their power, to ensure that an over-hasty majority does not ride roughshod over the legitimate interests of minorities and to make sure that democratic values are not abandoned at times of high fever. But the strength of our human rights legislation is that the judges cannot trump parliament, striking down legislation. The most they can do is declare laws or conduct by officials of the state or public bodies as incompatible with the Human Rights Act. Parliament then has to decide how to resolve the problem. This clever mechanism to maintain the ultimate supremacy of parliament was a formulation concocted by Derry Irvine, to his eternal credit. Yet some ministers still moan about the undermining of parliament and others caricature rights as the triumph of individualism to the detriment of communities.

Contemporary human rights are built upon a careful and sensitive balance between respect for the individual and support for communities. There are very few unconditional entitlements in the European Convention on Human Rights. Some rights, like the freedom from torture, are absolute but most rights involve a careful consideration of the rights of others: for example freedom of speech is offset by the requirement not to inflame racial hatred in a pluralist society. There are distinct provisions protecting our ability to form and sustain the human relationships that hold society together, whether the right to family life, freedom of religion, or freedom of assembly which protects our right to organise politically and in trade unions. Human rights do support communities but it should be recognised that sometimes communities can be oppressive – to homosexuals, strangers, women and those who are different.

In 2002 I acted for a young Bengali girl. She had been left behind in rural Bangladesh with her grandmother when her parents emigrated to Britain with a younger sibling. Another child was born and the older girl was brought over to join her parents. She was only 14 but was never sent to school, somehow slipping through the local authority net, and instead was used as a skivvy by the extended family. She never set foot out of doors, spoke no word of English and was sexually abused by her mother's brother. She was too frightened to tell anyone because of his threats and, even when she became pregnant, no one noticed and she remained silent. Early one morning she went into labour, crept to the tiny bathroom in the multi-storey council flat, biting into her own arm to staunch her moans, and delivered a baby girl. When she heard her father get up in an adjoining room, she was in such terror she threw the newborn out of the window.

The miracle was that the baby survived. Still covered in vernix and blood, with a long length of umbilical cord, the mite was found in a grass verge by some passers-by and the police were called. They worked out the trajectory of the fall and started to search the flats, dwelling after dwelling, until they found some blood-drenched clothing soaking in a bucket in the home of my young client's family. They asked them all to come to the police station, whereupon the father shouted and screamed at my little girl in Bengali, which none of the police understood. On the way the girl almost passed out from pain and was taken to hospital, where she delivered the afterbirth. She told an Asian woman doctor about being raped by her uncle and her terror of what would happen to her.

The girl, who was little more than a child herself, was charged with attempted murder. Her own mother refused to accept that her brother had violated her daughter and rejected her so that she had to be taken into care. The father tried to persuade the police to let him send her back to Bangladesh as she was now worthless, not only unmarriageable but she had also dishonoured the family. The baby, who had a fracture to her skull, seemed to be developing well but also had to be taken into care because she was unwanted by the family. The uncle, who had sexually exploited and terrorised the girl, disappeared into the ether, hidden by members of his community so that no DNA could be taken and he could avoid arrest.

I contacted the prosecution authorities to find out why a child who was the victim of crime was being prosecuted on such a serious charge and met the explanation that it was important to send out a message to the community that babies had a right to life under the Human Rights Act. None of us needed the Human Rights Act to know this but the more pressing message to the community had to be rather different even if it risked offending some of the elders.

The case came in front of a wonderful judge called Harold Wilson at the Old Bailey and the young girl was given a conditional discharge for attempted infanticide because it was recognised that what girl and baby needed were foster care and the support of social services for a long time to come. The judge made clear that others, including the parents, who were really guilty were escaping justice.

The whole wretched saga threw up a range of human rights issues: the entitlement of girls as well as boys to an education, the fact that no child should ever be held responsible for adult abuse, the low value attached to girl children and the lesser value attached to female testimony in some traditions.

I have represented a number of teenagers who have given birth secretly and killed their babies. This is not a phenomenon confined to any particular class or community. The protection of abusers or the blaming of victims is also not new to me and is also not culturally specific. However, the silence around these issues in some minority communities is deafening and the men can close ranks to prevent justice being done. It is imperative that respect for cultural difference does not become a mask for unwillingness to tackle difficult issues, especially if the elders of a community are men and may not speak for every part of the whole. If it were not for organisations like Southall Black Sisters and Newham Asian Women's Project, many minority women would have little support as they struggle against human rights abuses.

Acting for many battered women over the years, white and black, has taught me that communities should not be over-romanticised, since they often support practices which maintain the subordination of women. The language of human rights is a powerful lingua franca which is capable of drawing everyone into a consensus; it should be used at times to prevent communities from exerting unacceptable control over individuals in ways that deny them their right to flourish.

During the long campaign for a bill of rights throughout the 1980s and '90s people often debated whether British judges could be trusted with the new power they would wield under a charter of rights. I always argued that reform of the judiciary had to be a concomitant part of the process. Trust would require the creation of a judiciary which reflected society as a whole, rather than the white upper-middle-class men of public school background who dominated the higher echelons of the judges' ranks. However, I recall Professor Sir Bernard Crick saying that a bill of rights would change the way our judges judged – even the ones we had – and he was right. Judges are much more conscious that they have a responsibility to protect citizens, that they may have to hold government to account but must carefully balance community interests in the process.

Before the Second World War and the Nuremberg trials, judges the world over said it was not for them to decide what was unjust or immoral, their role was to interpret laws passed by parliament. However, events in Germany showed how a whole political and legal system could be corrupted. Judges and lawyers had sanctioned some of the worst crimes in history; they had provided a veneer of legality for the mass murder of Jews, homosexuals, gypsies, dissidents and many others and by doing so had legitimised a nation's surrender of its moral compass. They destroyed law and justice. After the war there was a growing international acceptance by governments and by lawyers that it was not enough that the rule of law should mean adherence by all to a nation's laws, properly passed by individual parliaments. Laws had to be tested against some other template. The role of those who administered justice had to be to say 'no' when the state overstepped the mark. Judges and lawyers had to become whistle-blowers, alerting us when boundaries are being crossed so that the slow process of corruption is cauterised before it takes hold. The challenge was to create a set of principles which would act as a safety net within every legal system. Our civil liberties may be vested in us as citizens but our human rights would be vested in our bare humanity, so that even when our civil and political rights are removed we should be able to appeal for protection on the basis of our rights simply as human beings.

In 1951 in *The Origins of Totalitarianism*, Hannah Arendt wrote: 'When we stand naked, as nothing but a human being, it is that bare humanity that all of us share which should call upon our compassion. That is what our claim to be civilised means.'

When people talk about rights, they often refer to a 'first wave' and a 'second wave'. The first wave of discussion came in the eighteenth century, at the time of the French and American revolutions, and in America the understanding of rights was enshrined in their constitution. The Founding Fathers invented a new purpose of government – to protect individual rights from community consensus. Americans today still refer to the concept of 'natural rights', implying that certain rights pre-exist human society; that rights are there to be discovered. The idea of natural rights also entails considerable hostility to state power – and resistance to the general encroachment of state power is a vital part of American culture. It is for this reason that the doctrine does not travel well outside the US. Rights are clearly not natural and different concepts of rights emerge from different societies. And in Britain and the rest of Europe it is recognised that the state can be an engine for change which is beneficial to communities. So, while the US Bill of Rights is seen as a landmark, it is a source of inspiration and not a model.

In America 200 years ago the colonising British state may have been the most significant power in people's lives, but in the modern world a multinational corporation capable of wiping out the employment prospects of a whole town might pose as many threats to individual rights as democratically elected government.

The American Bill of Rights has not had sufficient elasticity to engage adequately with changed circumstances. For example, the humorous commentator on the American way of life and most particularly on the inadequacy of gun control, Michael Moore, showed powerfully in his 2002 film, *Bowling for Columbine*, the huge social cost of his country's gun culture. The individual right to bear arms is privileged over any community interest in a way that could not happen in Europe, including here in Britain.

The attempt to exterminate the Jewish people in European gas chambers during the Second World War shocked people around the globe into a rethink of international law. The second wave of 'rights-thinking' followed. The difference between the notion of 'natural' and individual rights and the postwar human rights movement lies in the blending of individual rights and the concept of community. The star in the creation of a new legal order after the Holocaust was in fact an American, Eleanor Roosevelt, who held the first drafting meeting for an international charter in her Washington Square apartment in February 1947. The gathering was so eclectic it is hard to fathom how consensus was reached for such a visionary and brave project. There was a Chinese Confucian, a Lebanese Christian, a Stalinist from the Soviet Union, a devout Catholic Brazilian and a Canadian law professor. It is often claimed that if the meetings had taken place just five years later it would have been impossible to reach agreement because the Cold War had taken hold and China had become Maoist. However, the group struggled to create what Nadine Gordimer has called the 'creed of humanity that sums up all other creeds directing human behaviour' and in 1948 produced the draft for what was to become the Universal Declaration of Human Rights. The idea was ambitious, recognising that legal systems are distinct and draw upon the cultures from which they spring, but also believing that it was possible to establish a set of binding shared values to provide a backdrop of principle for them all. They had to create a secular document which had all the strengths of the great religions of the world but which spoke also for those who had no religion.

No nation came with clean hands to the table when the final signing of the Universal Declaration of Human Rights took place in 1948. Everyone had their own source of shame, just as today. These were pre-civil rights times and in the United States the legacy of slavery meant black people were still segregated from whites and racist legislation was still on the books. The Soviets were still conducting bloody purges of opponents, and for the British the effects of colonial rule still scarred relationships from Ireland to India.

The drafting committee was aware that the first wave of rights, which had been at the heart of the French and American revolutions in the eighteenth century, sought to set citizens free from the grip of the state and the Church. But these new post-Holocaust rights were striving to do something else – to create a better world for everyone. And for that to be possible it was not enough to guarantee 'liberty'. Individuals require protection from tyranny but they can also contribute to it: for example persecution because of your race could come from your neighbours. Tyrants do not have to wear jackboots. As I have pointed out myself, they sometimes wear Armani suits.

It was recognised that not only should restraints be put upon states to prevent the oppression of their citizens but ways also had to be found to require states to take a lead in preventing oppression from other sources. It should never again be possible for the state to claim democratic legitimacy or majority will for behaviour that denied any person's humanity. Violations by private companies or battering by husbands or cruel behaviour by any other individual – all these had to become the business of the state. That was the ideal, and any enlightened, imaginative politician with a vision for revitalising communities has the language at his or her disposal.

The Universal Declaration of Human Rights spawned a new generation of rights, more textured but just as far-reaching as those of the Enlightenment, based on the values of liberty and justice, dignity and equality, community and responsibility; they are at the heart of the European Convention of Human Rights and our own Human Rights Act.

So when the accusation is levied that the Act is all about rampant individualism it could not be more wrong. Contemporary human rights allow people to live in society free of discrimination or oppression but recognise that we all have duties to the community, as distinct from the state, 'in which alone the free and full development of personality is possible'. There are now over 50 international and regional human rights treaties and conventions which have developed out of the Universal Declaration and they all seek to balance collectivism and individualism. How could it have been otherwise when you look at the moment in time and the nature of the signatory parties, some of whom were collectivists with little commitment to the needs of the individual? This was the late 1940s: the woman chairing the process was a committed New Deal Democrat who believed the state had responsibilities to poor communities. This postwar period was also the generator of welfare state commitments all over Europe. The state's role was changing as it helped to provide welfare, health and education. The document's whole purpose was to balance the idea of the needs of the society as a whole with the rights of individuals.

Communitarian ideas in the United States are a direct response to this absence of second wave rights in the original United States constitution and due to the fact that although the US signed up to the Universal Declaration, it never took human rights thinking to its heart. Indeed it took Britain a long time, but a changed world has made engagement essential. What is now slowly developing in the United States is a campaign for contemporary European human rights not at government level but amongst community activists and academics. When David Blunkett plunders American thinkers for new ideas and is critical of human rights discourse because of its celebration of the individual, he is in fact failing to understand the difference between first and second wave rights.

We do need to foster traditions of 'community' in Britain, which like America has suffered as a consequence of unbridled consumerism. But this is not achieved by authoritarian threats or demands from the state. Encouraging the voluntary act of giving-back reaps far more dividends. We need to revitalise voluntarism – volunteers are needed to read with school-age children. We are needed at community centres to help with the literacy needs of Asian women, asylum seekers, young people who missed out in their schooling, ex-convicts who are saddled with unemployability because they have never been able to read properly either. Our work is needed at old people's homes, where we can visit the many elderly people who are lonely and infirm; it is needed in gutted neighbourhoods to help restore buildings, clean up parks, and convert brownfield sites into football pitches and running tracks. We need people to run youth clubs and youth sports teams. We need people prepared to visit prisoners and ferry children to visit imprisoned parents. And when we talk about responsibilities it should be to each other, not to Home Secretaries. Rights are not a quid pro quo for good behaviour and the mantra 'Rights and responsibilities' should not be abused.

An interesting gear change on human rights has happened since the end of the Cold War in 1989. The demise of communism was as much about human rights as the victory of free markets. Václav Havel speaks of the 'revolt of colour, authenticity and human individuality' which he saw at the heart of the waves of change in Eastern Europe.

Until the late 1960s the Universal Declaration of Human Rights was fairly toothless because of deference to the principle of state sovereignty. The UN ruled that it had 'no power to take any action with regard to human rights'. It was through non-governmental organisations like Amnesty International and Human Rights Watch, who brought cases before United Nations bodies and shamed states by bad publicity, that the concept really entered public consciousness. In the 1970s the UN itself began to authorise reports on specific countries like South Africa under apartheid and Greece under the Colonels, which undermined the self-confidence of those governments, sustained internal opposition organisations and encouraged international support for regime change. There have always been soft target states that the West is content to declare pariahs, like Iraq, Zimbabwe, North Korea and Iran. And then there are hard targets like the Soviet Union, now Russia, and China which are treated with kid gloves for political reasons. Double standards and hypocrisy abound, as Mary Robinson found when she was the UN Commissioner for Human Rights from 1997 to 2002. We may voice the notion that the standards are applicable to all countries no matter how powerful, but some powerful countries are happy to set the norms for others but consider themselves immune – like the United States itself. The failure to sign up to the International Criminal Court, which was established by the Rome Statute in 1998, is a prime example of American exceptionalism. The USA has not only decided not to be a participant but under a US law passed in 2002, it will cut off military aid from any state which fails to exempt American soldiers from ICC prosecution. Colombia, for instance, has been forced into issuing waivers so as not to lose nearly £600,000 million a year for its battle against guerrillas and drugs warlords. Similar threats have been issued to Eastern European countries: indeed I was present in the office of the Bosnian Foreign Minister in May 2003 when the call came through for her yea or nay. Needless to say, Bosnia felt obliged to agree. Croatia however was bold enough to refuse. And without any threats at all, the British government meekly signed up to a European agreement on American exemption.

The struggle to create internationally binding norms is greatly undermined when the one remaining superpower refuses to accept constraints upon its own behaviour. The affront to the rule of law and due process in detaining prisoners in Guantanamo Bay without access to lawyers, without charge for the vast majority, and with secret military commissions for the trial of some, makes a nonsense of attempts to draw other less developed democracies into law's embrace. The US is also the only developed country that has the death penalty in many of its states and uses it against children and those who suffer mental illness or mental impairment. It is impervious to any criticism of its domestic legal policies and ignores diplomatic efforts to intervene when foreign nationals are on death row. It dislikes the idea of being bound by laws other than those of its own or God's making

Yet, as the chief proponent of the global market, the USA has been anxious to export and globalise commercial law and bind others to it to protect commercial and property interests. Like Britain, it has been actively involved around the world in reforming legal systems to make them conducive to trading relationships and, just as our own big City law firms have offices now in Beijing and Moscow, so have the Wall Street firms and the great legal factories of Washington.

Globalisation taught nations like China that if they want to participate in international markets they must have systems of law which have the confidence of the corporations and trading entities with whom they wish to do business. The Chinese government invited organisations like the British Council to help create a commercial law base and train commercial lawyers; in the wake of that work British lawyers have assisted in the drafting of a criminal law code based on the presumption of innocence. The breakthrough is awesome. But it happened because of the well of trust which Britain has created with many nations over many years, even where history might have dictated otherwise. The progress may seem slow in China but a start has been made. The notion that impartial secular justice is essential to democracy should be remembered as a liberated Iraq takes form. Trust is the seedbed of good international relations and we may be depleting our store in the Islamic world.

So, commercialism has not travelled alone. But while the global market fosters new problems, it has also assisted the spread of human rights. Globalisation has stimulated the migration of people; nations are becoming increasingly multi-racial and the potential for intolerance of difference is great; advances in communication technologies accelerate the speed with which ideas are disseminated. Workers want to be protected from the indecencies of the market and human rights is one of the ways of taming and civilising a rampant global capitalism. This is why there is such ambivalence about this discourse in some quarters and why it matters so much. If we are to find a legal Esperanto which draws all nations into an acceptance of certain norms, a safety net must be provided for those who are most vulnerable. A call that echoes beyond citizenship and appeals to standards based on our common humanity is essential. And so it is that the asylum issue is the emblematic battleground on which the struggle for human rights is currently being fought.

Chairing the British Council has given me the opportunity to travel extensively in many parts of the world, often taking part in seminars and legal conferences. What has become clear to me is that the rule of law is even more fundamental than democracy and without it democracy is impossible. Visiting Bosnia, I saw that if the rule of law is not asserted immediately after a war or a military intervention, then organised crime and other malevolent forces fill the vacuum. Human rights principles create the bedrock, the fortifying base on which the many and varied societies around the world can build legal and social systems which will be respected. All the emerging democracies, whether in Eastern Europe, the former Soviet Union, Africa or elsewhere, will have a set of principles against which their legal systems will be judged. We can only take part in that vital international dialogue if we too have embraced those principles wholeheartedly. Until now Britain has been a model for the world and we should seek to maintain that role.

Whilst human rights are now higher on the agenda, the very words still create discomfort for some. To those who do not share my own political perspective I must emphasise that human rights are not owned by the left and nor should they be. They are the product of decent people on all parts of the political spectrum. How can we talk to the rest of the world about legal standards if we have not adopted the precepts and language ourselves?

No doubt a convergence of many factors explains why a human rights discourse has come of age. The fact that military generals now speak the language of human rights shows that the ideas have entered the mainstream. But although human rights should not be appropriated by the spin *meisters* and public relations advisers who people the offices of presidents and prime ministers, or deployed for strategic or tactical purposes or used to mask self-interest, sadly they are. After 11 September when the eyes of the West turned to Afghanistan, there was a sudden surge of concern about the treatment of women under the Taliban, a humanitarian urge which has subsided despite continuing abuses. Saddam Hussein's atrocities against his own people were loudly denounced when people wavered about military invasion: yet our own ministers ran hot and cold on the subject before the call for war.

It was reported in the *New Statesman* (December 2002) that an Iraqi opponent of Saddam who sought asylum in Britain had received a letter explaining Jack Straw's refusal of his application in 2001. It read as follows:

> The Secretary of State has at his disposal a wide range of information on Iraq which he has used to consider your claims. He is aware that Iraq, and in particular Iraqi security forces, would only convict and sentence a person in the courts with the provision of proper jurisdiction. He is satisfied, however, that if there are charges outstanding against you and if they were to be proceeded with on your return, you could expect to receive a fair trial under an independent and properly constituted judiciary.

Tell that to the families of those currently being exhumed from mass graves.

Disappointment is the word that springs to people's lips when they speak about Labour in government. The overall sense is that, despite their many important achievements, this government which took office with a huge majority and an extraordinary reservoir of goodwill has failed on too many fronts to meet expectations.

It is still a source of profound dismay that *our* government is allowing the agenda on law and order and asylum to be set by the right: removing long established safeguards from those accused of crime; failing to recognise that simple punitive measures drive the poor into further deprivation and do not prevent crime; overseeing the greatest rise in the prison population for over a hundred years; allowing racist police practices to persist despite anti-racist rhetoric; attacking judges and undermining their crucial role in maintaining the rule of law; cutting legal aid to the bone so that the poorest in our society suffer.

We see the government's failure particularly with the Human Rights Act. The original vision was that it would bring about a cultural change, but this has not been realised. As Yvette Cooper, a minister under Derry Irvine in what was then the Lord Chancellor's Department, has said publicly: 'The Human Rights Act and the approach it takes are far from embedded across society at this stage.' She pointed out that many people still misunderstood the central concepts and harboured misconceptions that needed to be challenged by the government which should be 'championing' the Act. However, sometimes it is government ministers themselves who misunderstand.

When asylum seekers have been persecuted by parties other than the state, and their state has failed to protect them from such persecution, British courts have determined that this fulfils the legal requirements for refugee status. This is a different interpretation from the legalistic one, which has been preferred by other European countries, where only persecution by the state is acknowledged to fulfil their responsibilities under the Refugee Convention. For example, in Somalia there is no recognisable state but one clan can threaten the very existence of another one and people flee to escape the torture. In the case of *Shah and Islam* v. *Home Secretary*, women were fleeing wife-burning in Pakistan and the argument was successfully made that gender persecution ignored by the state was clearly persecution. It is crucial that the special persecution which is inflicted on women, such as rape and stoning, is recognised. The British courts have followed the human rights approach taken in other jurisdictions like Canada, yet rather than taking pride in such a progressive approach, some politicians have been angered by this widening of the definition, because it is out of kilter with the judicial interpretations in Germany and France.

As Yvette Cooper MP made clear, a failure to root the Act deeply in public acceptance means that 'we risk creating a climate in which a reactionary government can get away with pulling out'.

Parliament's Joint Committee on Human Rights carried out a two-year inquiry into the implementation of the Act and found that the initial burst of enthusiasm had dissolved and there was evidence of widespread human rights abuse in care homes and other institutions responsible for the vulnerable. Its report, published in May 2003, gave a blunt warning that if the courts were not supported by other agencies, the original vision of the Act would not be realised.

> Litigation is an essential last resort in protecting the rights of the individual or groups, but it is not the most effective means of developing a culture of human rights . . . In their decision making and their service delivery, central government, local authorities, schools, hospitals, police forces and other organs and agencies of the state should ensure full respect for the rights of all those involved.

The committee did not find much evidence of increasing awareness of human rights and their implications for society, and where there was awareness it was often partial and ill-informed. There was also evidence of widespread lack of respect for the rights of those who use public services, especially those who need most protection. This failure has come about because no energy has gone into firing the boilers either in government departments or in public bodies with the belief that human rights is about how we all behave every day. Respect for human rights is not to be seen as a burden to be shouldered but as a common good in which we can take pride.

The joint committee strongly recommended a move to create an integrated body which would combine the idea of a human rights commission with the single equality body that the government has already unveiled to enforce anti-discrimination laws. The government announced on 29 October 2003 that it will create a single commission.

In this book I have tried to argue that whatever we face in the modern world, the sacrifice of civil liberties and human rights is a folly. I have tried to bring together the losses that have taken place so far, the government mindset that underpins the retreats from principle and the impact of those erosions when taken collectively. By eating away at the different elements of our justice system we are destroying the trust between citizens and the state; it prevents people having fulfilling and free lives.

We need to be wary of rhetoric, whether it comes from government or from the newsmongers of the media, and ensure that law and legal judgments are not unduly influenced by false public perceptions, or opportunistic political agendas. We need to think hard about the way the courts treat vulnerable witnesses, about the problems caused by ill thought-out sentencing, and the crisis in our prisons. We need to safeguard the role of the jury, and the integrity and independence of the judiciary. And above all we need to test each new proposal that affects the law in any way against the touchstones of civil liberties and human rights. The law is not only for lawyers – it belongs to and affects all of us, and as I write a serious justice gap is in the making.

The political personalities to whom I have referred in this book will move on. There will be new Prime Ministers, new Home

Secretaries, new Secretaries of State for Constitutional Affairs but the problems and challenges are likely to remain. Globalisation poses many new challenges and the law will have to take account of the social and economic factors which may lay claim to the future. Greater numbers of older people will create the need for increased immigration, despite the current panics over asylum seekers. If not well handled, the arrival of new migrants could create social unrest, and serious intolerance. States are also going to be more susceptible to global market fluctuation and economic recession, which may mean financial crisis and the consequent risk of social conflict. There is always more crime, and more social problems, when people are unemployed and experiencing hardship. Demographics show us that while Western nations are ageing, there are increasingly high numbers of young men in the developing world who are unemployed and living without any prospects. Unless we institute a fairer distribution of resources their disenchantment may fuel a rise in international terrorism. We can live in hope that none of these events come to pass but a framework of just law and civil liberties provides important protections for the tough times. A belief that governments will always be benign is wishful thinking.

Law translates standards of human rights into reality. Creating a world that is respectful of law is a journey, a utopian journey, and we are still not absolutely sure how to get there. But just as democratic rights were the big idea at the beginning of the twentieth century so human rights are the big idea of the century we have recently entered. They have the potential of radically affecting the way in which we relate to each other as nations and as next-door neighbours. Human rights is where the law becomes poetry. In many ways laws are the autobiography of a nation and in Britain we have many proud stories to tell but we also have shameful chapters. This book is meant to be an alarm call about the way our liberties are being eroded. A serious abandonment of principle is in train; all of us have to say it's time to stop.

FURTHER READING

Abramsom, Jeffrey. *We, the Jury: The Jury System and the Ideal of Democracy*, Basic Books, 1994

Akester, Kate. 'Restorative Justice. Victims' Rights and the Future', *Legal Action Magazine*, Legal Action Group, January 2002

Arendt, Hannah. *The Origins of Totalitarianism*, Harcourt Press, 1951

Auld, Lord Justice. *Review of the Criminal Courts of England and Wales*, The Stationery Office, 2002

Baron-Cohen, Simon. *The Essential Difference: Men, Women and the Extreme Male Brain*, Allen Lane, 2003

Blunkett, David. *Politics and Progress*, Demos, 2001

Bobbitt, Philip. *The Shield of Achilles*, Allen Lane, 2002

Carlen, Pat (ed.) *Women and Punishment: The Struggle for Justice*, Willan Publishing, 2002

—*Criminal Justice*, Sage Publications, 2002

Coyle, Andrew. *A Human Rights Approach to Prison Management*, ICPS, 2002

Crouch, Colin. *Coping with Post Democracy*, Fabian Society, 2001

Dershowitz, Alan. *Why Terrorism Works*, Yale University Press, 2002

Finkel, Norman. *Commonsense Justice*, Harvard University Press, 1995

Fukuyama, Francis. *The End of History and the Last Man*, Simon & Schuster, 1992

Gearty, C.A. and Kimbell, John. *Terrorism and the Rule of Law: A Report on the Laws Relating to Political Violence in Great Britain and Northern Ireland*, Civil Liberties Research Unit, 1995

Genn, Hazell. *Paths to Justice: What People Do and Think about Going to Law*, Hart Publishing, 1999

Giddens, Anthony. *Where Now for New Labour?* Blackwell, 2002
Giddens, Anthony. *The Third Way,* Blackwell, 1998
Giuliani, Rudolph. *Leadership,* Miramax Books, 2002
Graef, Roger. *Why Restorative Justice? Repairing the Harm Caused by Crime,* Calouste Gulbenkian Foundation, 2001
Griffith, J.A.G. *The Politicians of the Judiciary,* Fontana Press, 1997
Grove, Trevor. *The Juryman's Tale,* Bloomsbury, 1998
Higgins, Rosalyn and Flory, Maurice (eds). *Terrorism and International Law,* Routledge, 2002
Human Genetics Commission. *Inside Information,* Human Genetics Commission, 2002
International Bar Association. *International Terrorism: Legal Challenges and Responses,* Transnational Publishers, 2003
Kennedy, Helena. *Eve was Framed,* Chatto & Windus, 1991
Klug, Francesca. *Values for a Godless Age,* Penguin Books, 2000
Lees, Sue. *Carnal Knowledge,* Hamish Hamilton, 1996
Power, Samantha. *A Problem from Hell,* Flamingo, 2003
Putnam, Robert D. *Bowling Alone,* Touchstone, 2000
Putnam, Robert D., Leonardi, Robert and Nanetti, Raffaella, Y. *Making Democracy Work,* Princeton University Press, 1994
Ramesh, Randeep (ed.) *The War We Could Not Stop,* Faber & Faber, 2003
Rieff, David. *A Bed for the Night: Humanitarianism in Crisis,* Vintage, 2002
Robertson, Geoffrey. *Crimes against Humanity,* 2nd edn, Penguin Books, 2002
Rose, David. *In the Name of the Law,* Jonathan Cape, 1996
Sereny, Gita. *Cries Unheard: The Story of Mary Bell,* Macmillan, 1998
Shawcross, William. *Deliver Us from Evil,* Bloomsbury, 2000
Stern, Vivien. *A Sin against the Future,* Penguin Books, 1998
Steyn, The Rt. Hon. Lord. 'The Case for a Supreme Court', *Law Quarterly Review,* July 2002
—*Human Rights: The Legacy of Mrs Roosevelt,* The Holdsworth Club of the University of Birmingham, 2001
Timmins, Nicholas. *The Five Giants: A Biography of the Welfare State,* Fontana Press, 1996
Victory, Patrick. *Justice and Truth,* Sinclair-Stevenson, 2002
www.prisonstudies.org World Prison Brief
Woolf, The Rt. Hon. Lord. 'Human Rights: Have the Public Benefited?' The British Academy, 15 October 2002

INDEX